TRAVELS IN ARABY

GOOD READ

ABOUT THE BOOK

Aristocrat, Prime Minister William Pitt's niece, Lady Hester Stanhope grew up at Chevening in Kent, the home of the Earls of Stanhope (now the residence of The Prince of Wales).

100 years before Lawrence of Arabia, she travelled throughout the Arab world on her own, adopting the customs, tongues, and dress of her exotic Arab companions. Shipwrecked off Rhodes, attacked by Bedouins at night in the Syrian desert, the first European woman to visit Palmyra, nearly killed by the Plague, she courted extraordinary adventures and surrounded herself with extraordinary people. Before her death her reputation was so great that not even the Sultan dared defy her. She became an oriental potentate in her own right.

ABOUT THE AUTHOR

John Watney, who descends from a brewery-owning family, was born in London and grew up in France. He has written many novels, *The Enemy Within, The Unexpected Angel, The Quarrelling Room, The Glass Façade*, a volume of war memoirs and most recently a remarkable biography of the empire-builder *Clive of India*.

John Watney

TRAVELS IN ARABY OF LADY HESTER STANHOPE

GORDON CREMONESI

BRANCHES

Designed by Heather Gordon-Cremonesi
Produced by Chris Pye
Set by Preface Ltd, Salisbury
Printed in Great Britain by
The Garden City Press Limited

The publishers wish to thank
The Witch Ball Print Shop, Brighton
for their help in finding illustrations

ISBN 0-86033-005-2

Gordon Cremonesi Publishers
New River House
34 Seymour Road
London N8 0BE

CONTENTS

Part I   The Making of a Traveller
Chapter 1   A Traveller Is Born   3
Chapter 2   Stanhopes and Pitts   9
Chapter 3   In Search Of Escape   17
Chapter 4   The First Get-Away   25
Chapter 5   Another Escape   38
Chapter 6   Invasion Scare   56
Chapter 7   Gains and Losses   74

Part II   A Wanderer In Araby
Chapter 8   Departure   99
Chapter 9   Malta and Greece   107
Chapter 10   Constantinople   123
Chapter 11   Shipwreck   137
Chapter 12   Egypt and the Holy Land   147
Chapter 13   The Great Expedition To Palmyra   167
Chapter 14   Love and the Plague   183
Chapter 15   The Riches Of Ascalon   198
Chapter 16   Farewell, My Once Dearest B   213

Part III   The Queen
Chapter 17   Dar Djoun   225
Chapter 18   Retreat   248
Chapter 19   The Final Escape   261
Chapter 20   Not Easily To Submit To Fate   280

Index   290

PART ONE

THE MAKING OF A TRAVELLER

CHAPTER ONE

A TRAVELLER IS BORN

On 12th March 1776 the great house of Chevening, a few miles
north of Sevenoaks in Kent, awaited the birth of the first child to
Lord and Lady Charles Mahon. The expectant mother was Charles's
cousin, Hester Pitt, daughter of the Earl of Chatham, "the Great
Commoner", who, in 1757, on becoming Secretary of State, when
England's fortunes were at a particularly low ebb, had said, "I
know that I can save England, and that no one else can". And he
had.

She had two brothers, both younger than herself. One, John,
born in 1756, was the heir-apparent to the Chatham title. When
the Great Commoner had accepted, against all expectations, the
title and £3,000 a year in 1761, his admirers had been so upset
that they had referred to his wife as "Lady Cheat'em", but that
was a long time ago. Chatham was now an elder statesman; and
young John looked forward to the day when he, too, would
become the Earl of Chatham.

Of a very different character was the younger brother, William.
Born in 1759 he was already showing himself, at the age of
seventeen, to have qualities far above those of an ordinary young
man of his age, but even the most sanguine of his early admirers
could not have guessed that within seven years he was to rise to
the highest political post in the land.

While their twenty-year-old sister waited for the birth of her
first child, her husband Charles marched, in his usual erratic
arm-swinging way, about the grounds of Chevening. He was a

strange looking person; gaunt, tall, with a hooked nose and angular face. According to Sir N. W. Wraxall, a contemporary, he looked more like one of Cromwell's Puritan secretaries than a nobleman. But then his upbringing had been somewhat unusual.

His father, Philip (the 2nd Earl), was a gentle and retiring man, more concerned with mathematical than political problems. When he reluctantly took his seat in the House of Lords on 15th January 1736 he made no impression whatsoever. Even when he was twenty-nine it was reported that he spoke "with great tremblings and agitations". He preferred Euclid to the House of Lords.

It was not until he was thirty-two that "he lifted up his eyes from Euclid and directed them to matrimony" — to quote the sharp witted Horace Walpole. The woman he chose was Grizel Hamilton, grand-daughter of the 6th Earl of Haddington.

She met Philip when she was twelve years old, in Rome and Bologna, when he was on the Grand Tour, and spent most of the time arguing with him and another friend. She was a sensible, Scottish girl who was destined to live to the age of ninety-two and be very much concerned with the upbringing of her turbulent young grand-daughter — Lady Hester Stanhope.

But in 1744, at the age of twenty-six and without a dowry, it did not look as though she would marry at all. Then quite suddenly in May of that year the shy 2nd Earl, after a few brief visits to her family, finally proposed to her by letter. She replied:

"My Lord,

Mama gave me your letter which surprised me very much, as I am sensible I am unworthy of so long and true a friendship as you show for me. I have always had the greatest regard and esteem for your Lordship, but marriage never came into my head, and that is a thing of so serious a nature that I can't suddenly determine whether I am capable of making you as happy as I wish you. You have a better opinion of me than I deserve, and may be disappointed which always will give me concern. Mama and all my friends have left it entirely in my own determination which I am almost afraid to do upon your account, not my own, being persuaded that you'll do all in your power to make me happy as I should expect to be with a person of so much honour and integrity. I hope you'll consider that I have no fortune. I am, My Lord,

Your most obedient servant,
Grizel Hamilton."

Philip had his suit embroidered by Elizabeth Parr for £42, paying £30 for the gold lace itself. He got himself a new hat from David Allen for £1.1.0, paid one shilling for a bow to be sewn on, gave fifteen of his servants new gloves and married his Grizel, at the end of July, paying on 25th July, "Mr Williamson for marrying me to Miss Hamilton £21.00". His "endowing purse" to his wife was £105. This started a marriage that was, on the personal level at least, to be long and happy.

Not so smooth-running was the question of an heir. A son, named Philip after his father, was born in 1746, but he was weak and had inherited Grizel's father's consumption. His persistent cough worried the whole close-knit family. By January 1763 the boy's condition had got so bad that Grizel and Philip took him to Geneva in the hope that the Swiss climate might cure the over-tall, thin, consumptive youth. But he died on 6th July of the same year.

So it was that their second and now only son, Charles, a sturdy eleven-year-old schoolboy at Eton, became Lord Mahon, and heir to the Stanhope title. It was essential that he, in his turn, should have a son to keep the title in the direct line. And as he waited anxiously for his pretty, sweet, young wife to give birth on that early March day, perhaps his thoughts were all on his future son. Or perhaps not — for he was a very unusual heir to an earldom, because ten years spent in Geneva had a profound effect on him.

Switzerland was then the centre of extreme radical thought. The works of Jean Jacques Rousseau formed the basis of many social ideas. (Man was vile, only nature was pure.) Added to this simple agrarian thought were the revolutionary theories of Voltaire and others; all men were born equal, inherited titles and ranks were morally, socially and politically wrong. The impressionable young Lord Mahon absorbed this climate of opinion with all the grave and serious concentration of his nature.

He was extremely intelligent. His father, who was in charge of his education, taught him Greek, while a Swiss mathematician called Le Sage gave him his knowledge of mathematics. Other tutors would keep him busy for the other eight hours of a day; he was fond of and good at painting.

At the same time he concentrated on outdoor games. He liked skating and other pastimes. His mother reported in 1768, when he was a tall, thin, fifteen-year-old boy, that he filled up some of his time with cricket. She even sent to England for a cricket bat and balls, so that, "he may not forget that he is a Kentish man".

Eight months later, she records that he attended his first dance, which he did not seem to like, but she added hopefully: "I believe he'll dance well." Soon he seems to have liked dancing well enough to start flirting.

But it was in the world of invention that his main interest already lay. In 1769, an English visitor to the Stanhopes, Lady Mary Coke, wrote to a friend: "He has invented, I was told, a mathematical instrument which I was assured is better for the purpose it is intended than any other of the kind; yet he is but seventeen years of age."

Though he became a member of the Genevese Council of Two Hundred, and thus learnt more radical political views, and a Commander of the Company of Archers (which cost him £573 in feasts in the first year alone) his interest in inventions broadened and deepened. By the time he was in his twenties, his mother wrote: "At present the passion is a pyrometer of his own invention to try the contraction and dilation of metals . . . "

He was now a thin young man of five feet eleven. Grizel's sister, Rachel Hamilton, viewing him with shrewd Scottish eyes during a visit to Geneva in the autumn of 1773, records " . . . he is not formed in his person, very shambling . . . ". A week later she writes: "Charley improves upon one every hour, he is so unformed in his person that he does not strike you at first . . . ." He tended to mumble, but she was astonished at the influence he seemed to have on Genevese public affairs. Like everyone else who met him, she commented on his extraordinary capacity for invention: "People of judgement", she added, "say all his inventions are good."

His parents decided that the time had now come for him to return to England so that he could take up his expected position in society. The family travelled back via Paris, where Charles stayed until the early summer. Despite his gawkiness, he conformed with the requirements of society, wearing laced clothes, ruffles and the fashionable white feathers in his head. But he refused to powder his hair as all smart young men did. He said it gave him a headache.

On arriving back in England he was presented at Court, where his dark unpowdered hair caused something of a sensation. One rumour had it that he left it unpowdered because of his radical views, and that he was protesting against the high cost of wheat; others thought he had just gone wild, living abroad so long. No-one realized that it was because powder gave him a head-ache — on such flimsy matters reputations are often made. Horace Walpole, that cruel but acute witness of social affairs described him, because of his dark hair and the white feathers he wore, as being "tarred and feathered". Charles Mahon seemed not to care.

He was, anyhow, soon far too busy courting his attractive sixteen-year-old cousin Lady Hester Pitt, and seeking with the help of John Wilkes, whom he had met earlier in Geneva, a seat in Parliament as a "radical" candidate. Although he withdrew his candidature half way through the contest, he made a considerable impression, favourable or unfavourable according to one's political views, on society at the time.

His coming marriage with Hester Pitt was approved of by the Pitt family. The Earl of Chatham liked the gawky young man, comparing him to a mine which was full of "invaluable treasures". Charles Mahon had, Chatham wrote, "a Head to contrive, a Heart to conceive, and a hand to execute whatever is good, lovely or of fair repute".

Lady Chatham was equally pleased. She had been Lady Hester Grenville, a member of that proud, wealthy and cold family that had "adopted" the great Chatham before he was even Secretary of State. She and Grizel Stanhope, Charles' mother, had been friends for years. All through Grizel's long exile in Switzerland, the two had corresponded, warmly and intimately.

Finally, Grizel herself was delighted. She wrote ecstatically to Lady Chatham. "I wish I could find words to express what I feel at this moment, but I can only say, that my dear child had made a *wise* choice, and the same that would have been mine had I been to choose for him . . ." and then, on a less formal and more emotional note, added: "I often wished that I had had a daughter, and in her I think I shall have one as dear to me as if so by birth."

So Charles Mahon, at the age of twenty-one, married his young cousin. The great Earl of Chatham, too debt-ridden, could not give his daughter a suitable wedding present. It was left to his wife's family, the Grenvilles, to provide the jewellery and £1,000 endowment gift to the young bride.

The newly weds divided their time between their house in London and Chevening, while Mahon strove, unsuccessfully, to get himself elected to Parliament. When not seeking an elusive radical seat, he spent the time happily with his philosophical and scientific enquiries.

But the baby, when it was born, turned out to be a girl. Christened Hester after her mother, she was to be known to the world one day as Lady Hester Stanhope, but at this point of time she was merely a baby girl who should have been a boy.

CHAPTER TWO

STANHOPES AND PITTS

Hester, a strong healthy baby, gave very little trouble and was an enterprising child. One day, still only two, she made herself a straw hat of a type that was fashionable then. She took out the crown of an ordinary hat, and put instead a piece of puffed up satin. It was so realistic looking and considered such an achievement for such a young child that her grandfather made a little paper box to hold it, and put the day and month of Hester's age on it.

This, at least, was the story she told her doctor many years later, when she liked to spend the evening, or the whole night, reminiscing. No doubt there was some exaggeration; and the baby girl was probably helped by an understanding grown-up; but the story of Hester making a hat persisted.

She spent much of her time at Chevening with her grandparents, the gentle 2nd Earl and his capable wife, Griselda. The first Earl, James Stanhope, had bought Chevening, the Stanhopes coming originally from County Durham, and there are references to the family as far back as the thirteenth century. They had taken their name from the township of Stanhope in County Durham, but had moved south during the fourteenth century. James's father, Alexander, was the twelfth son of the Earl of Chesterfield; a not very enviable position. Alexander had pursued a moderately unsuccessful diplomatic career (due mainly to his inherent dislike of foreigners) and had forced his four sons to enter the services, two for the army and two for the navy.

Only the eldest, James, achieved a modicum of success. He served with Marlborough for a while; and then, on 14th September 1708 began landing troops, despite the fact that the navy refused to support him, on the island of Minorca. By 30th September he had captured Fort Mahon, the main enemy stronghold; the island surrendered and Stanhope became a hero.

Unfortunately his strategical grasp was not as good as his courage and tactical ability. In 1710, when he was in charge of the British troops in Spain, under the command of the Austrian general, Starhemberg, he allowed a combined French–Spanish army, under Vendome, to isolate him at Brighuega. Stanhope surrendered with his army; in order, he wrote, to ". . . try and save so many brave men who had given service to the Queen [Anne] and will, I hope, live to do again". In his letter to the Secretary of State, dated 2nd January 1711, he added: "I cannot express to your Lordship how much this blow has broken my spirits which I shall never recover."

He was kept a prisoner of the Spaniards for twenty-one months, and was finally exchanged for the Duke of Escalona. By the time he returned to England his last remaining brother had been killed in action in Spain, and the war had anyhow petered out.

But it wasn't the end for James Stanhope. His military career destroyed, he turned to politics. Walpole, that astute politician, saw in Stanhope a useful addition to the Whig cause. For though Stanhope had been defeated, he was still a popular and handsome hero. A political future, more brilliant than his military one, seemed to lie ahead.

It was soon after his return from Spain that he met Lucy Pitt, "Diamond" Pitt's daughter, a sweet tempered girl of twenty-two, with a dowry of £6,000. She and the dashing forty-year-old soldier–politician fell in love and were married on 24th February 1713, thus creating the first link that was to endure for over a hundred years. In time it was to have a decisive effect on young Hester Stanhope's life.

As soon as James Stanhope married his beautiful Lucy, he set about looking for a suitable home for himself, his family and his new position in Society; for on 3rd July 1717, he had been created Baron Stanhope of Elvaston [Elvaston was his father's birthplace] in the County of Derby and Viscount Stanhope of Mahon, in Minorca [thus assuring the title of Mahon to his heir].

He found his home at Chevening, at what was then a crossroads a few miles north of Sevenoaks. It was a large square house originally designed by Inigo Jones. In Harris's "History of the County of Kent" published in 1719 it is shown with its two wings, enclosed courtyard, grill-like gates and high railings; a solid, compact, square place spreading out its arms as if to encompass all who lived there.

Behind the house lay the complex and extensive gardens. They had been laid out on a formal pattern of box-hedges, yew trees and straight alleys bisecting each other at regular intervals; a copy of the static classical gardens of the great French châteaux. "Capability" Brown had not yet arrived to give the English country house its destinctive style. Beyond the gardens, the empty, undulating hills of Kent broke the wide horizon.

While James Stanhope, now Secretary of State, travelled between England and Europe on his country's business and added an Earldom to his other titles, Lucy settled herself at Chevening. She supervised the extensive alterations ordered by James, and gave birth in quick succession to four of her seven children.

By 1720, James Stanhope's position seemed unassailable. He was politically secure both in Parliament and abroad. He had a beautiful wife, fine children, a title and a wonderful house.

Then the South Sea Bubble burst.

For some time speculators had been floating bogus companies with shares known as South Sea stock. Investment fever grasped almost everyone who had any money. Shares changed hands at ever increasing prices. No attempt was made to verify whether the South Sea companies actually existed, and when the crash came, many people were ruined. Worse still, it was discovered that politicians, including many ministers and colleagues of Stanhope, were implicated.

Though not directly involved in the ensuing scandals he became disgusted with political life. There were rumours that he would return to the army as Captain-General in place of the old and now ailing Duke of Marlborough. However, on 4th February 1721 the young and dissolute Duke of Wharton launched a violent and personal attack against Stanhope.

Stanhope replying with equal violence was taken suddenly ill with headache and carried home to his London house. The next day while an apothecary was getting ready to bleed him (the

almost universal remedy of that time for any illness) Stanhope suddenly shouted "I shall have no occasion for your assistance" and fell back dead. He had broken a blood vessel and died of haemorrhage, aged forty-eight.

Thus, by the time Hester was born, the Stanhopes had attained, within two generations, a position of some importance in the military, political and social life of the eighteenth century.

Charles Mahon, Hester's father, was determined to continue the tradition of service to his country, but owing to his foreign upbringing and brilliant mathematical brain, his approach was difficult. He refused any kind of safe Whig seat, but tried, unsuccessfully, to get himself elected as a radical.

At the same time he was busy inventing a fireproof material, which by September 1777 had been perfected and he decided to put it to the test. He built a wooden two-room, two-storey house, fireproofed the upper room, floor and supports, and then invited a number of distinguished guests, including the Lord Mayor and the President of the Royal Society, to take ice-creams in the upper room.

The lower room was filled with combustible materials and as soon as the guests assembled he set fire to it. The heat was so intense that the glass windows melted like sealing-wax and ran down the blazing walls; yet to the amazement and, no doubt, relief of those standing immediately above, not a flicker of heat was felt, and the floor remained as cool as if there were no fire underneath. Even the ice-creams did not melt. Equally successful were his ingenious calculating machines, two of which can be seen to this day in the Science Museum in London.

But more serious events were to distract him. The American colonists had declared for independence, Boston fell, and Lady Chatham was distraught because her eldest son, Lord Pitt, was serving in Canada. The Earl of Chatham was even more concerned since he always believed that Lord North's handling of the American colonists had been disastrous. Force *would* not, *could* not succeed; he believed they should be allowed to arrange their own affairs and govern themselves, otherwise all would be lost.

But he was out of office, ill and in his usual desperate financial state. With the help of his younger son, William, recently down from Pembroke College, Oxford, he managed to get to the House of Lords, where, leaning heavily on his stick, he said: "You cannot conquer the Americans. You talk of your powerful forces to disperse their army, but I might as well talk of driving them before me with this crutch."

They would not listen.

The following year, on 7th April 1778, he went to the House of Lords again. Now very weak, he was supported by William on one side, and Charles Mahon on the other. Two of his other sons were also in attendance. Hardly able to speak, his voice was sometimes but a whisper, only occasionally rising to the old power. The real enemy was not America but France. "Shall a people that fifteen years ago was the terror of the world now stoop, so low as to tell its ancient inveterate enemy, 'Take away all we have; only give us peace'?" and finally, before sinking back exhausted, and it seemed to many, dying, he managed to cry out "Let us at least make an effort; and if we must fall, let us fall like men."

He was taken back to his home in Hayes, Kent, where he constantly asked his son William to read the account of Hector's death in the Iliad. He died 11th May 1778 and was buried at Westminster Abbey.

But Lady Mahon was soon expecting again, and in February 1780, a month before Hester's fourth birthday, she gave birth to a third daughter, who was christened Lucy. Though still only in her twenty-fifth year, the poor mother, exhausted by continual childbearing, seemed unable to throw off the effects of Lucy's birth. She rallied slightly with the coming of spring, but relapsed again early in the summer. She died on 18th July 1780, leaving behind her three small daughters, of which the eldest, Hester, was only four.

Charles Mahon was almost driven mad with grief. He would stride about the place, more dishevelled and wild-looking than ever. He could hardly bear to have his daughters in his sight. To him it seemed that they had killed his lovely young wife. His mother, Grizel, took over complete charge. On Charles' behalf she wrote to his friends telling them of the young wife's death. It was she who tried to comfort Charles himself, and who took responsibility for looking after the three young girls. They had, in the way that children do, survived the grown-up tragedy with remarkable ease. They had, anyhow, as was the usual custom among the aristocracy, been in the care of nurses and servants from birth. Only Grizel Stanhope noted their progress: "The sweet children", she wrote on 6th August 1780, to her old friend Lady Chatham, "are perfectly well and thrive amazingly in the good air."

Despite his grief (or perhaps because of it) Charles Mahon increased his efforts at getting into Parliament. He travelled the country and canvassed wildly, keeping himself busy, too busy to think of his deceased wife. At last, in October 1780, he was elected, not, as he had hoped, as a radical, but for the pocket borough of High Wycombe. He immediately threw himself with his accustomed and awkward energy into attacking the Government, and declared that he would oppose every measure put forward.

In November 1780 his mother wrote again to her old friend, Lady Chatham:

> "I am interrupted by Hester who wants me to put up her Doll's new bed, but as she is much handier than I am, I won't attempt it. Grizelda wants me to carry her to the top of the House to see the snow. She now chatters and imitates her sister in all, good or bad. Sweet Lucy has indifferent nights with her teeth, but is not ill, none yet cut."

Charles Mahon eventually decided to remarry. He still had no male heir, and his mother could not be expected to look after his three young daughters for ever, and as a Member of Parliament he also needed the solidity of matrimony. Once again he kept within the family orbit. One of Lady Chatham's younger brothers had a daughter named Louisa, who though beautiful had much of the famous Grenville haughtiness. Charles Mahon decided to marry her.

It was a delicate business, for he was substituting Lady Chatham's daughter for her niece. He would obviously have to explain to the old lady how he could apparently forget her daughter so quickly, and take on the new woman. Louisa was of a cold nature, and not Lady Chatham's favourite.

With unusual tactfulness Charles Mahon wrote on 1st February 1781:

> "My dearest Lady Chatham,
>   From the affectionate kindness you have always shown me I know you will not be insensible to anything that materially

relates to my welfare and happiness, which what I am going to mention particularly does. The very melancholy state, in which I had been left by the great trying misfortune I experienced last year, and the strong effect it produced upon me, has made me desire not to continue in a solitary situation in which, both for my own sake in all respects and for that of my children I must wish not always to remain. The pure happiness I once experienced, which I so gratefully felt, and which I shall ever gratefully remember, is a persuasive reason upon my mind, to engage me to think of settling again. There is a person, whose gentle temper and other amiable qualities I have known from a child; and of whom I have had, since that time, many additional reasons to have a favourable opinion; I mean your respectable brother's daughter, Miss Louisa Grenville. I trust my dearest Lady Chatham you will not disapprove either of my resolution or my choice. Sure I am she is the niece of one of the finest and most valuable women that ever existed."

Whatever private misgivings Lady Chatham might have had, there was little that she or anyone else could do. It was obviously sensible that Mahon should marry again, and by keeping it in the family he at least assured a continuity of in-laws. Charles and Louisa were married in March 1781.

The new Lady Mahon was never popular either with the daughters of her predecessor, or, it would seem, with her descendants. Her granddaughter, the Duchess of Cleveland, was to write somewhat contemptuously of her: "She was a worthy and well-meaning woman; but as I remember her, stiff and frigid, with a chilly and conventional manner." The Duchess was writing then of a young person's memory of an older woman. When Louisa married Charles Mahon she was twenty-three, and it must have been a daunting experience to follow a much loved and popular wife and find herself suddenly responsible for three very young stepdaughters. Louisa, with a background of devotional reading to sustain her, undoubtedly attempted in the beginning to fulfil her new and unexpected role. It was the basic narrowness of her character that made failure almost certain; that, and the almost certain knowledge that Charles still loved his dead wife.

However, in one particular sphere she was completely success-ful: before the year in which she was married was out, she gave birth to a son. He was christened Philip Henry, and Lord Mahon at last had a son and heir.

Charles was now extremely busy, politically. His London house was in Harley Street, but he now found that it was too far from the House of Commons, so he moved to Downing Street. He was a strong supporter of his cousin William Pitt who had entered Parliament on 23rd January 1781 at the age of twenty-one. Charles, seven years the elder, was pleased to give Pitt, throughout his early time in Parliament, the benefit of his experience.

Then, quite unexpectedly, on 19th December 1783, Pitt became Prime Minister at the unbelievably early age of twenty-four. Charles Mahon continued to support him for a while and on one occasion, after Pitt had reduced the tea duties in 1784, Charles rose and, in his usual stentorian voice and gesticulating wildly, praised Pitt for having knocked "smuggling on the head at one blow". Whereupon, with brilliant mistiming, he brought his order paper smartly down on top of Pitt's head. It almost brought the House down; but Charles Mahon seemed unaware of anything unusual and went on speaking with his usual vehemence.

Chevening, near Sevenoaks in Kent, the home of the Stanhopes for 250 years. Hester was born and spent her childhood here. When the Stanhope title recently became extinct, the house was offered to the Prince of Wales, as was the wish of the 6th and last Earl of Stanhope. (*The Times*)

CHAPTER THREE

IN SEARCH OF ESCAPE

Meanwhile Hester and her sisters were growing up at Chevening, though still very young. Their grandmother Grizel and a governess were in charge of them, but the relationship between Grizel and the girls was undergoing a change. Hester was beginning already to show a determination of spirit unusual in a young girl. There were times when she and her grandmother clashed temperamentally. They always made it up; but although Grizel used the word "sweet" when talking about Grizelda and especially Lucy, prettiest of the three, she never did when referring to Hester. Already, perhaps unconsciously, perhaps deliberately, Hester was taking charge of her two younger sisters.

Already the lure of France and "abroad" had taken hold of her. She recalled the moment, later, to her physician–biographer, Dr Charles Meryon:

> "Just before the French Revolution broke out, the ambassador from Paris to the English Court was the Comte d'Adhémar. That nobleman had some influence on my fate as far as regarded my wish to go abroad, which, however, I was not able to gratify until many years afterwards. I was but seven or eight years old when I saw him; and, when he came by invitation to pay a visit to my papa at Chevening, there was such a fuss with the fine footmen with feathers in their hats, and the count's bows and French manners, and I know not what, that, a short time aferwards, when I was sent to

17

Hastings with the governess and my sisters, nothing would satisfy me but I must go and see what sort of a place France was. So I got into a boat one day unobserved, that was floating close to the beach, let loose the rope myself, and off I went. Yes, Doctor, I literally pushed a boat off, and meant to go, as I thought, to France. Did you ever hear of such a mad scheme?"

No doubt, the incident was romanticized by the passage of time, but it is not difficult to imagine the sturdy independent minded little girl, already something of a bother to her grandmother, doing just that, in order to satisfy her curiosity about the marvellous foreigners she had met at her father's house.

Her stepmother, Louisa, after the first half-hearted attempt to be "mother" to the three little girls, soon gave up the attempt, and left them to Grizel's care. Louisa was anyhow too busy producing further children for Charles Mahon. She presented him with a second boy, who died at birth, in 1784, and a third, Charles Banks, in 1785.

But now a family death occurred that once more changed the course of all their lives. On 7th March 1786, the self-effacing and erudite 2nd Earl died. Charles Mahon became the 3rd Earl, and had to leave the House of Commons, where he was already becoming critical of some of Pitt's financial proposals, and moved to the House of Lords. Louisa now became the Countess of Stanhope, and her eldest son, Philip Henry, aged four, the new Lord Mahon. Most importnat of all, from the point of view of the three sisters, Grizel, as was expected of her, left Chevening and retired to the Dower House at Ovenden. Admittedly, it was just across the park, and she saw the children frequently, but she was no longer directly in charge of them. They were now the sole concern of the 3rd Earl and his wife.

Charles started off his political career in the House of Lords exactly as he had started in the House of Commons: by attacking the Government of the day. But this time it was led by his cousin William Pitt. Charles objected to Pitt's suggestion that a sinking fund should be set up to lessen the National Debt. As a result, the one time close association between the two cousins was lost. They drifted apart politically and socially.

In any event, Charles found himself much more isolated in the more traditional atmosphere of the House of Lords. There was no one anywhere near as radical as himself. He knew too that as a peer and a radical one at that, he stood little chance of real advancement. He therefore turned once more to his first interest: invention.

He wanted to invent a ship that could move without the help of wind or tide. Indeed, that could, incredibly, move *against* both tide and wind. He began making models of possible ships, abandoning the bulbous shape then popular, for a narrower, pointed and therefore faster shape. He would try these models out on the great lake in the gardens behind Chevening. In order not to be disturbed he forbade the children to use it.

He had long been fascinated by electricity and had already published a book on the subject. He was particularly concerned with the possibility of lightning striking the same place again. He suggested that lightning conductors should be used extensively throughout the country. After a recent death from lightning in Scotland, he gave to the Royal Society, on 15th February 1787, a lecture on the danger of the returning stroke of lightning.

The children saw very little of the 3rd Earl and even less of his wife. The memory of that childhood isolation remained with Hester all her life. Years later, on speaking of her childhood, she recalled: ". . . we were left to the governesses. Lady Stanhope got up at ten o'clock, went out, and then returned to be dressed, if in London, by the hair-dresser; and there were only two in London, both of them Frenchmen, who could dress her. Then she went out to dinner, and from dinner to the Opera, and from the Opera to parties, seldom returning until just before daylight. Lord Stanhope was engaged in his philosophical pursuits: and thus we children saw neither the one nor the other. Lucy used to say, that if she had met her mother-in-law [stepmother] in the streets, she would not have known her. Why, my father once followed to our own door in London a woman who happened to drop her glove, which he picked up. It was our governess; but, as he had never seen her in the house, he did not know her in the street."

Even in a society and period where children were normally isolated from their parents, the conduct of the 3rd Earl and his wife was exceptional. It is not surprising therefore that the children became more and more of a separate entity, under the increasingly dominating control of the eldest girl, Hester. Her own mother dead, and the boy's mother indifferent to the fate of her own sons as much as her stepdaughters, Hester must have begun to feel that all their futures depended entirely upon her.

Meanwhile, the 3rd Earl was becoming odder and odder. "He slept", Hester gleefully told Dr Meryon many years later, "with twelve blankets on his bed, with no night cap, and his window wide open: how you would have laughed had you seen him! He used to get out of bed, and put on a thin dressing-gown, with a pair of silk breeches that he had worn overnight, with slippers, and no stockings: and then he would sit in a part of the room which had no carpet, and take his tea with a bit of brown bread."

No wonder the fastidious Louisa got more and more bored with his peculiarities and spent as much of her time as possible with her more "civilized" London friends. But before doing so, however, she gave birth to yet one more boy, James, in 1788; and then was seen by her stepchildren even less than before.

The governesses were now supreme. Hester so disliked them, that she retained a hatred for them all her life and swore "eternal warfare against Swiss and French governesses". One governess, she recalled later: "had our backs pinched in by boards, that were drawn tight with all the force the maid could use; and as for me, they would have squeezed me to the size of a puny miss – a thing impossible".

She was very proud, even at an early age, of what she considered her high breeding. Once again, the unfortunate governesses came in for her contempt and dislike: "My instep", she declared, "by nature so high, that a little kitten could walk under the sole of my foot, they used to bend down in order to flatten it, although that is one of the things that shows my high breeding."

Not that life at Chevening was, at least at this time, unhappy for the children. It was a world in itself. There were at least a hundred people, tenants and servants, who were dependent for their existence on it. The complex business of running the house had been in Grizel's capable hands while her husband was alive, and after his death the organization she created continued to run smoothly enough, even though Louisa was so often away in London. The housekeeper was the central figure in the house. Her orders covered every housekeeping activity: the weekly killing of an ox and the daily killing of a sheep for the kitchens; the washing on four stone troughs of the thousand pieces of dirty linen collected every week; the lowering and heaving up of the false ceiling in the laundry, so that the clean linen, beautifully embroidered table-cloths and towels could be dried; and for the lighting, on wet days, of the three drying stoves.

She also made sure that staff rules and regulations were carried out. There was a strict sense of hierarchy. Each tenant, servant and labourer had his or her allotted place. There were privileges to be awarded, restrictions to be enforced. A lady's maid, for example, could wear heels of a certain height only. She was not allowed to wear white clothes or curl her hair. A special pair of scissors was kept, so that the locks of any daring lady's maid who infringed this rule could be cut off immediately. In obdurate cases a rod to lightly but effectively whip the culprit was also at hand.

In times of sickness the housekeeper, accompanied by the still-room maid (the equivalent of a hospital nurse), would bring medicine, gruel or barley water to the invalid; and then see that the doctor's instructions were carried out. When a woman on the estate was expecting a baby, two guineas were sent to her, as well as a number of goods which included baby linen and blankets; and, perhaps for the husband's benefit as much as his wife's, two bottles of wine.

The world outside the house was equally hard working and carefully organized. The washerwomen would start work at their outdoor troughs before 1.00 a.m. every Monday morning. They would soap, beat and rinse the whole of that day, and the whole of the next, stopping only for meals. By midnight on Tuesday, the washing would be done, and they would be allowed to leave the estate.

Sheep grazed on the open land beyond the gardens and the shepherd and the whole of his family, including his daughters, would be engaged in looking after the flocks. It was a common sight to see a hefty shepherdess carrying a large struggling sheep from one pasture to another. There was also the post-boy. He would generally be about twelve years of age, and his job was to ride into Sevenoaks, on horse-back, to fetch the letters, every day except Sunday. It did not matter how bad the weather was, or how impassable the roads, that was his responsibility. Sometimes, in the winter when the snow was on the ground, and the earth as hard with frost as metal, he would return, his fingers so numb with cold, that he could not even dismount from his horse. He would have to be lifted down before the letters could be taken off him. Even then, he could not walk, or feel anything, but would have to have his face and hands rubbed with snow to warm them, and be frog-marched up and down the courtyard before the circulation returned to his limbs, enabling him, at last, to make for the servant's hall, where a well-earned hot meal was waiting for him.

The six Stanhope children formed a compact, self-contained unit in this complex, almost feudal organization. By 1788, when Hester was twelve, they were a recognizable force. Hester was their undisputed leader and showed a remarkable mastery of the others. Although not highly educated – the 3rd Earl did not allow the children access to his large library, believing, despite his own reliance on books, that they were harmful to the development of the mind – she could and did discuss "philosophy" with her father, the only one of his children he ever cared to have in his company.

She was a tall, strong young girl, full of enormous energy, keen on riding and outdoor life. Her high instep, intact despite the efforts of her governesses, gave her a springy attractive walk. At times she looked and behaved more like a boy than a girl. Her voice was deep and resonant. Since the year before she had been learning, not very successfully, to play the guitar and to sing. As Grizel noted in one of her many letters to Lady Chatham: "The first amuses her, and the latter I hope will be of use to me in softening her voice, which from her strength was rather unmusical and masculine." She admired courage and tenacity. It was perhaps for this reason that she and her father got on well together.

Griselda, two years younger, was a clever, plain and not very endearing child. She wanted to dominate the group, but had none of Hester's natural authority. She imitated her elder sister but at the same time was jealous of her. Nobody seems to have liked poor Griselda, least of all her father. Lucy on the other hand was the prettiest of them all, but also the least intelligent. She had a small round face, bright eyes and an endearing nature. She was always "sweet" Lucy to all and sundry. But though her father liked her appearance, he found her continual company tiring. "Now Papa is going to study," he would say, "so you may go to your room." And to her room sweet Lucy would go.

Even though Hester was fond enough of her sisters she would

never allow them to come to her room unless they had first sent a servant to enquire whether it was all right to do so. She must always have been, subconsciously, aware of what the early death of her mother meant to the three of them. Children who lose their mother early tend to become suspicious of life, withdrawn and independent. It is as if the loss of such an essential prop can never be replaced. Hester showed, as can be seen by her grandmother's remarks, an unusual degree of self-sufficiency and autonomy. As the eldest she undoubtedly felt responsible for her two younger sisters. She undertook her self-imposed duties briskly and efficiently. One feels, in fact, that she enjoyed bossing her sisters about.

All her later comments and actions show, too, that she felt equally responsible for her young half-brothers. They, too, had "lost" their mother, not through physical death, but through the living death of the world of governesses. Seeing them so deserted she added them to her list of "children". By 1788, when Hester was twelve, the eldest boy, Philip Henry, was already Lord Mahon, and was always referred to by the family as Mahon, as if it were his christian name. He was a sturdy, good looking boy of seven. Charles, the next boy was three, and James a baby.

Meanwhile, the 3rd Earl was busy with Wilberforce over the anti-Slave Trade Bill. It was Stanhope, the passionate believer in freedom, who presented it to the House of Lords, and managed, despite opposition, to get it through in July 1788. In this year too there started a great trial that was to drag on for years – the impeachment of Warren Hastings for alleged misappropriation of funds while he was Governor of Bengal. Though Stanhope was neither for nor against Warren Hastings as a person, he attended the trial regularly as a self-appointed watch-dog to see that the proceedings were properly carried out. For, wherever freedom of expression was concerned, and it was very much so in this trial, the 3rd Earl felt it his duty to be there.

Hester also went to the trial; but her reactions were somewhat different; and her recollections, as told to Dr. Meryon many years later, had a different significance:

"I can recollect, when I was ten or twelve years old, going to Hastings's trial. My garter somehow came off, and was picked up by Lord Grey, then a young man. At this hour, as if it were before me in a picture, I can see his handsome but very pale face, his broad forehead; his corbeau coat, with cut-steel buttons; his white satin waistcoat and breeches, and the buckles in his shoes. He saw from whom the garter fell, but, observing my confusion, did not wish to increase it, and, with infinite delicacy, gave the garter to the person who sat there to serve tea and coffee.''

To the lure of France was being added a new one: the fascination of handsome men. Like her love for foreign countries, this fascination was to last a long time.

Charles, 3rd Earl Stanhope. An eccentric, possibly a genius. His very left-wing political ideas brought him trouble. He was a great one for "freedom", yet ruled his family like a despot. (*Frank Hemel*)

CHAPTER FOUR

THE FIRST GET-AWAY

On 14th July 1789 a Parisian mob stormed the great fortress of the Bastille and captured it after a fierce struggle. It had long been used as a political prison, and the victorious attackers immediately opened all the cells to free the prisoners. Those who opposed the Ancien Régime, or had merely fallen into disfavour with the Monarch — or more often (especially in the time of Louis XV) his mistresses — were thrown, usually without trial, into the Bastille; there they were left to languish for years, sometimes for life. When the more moderate Louis XVI succeeded to the throne some of the worst practices of his predecessor were abandoned, but even Louis XVI could not close the Bastille.

It needed a wild mob to strike this symbolic blow against the established order in France, and the effect upon France's neighbours was immediate. Left-wing elements, who for years had been absorbing the radical teachings of republican preachers, felt the time had at last come for a complete reversal of the old order and for its replacement by new liberal ideas. Poets like the nineteen-year-old William Wordsworth, and artists like thirty-two-year-old William Blake, joined with left-wing politicians to greet the new spirit of liberty; and among the most vociferous Charles, 3rd Earl of Stanhope. It was the culmination of all his hopes, and was to have a devastating effect upon the lives of his children.

On 4th November 1789, the Revolution Society, of which Stanhope was a prominent member, met in order to welcome the Revolution in France and passed a resolution expressing the hope

25

that the relationship between England and France would be improved by the advent of the new spirit of liberty in France. On 14th July 1790, first anniversary of the Fall of the Bastille, the Society went even further. Six-hundred-and-fifty-two members met for dinner at the Crown and Anchor Tavern. Each wore the red, white and blue cockade of the Revolution; and the centre piece of the main table was a large stone brought over to England from the ruins of the old Bastille fortress. Stanhope was Chairman and made what was called at the time "a pointed speech" in praise of the new regime in France; while the playwright Sheridan proposed a resolution rejoicing in "the establishment and confirmation of liberty in France", noting with pleasure "the sentiments of amity and goodwill which appear to pervade that country towards this". Horne Tooke and others made their contributions. Charles Stanhope's health was drunk and the exuberant aristocrat sent off to the Duc de la Rochefoucauld a letter of congratulations from the Society, and asked the Duke to present it to the National Assembly in Paris.

Treilhard, President of the National Assembly, replied on 28th July 1790:

> "It is fitting, my Lord, in a country in which liberty may be said to be a natural inheritance that the French Revolution should be correctly appreciated. Shall we see the glorious day when governments will be animated only by humbleness and good faith? It is men like you, my Lord, and the fine members of your Society who will hasten this new revolution. Your lofty thoughts will then encompass the world."

Despite these fine words, however, the touchy 3rd Earl soon quarrelled with the Revolution Society over a General Meeting resolution automatically binding all members to the views of the Society whether they really approved of them or not. This did not mean that he changed his revolutionary views. On the contrary, they were increased. He began to put some of them into practice where his family and children were concerned. Whereas he had long believed that book education was bad for children, especially girls, he now preached that only manual labour was honourable.

He stopped what little education his children were receiving and encouraged them into taking an interest in manual work, and on a few occasions obliged Hester to go out on to the common and help look after the turkeys. This was, no doubt, for educational rather than practical reasons, so that this over well-bred young lady could see how "the other half" lived. In the same way, he apprenticed his eldest son to the local blacksmith so that he could master a useful trade. These token enforcements remained, however, in the minds of his children for life.

More distressing, perhaps, was his insistence that the girls should wear plain and unattractive clothes. Liberty, equality and fraternity could not, he felt, go hand in hand with fine clothes. This great freedom-lover of a man, was, where his family was concerned, the greatest despot imaginable. "My father", recorded Hester, "always checked any propensity to finery in dress. If any of us happened to look better than usual in a particular hat or frock, he was sure to have it put away the next day, and to have something coarse substituted in its place."

Sometimes, in what the family called "one of his republican fits", he would go really too far; such as, for example, when he decided that he would no longer keep any carriages or horses. Hester told her doctor:

> "Poor Lady Stanhope was quite unhappy about it: but when the whole family was looking glum and sulky, I thought of a way to set all right again. I got myself a pair of stilts, and out I stumped down a dirty lane, where my father, who was always spying about through his glass, could see me.
>
> "So when I came home, he said to me:
>
> " 'Why little girl, what have you been about? Where was it I saw you going upon a pair of — the devil knows what? — eh, girl?'
>
> "Oh! papa, I thought, as you had laid down your horses, I would take a walk through the mud on stilts; for you know, Papa, I don't mind mud or anything — 'tis poor Lady Stanhope who feels these things; for she has always been accustomed to her carriage, and her health is not very good.
>
> "'What's that you say, little girl', said my father, turning his eyes away from me; and, after a pause, 'Well, little girl, what would you say if I brought a carriage again for Lady Stanhope?'
>
> "Why papa, I would say it was very kind of you.

" 'Well, well', he observed, 'we will see; but, damn it! no armorial bearings.'

"So, some time afterwards, down came a new carriage and new horses from London; and thus, by a little innocent frolic, I made all parties happy again."

It is not surprising that the aristocratic families in the neighbourhood began calling the house "Democracy Hall"; while the 3rd Earl's friends as well as his enemies referred to him as "The Jacobin Earl". He, himself, however, preferred to call himself "Citizen Stanhope", and indeed signed his letters "fellow-citizen".

But the early euphoria engendered by the French Revolution soon evaporated. Mirabeau, who might have kept the Revolution on constitutional lines, died. Foolish Louis XVI attempted to flee Paris on 21st June 1791 and was arrested at Varennes near the Belgian frontier. War broke out between France and Austria in April 1792, and when Talleyrand, the French envoy in London, asked Stanhope to find out whether England would mediate between the warring nations Pitt would not consider the idea. The situation was too grave for an "outsider" such as the 3rd Earl to have influence. Both England and Revolutionary France were on a collision course. Each event brought war closer. The execution of Louis XVI on 21st January 1793, the invasion of the Austrian-held Netherlands, where Britain had an obligation under the Treaty of Utrecht, and finally the opening of the Scheldt by the French, in defiance of the Peace of Westphalia, made war inevitable. In February 1793 France declared war on Great Britain and Holland; and found herself almost at once fighting fifteen countries including, in addition to England, Holland, Austria, Prussia, Spain and Sardinia, then an independent and somewhat powerful country.

Though the 3rd Earl's sympathies were with the French, he was still busy with his scientific experiments. Watt's steam engine had appeared in 1782, and Charles Stanhope was fascinated by its possibilities. He had already produced, a few years before war broke out, a steam carriage. It had been tested, for some odd reason, on the Calais–Boulogne road. Lord Holland had been unkind enough to say that it "ran uphill with extraordinary rapidity, got along with some difficulty on plain ground, but came to a dead stop at every descent". It never got beyond the experimental stage.

But the Earl's real interest was in the ships he tested on the lake at Chevening. He was still hoping to produce a ship that could move without the assistance of wind or tide. He had experimented with a "vibrator" or "self-feathering paddle", which, as its name indicated, was a huge machine-driven paddle that opened out when being pushed back, thus forcing away the greatest amount of water; and folded back on the return stroke, thus affording the least resistance to the forward-gliding ship. It was ingenious, but slow and extremely cumbersome.

He had communicated with Boulton and Watt on the use of steam in ships in 1789, and by 1793, with the help of Robert Walker, designed a steam-driven boat. He had even managed to interest the Admiralty in the project; and got permission to build his ship, but only on condition that he put up £6,000 of his own money as a guarantee, which would be forfeited if it did not work.

His ship, the "Kent" (200 tons), was finally lauched on 30th March 1793. Grizel, Dowager Lady Stanhope, now 74, wrote to her old pen-friend Lady Chatham:

> ". . . the expected ship was launched yesterday at Rother-hythe with great success and named the "Kent". The indefatigable inventor and builder, with Lady Stanhope and all his young family present, and all happy and pleased . . ."

Although proud of her son's achievement, the astute old lady added that she thought it would probably be of great public use. "I say probably for who'll venture to say more of any thing." Whatever her misgivings about the practical value of her gifted son's inventions, she had no doubt of the happiness it brought to Hester, her sisters and half-brothers. In the same letter to Lady Chatham she wrote:

> "I fancy you'll easily suppose the joy of the young people to show their eagerness for its succeeding, having been witness to great part of the fatigue and trouble it had given their father, the being on the Thames in a boat down to Greenwich where he accompanied them, after he had sailed in his ship, in short the whole may perhaps be marked in their calendar as one of the happiest days of their lives."

It would be two years before even the boilers were installed in the "Kent", that Charles Stanhope would have to raise his bond from £6,000 to £9,000, which he never recovered; and that the sharp, ever critical Lord Holland was to remark that Stanhope was building a ship to carry coal from Newcastle to London, which would use up all its cargo before it reached its destination.

But in 1794 a new trouble was to beset the family. Charles Stanhope had engaged as secretary a revolutionary and controversial clergyman called Jeremiah Joyce, the author of "Scientific Dialogues". This gentleman, apart from his secretarial work, was responsible for the education of Stanhope's sons, including Mahon, the heir. Charles Stanhope refused to send any of them to school, believing that schools, particularly public schools like Eton, distorted young minds. Jeremiah Joyce, with his good republican principles, would give the boys what formal education they required.

One morning, as Joyce was getting up and as Hester later put it "was just blowing his nose, as people do the moment before they come down to breakfast" there was a loud knock on the front door, and immediately two Government officers broke into the house. Armed with a warrant they arrested the unfortunate Jeremiah Joyce on a charge of treason. The war with France was then going extremely badly and anyone suspected of French or revolutionary opinions was in danger of arrest and worse. Joyce was found guilty of the charge — though he was almost certainly innocent — and sent to prison.

Stanhope also came under suspicion of treason and Pitt warned him to keep away from revolutionary meetings. One day, on returning to the house in Mansfield Street which Stanhope now owned, he found it surrounded by a mob of incensed citizens, demonstrating against him. He tried to remonstrate with them, but they hurled themselves at the house, broke into it and set it on fire. The 3rd Earl only managed to escape by clambering over the roofs.

This violent incident had an enormous effect on Hester. Although she was not there at the time, she heard all about it at Chevening. Somewhere in her young girl's mind began to grow the belief, soon to be a conviction, that her father would one day go too far, and find himself, like poor Jeremiah Joyce, behind bars for his political views. She was already firmly convinced that the future well-being of her sisters and half-brothers depended solely upon her; now, to her heavy, if self-imposed, family responsibilities, she added that of her wayward father. She was particularly afraid that he would share the fate of Lord Thanet, Ferguson and others who were thrown into gaol for treason. She explained this fear, many years later, to Dr. Meryon, adding: ". . . and I said, 'If my father has not a prop somewhere, he will share the same fate.' " She did not mean that she was to be his prop, but it was up to her to find one for him, in order to stop him damaging himself.

But her father continued doggedly on his way. When, in May 1794, at the height of Warren Hastings' impeachment, the Government abolished for a time the Habeas Corpus Act, Stanhope refused to attend the trial any longer, declaring that "in a country where there is no security of personal freedom, courts of justice lose all their native dignity and become the shadows and forms only of what they represent".

When Joyce was finally released in December 1794, Charles Stanhope immediately gave a huge ball at Chevening to celebrate the fact. There were 400 guests, mainly local county families, and dancing and feasting went on all night. In the centre of the ballroom was a group of emblematic figures, with the words THE RIGHTS OF JURIES inscribed above them. It was, as the "Gentleman's Magazine" recorded at the time, "a display of Old English hospitality, revived with the best characteristic of Englishmen, the love of liberty". It was also Hester's "coming out" party. She was now twenty and it seemed to the 3rd Earl an excellent opportunity to launch his eldest daughter on society; for, though he held such strong republican views, he expected that the least his daughters could do was to marry well.

The following year, in January 1795, he put up a motion in the House of Lords declaring that "this country ought not, and will not, interfere in the internal affairs of France . . .". He came under violent verbal attack. Not only his views but his character and habits were abused. Doubts were voiced on his right to call himself a peer and an Englishman. Jacobism, it was claimed, had deprived him of his senses. Even his friends, in the House of Lords, who accepted that his views were "pure" took fright and refused to vote for him.

When it came to the vote, he lost the division by 61 to 1, the 1 being himself. From then onwards he referred to himself as The Minority of One. A medal was struck containing the words "Stanhope the friend of Trial by Jury, Liberty of the Press, Parliamentary Reform, Annual Parliaments, Habeas Corpus Act, Abolition of Sinecures, and of a Speedy Peace with France". In protest against Parliament, he then withdrew (his Minority of One proudly intact) and took no further active interest in the House of Lords for the next five years.

But he had not finished with Jeremiah Joyce. The Chevening Ball had shown the country where his sympathies lay. Now it was time to show the town. He engaged a room at the Crown and Anchor Tavern and invited Joyce and other suspects who had been unconditionally released to dinner. As President, he made a speech rejoicing in the release of the innocent men, reaffirming his belief in the freedoms contained on the Stanhope medal.

To Hester, however, these new activities, and the increasing political isolation of her father, only added to her apprehension. She felt sure now that the whole future of the family lay in her hands. Grizel, her grandmother on her father's side, was too old and easy-going to take up the challenge; Lady Chatham, her grandmother on her mother's side, too far away in Somerset; and Louise, her stepmother, too interested in her social round, and too remote even to be approached.

In 1796 the County of Kent resounded with the news that Lord Romney was to hold a Review. It was to be the social highlight of the season, for the King and Queen would be there. Hester was determined to go. The 3rd Earl was equally determined that she should not go, for he objected, on principle, to military displays. So Hester had to resort to subterfuge. "Nobody ever saw much of me", she confided many years later to Dr. Meryon, "until Lord Romney's review. I was obliged to play a trick on my father to get there. I pretended the day before, that I wanted to pay a visit to the Miss Crumps, and then went from their house to Lord Romney's. Though all the gentry of Kent was there, my father never knew, or was supposed not to have known, that I had been there."

It was her first appearance in high society, and she was a sensation. Her youthfulness, her height (she was six feet tall), her enormous energy, freshness and a kind of disarming directness of approach, made her stand out in that bewigged, powdered and snide society.

To her it was a wonderful world, full of lovely girls of the time, attracted to these gaily attired men, so different with their manliness, panache and dash, to the staid gentry of her county, or the innuendo-speaking courtiers. But whereas most young ladies adopted a simpering eyelid fluttering attitude in the hope of attracting their attention, Hester's approach was very different, as the following incident, which she subsequently recounted to Dr. Meryon, shows only too well:

"It was at that review that I was talking to some officers and something led me to saying: 'I can't bear men who are governed by their wives, as Sir A. H. . . . is; a woman of sense, even if she did govern her husband, would not let it be seen: it is odious in my opinion.'

"And I went on in this strain, whilst poor Sir A himself, whom I did not know, but had only heard spoken of, was standing by all the time. I saw a dreadful consternation in the bystanders, but I went on.

"At last someone – taking commiseration on him, I suppose – said, 'Lady Hester, will you allow me to introduce Sir A. H. . . . to you, who is desirous of making your acquaintance.'

"Sir A very politely thanked me for the advice I had given him; and I answered something about the regard my brother had for him, and there the matter ended."

"The King" [she added] "took great notice of me, and, I believe, always after liked me personally. Whenever I was talking to the dukes, he was sure to come towards us. 'Where is she?', he would cry; 'Where is she? I hear them laugh, and where they are laughing I must go too.'

"Then, as he came nearer, he would observe, 'If you have anything to finish I won't come yet – I'll come in a quarter of an hour.'

"When he was going away from Lord Romney's, he wanted to put me bodkin [i.e. squeezed between two people] between himself and the Queen; and when the Queen had got into the carriage, he said to her, 'My dear, Lady Hester is going to ride bodkin with us: I am going to take her away from Democracy Hall.'

"But the old Queen observed in a rather prim manner, that I had not got my maid with me, and that it would be inconvenient for me to go at such a short notice: so I remained."

Despite the King's joking suggestion that he would take her away from Democracy Hall, Hester liked the country. "At the back of the inn, on Sevenoaks Common", she later told her doctor, "stood a house, which, for a residence for myself, I should prefer to any one I have ever yet seen. It was a perfectly elegant, light, and commodious building, with an oval drawing-room, and two boudoirs in the corners, with a window to each on the conservatory. When I visited there, it was inhabited by three old maids, one of whom was my friend. What good ale and nice luncheons I have had there many a time! What good cheese, what excellent apples and pears, and what rounds of boiled beef!"

So perhaps it was the warm welcome and excellent fare that attracted her as much as the house itself. She was, anyhow, accustomed to travelling about the countryside on horseback, accompanied only by her groom.

That she must have been a fine horsewoman, can be gathered from the following account of an incident on one of these journeys:

"I remember, when Colonel Shadwell commanded the district, that, one day, in a pelting shower of rain, he was riding up Madamscourt Hill, as I was crossing at the bottom, going home towards Chevening with my handsome groom, Tom, a boy who was the natural son of a baronet. I saw Colonel Shadwell's groom's horse about a couple of hundred yards from me, and, struck with its beauty, I turned up the hill, resolving to pass them and get a look at it. I accordingly quickened my pace, and, in going by, gave a good look at the horse, then at the grrom, then at the master, who was on a sorry nag. The colonel eyed me as I passed; and I, taking advantage of a low part in the hedge, put my horse to it, leaped over, and disappeared in an instant. The colonel found out who I was, and afterwards made such a fuss at the mess about my equestrian powers, that nothing could be like it. I was toasted there every day."

It was Lucy, the Madonna-like, pretty, sweet, sixteen-year-old girl who, in the end, was the first to break away from the

Chevening thraldom. For some time now, a twenty-seven-year-old apothecary, or pharmaceutical chemist, called Thomas Taylor, came to Chevening to give drugs and supervise any of the numerous bleedings among the staff that were thought necessary. At a time when even doctors were considered little more than servants — the days of the saw-bone and quack were still very close — a chemist's assistant from Sevenoaks was less than nothing. However, when Lucy announced her intention of marrying Taylor, the 3rd Earl wrote to a friend of his, William Smith, a Member of Parliament, on 25th January 1796: "My youngest daughter Lucy is soon going to be married to a most worthy young man of her own choosing. Her mind is liberal, and she despises Rank and *Aristocracy*, as much as I do. I have seen much, both here and abroad, of the middling classes; and I have observed, by far, more happiness there, as well as virtue, than amongst those Ranks of Men who insolently term themselves their *betters*. Her object is Felicity, and I trust she will find it. She has behaved with the greatest propriety, and with a becoming confidence due to an affectionate Father."

James Gilray, in a brilliant but unkind cartoon of the time, shows the lean-faced 3rd Earl handing Lucy over in marriage to young Taylor, who is represented by a chemist's mortar and pestle which had been given legs and arms, but no head. Behind, dressed as a clergyman and holding a "bible" entitled "Rights of Man" stands Charles James Fox, while to the right is his "assistant" Richard Sheridan. On the wall behind is a picture entitled "Shrine of Equality" depicting a guillontine at work. The whole cartoon is entitled "Democratic Levelling — Alliance à la Francaise or The Union of the Coronet and Clyster Pipe".

Hester, in her search for help for her family, now turned to the one man who could, in fact, help her — her mother's brother, William Pitt, the Prime Minister. He was then thirty-seven, unmarried and had been Prime Minister for the past thirteen years; ever since, in fact, that extraordinary day in 1783 when, to the shouts of derision of the Opposition, he had agreed to form a Government at the age of twenty-four. Very few Members of Parliament, his rivals Fox and North least of all, had thought he would last more than a few weeks. Now he was almost Parliament itself.

He still retained the haughty look he had inherited from the Grenvilles and was still tall and slim. With his "egg-head" forehead, and sardonic slightly turned down mouth, he gave the impression of cool, perpetual self-control, as if her were surveying the world around him from a great and special distance. Yet the wit that was always close to the surface, and the sharp intelligence of his eye captivated all who met him.

Pitt responded to Hester's appeal. The plight of the three young girls, left to Louisa's uncaring attention, and having to endure in private the vagaries of the 3rd Earl that he, Pitt, had endured in public, touched him. He allowed Griselda to stay at a cottage on his estate at Walmer Castle, and to there she fled in the same year that Lucy got married; a fact that made the 3rd Earl compare himself, rather inappropriately, to Lear.

It was while Griselda was on a visit to Ramsgate that she met an army officer named John Tickell, or Tekell as his name was sometimes spelt. They fell in love and decided to get married. Griselda wrote to her Chatham grandmother about the proposed event in March 1800:

> "My dear Lady Chatham,
>
>   I wrote to Papa yesterday morning; I said I did not come to a decision of importance without thinking it proper to inform him of it, that I was going to be married to Mr. T whom I had seen at Ramsgate, and where the acquaintance between us was formed that has since been renewed, that I would be obliged to him to inform Grandmama & I earnestly hoped it would meet with his approbation, & I'd be happy to hear from him."

Although the 3rd Earl did not appear to be enthusiastic over the choice of his second daughter, he wrote that he wished she "may be happy"; he added: "He is nearly a Stranger to me. I know nothing about his character, his Principles either public or private, his companions, his circumstances." However, he thought he was a "very good-natured man, which is a most valuable and important quality".

The "good-natured man", however, had a flaw. He had made out that he had a considerable income, whereas, in fact, he had none; and there was some trouble over £10,000 that disappeared, or perhaps never existed. Griselda broke off the engagement, and in an undated letter to Pitt, though obviously written at the time,

Griselda's younger sister, Lucy, wrote:

"Having heard from Hester within these few days that a message has been sent to G. mama & Mrs. Stapleton by an old friend of theirs stating that Mr. Tekell is a man of lost character, has spent all he has, sold the reversion of all he is ever likely to have, one sister married very low, & the other an improper character, and that you are likewise informed of these particulars I think it is incumbent on me to inform you how I conceive the affair stood when Griselda left Wickham; being totally ignorant of what passed between you when she was last in Town.

"After parting with Mr. T she told me, in tears, she was the most unfortunate of beings; for at the very moment she saw the necessity of their parting her esteem was doubled for him. She added that altho' she was determined never to marry him Till [since] she saw there was no longer a chance of Them being left, with what she considered not a bare sufficiency, her ever settling was entirely out of the question."

However, despite Griselda's strong affirmation that she would never marry, Lucy did not feel too sure. She continued her letter to Pitt:

"I have other reasons for wishing her to be informed of the truth as I conceive if she *now* continues seeing him it may prove a detriment to her in the world. When he took leave of her here he promised her it shd be for the last time, yet if he is the sort of man report says he is, you may judge if he is likely to keep his word."

Pitt, however, was not as worried as Lucy was about Griselda's choice. Realizing, perhaps, that an imperfect Tickell was better than no Tickell, he persuaded a not unwilling Griselda to change her mind; and they were duly and happily married.

CHAPTER FIVE

ANOTHER ESCAPE

Following the escape of the two younger girls from "Democracy" Hall Hester's life became more liberal. She continued to live at Chevening, mainly to keep guard over her three half-brothers. Mahon, "incomparable" Mahon as she called him, was growing into a young man. Tall and lanky like his father, he had the same arrogance, but in his case there was nothing to be arrogant about. The 3rd Earl had deliberately kept him under-educated. Apart from apprenticing him to the local blacksmith, he had made quite sure that the young man should have no right-wing views by giving him left-wing tutors like Jeremiah Joyce, or ridiculous ones like Dr. Cranford, nicknamed "Old Chrystalpate" by the boys, who swore continuously at his pupils or strode purposefully across the countryside like, as grandmother Grizel put it, a packman − indeed she was convinced he had once been one.

The 3rd Earl's reason for keeping his son and heir under-educated was simple: he wanted to be rid once and for all of the title. But he alone could not renounce it. His heir also had to agree that it should be discontinued, and the heir could only do this after the age of twenty-one. In the meantime, Mahon had to be kept under control.

Hester lost no time. She had already persuaded Pitt to find her sister Lucy's husband, ex-apothecary Thomas Taylor, the position of Controller-General in the Customs Service. This incensed the 3rd Earl, for he disapproved, as he never ceased to proclaim to all and sundry, of any form of government office. So annoyed was he, in fact, that he broke off all relationships with his youngest daughter and her husband, a fact that did not seem to trouble the young couple, for they remained as happy together as ever. Hester also appealed to Pitt for help with the difficult Griselda and her awkward, impoverished husband. Pitt gave the couple money, and allowed them to stay on indefinitely at the cottage at Walmer.

But Mahon was the main problem. The poor young man was so circumscribed, that he could not even call on his half-sister Griselda at her Walmer cottage without pretending that he was hunting butterflies. Not that Griselda could do much except offer sympathy. It was to Hester that he turned for help; and through Hester, to William Pitt. He advised the young man to refuse to give his permission to break the entailment on the Chevening Estate. Hester, at the same time encouraged him to keep his independence. She felt herself personally responsible for his future and that of the two younger brothers, and although she could not see what, at the moment, could be done about them, she would not abandon them.

Thus began, at Chevening, a curious duplicity. While Mahon and his brothers ostensibly followed the line of conduct laid down by the 3rd Earl and their tutors, and Hester behaved with all the correctness of a dutiful elder daughter, Hester organized secret meetings at Chevening between the four of them. Plans for the "release of the prisoners" were discussed, and messages from Pitt and other members of the family were delivered by Hester. Replies were composed and given to the elder sister to be conveyed back to those who sent them. Hester enjoyed the intrigue, and the sense of importance and power she had. She was also genuinely concerned about her half-brothers, and felt that her father's treatment of them was another folly to be corrected. The only member of the family who appears not to have been in the conspiracy was Grizel Stanhope, at the Dower House across the Park. Although she loved her grandchildren, she would not put their interest above that of her beloved son, Charles, however erratic the 3rd Earl might appear to be.

When Hester was in London, Mahon would write secretly to her reminding her of his need for help, ". . . I desire more anxiously", he wrote on one occasion, "and even more ardently than ever to be *freed* from this bondage under which I have so long groaned". Meanwhile she continued to be seen at London dances and social gatherings, cheerfully making female enemies wherever she went. La Duchesse de Gontant, an aristocratic refugee from France, recounts in her memoirs how she met Hester at a fancy dress party given by Lady Stafford in her gardens overlooking the Thames:

"We had gone disguised as fortune-tellers. Mrs. Wilmot carried off her role with great verve, but had the unfortunate idea of bringing a real live donkey with her. The music frightened the animal, and it began to bray so loudly that Mrs. Wilmot could not get out a single word. Everyone around us began laughing, but all we could do was to hide our blushes.

"But this wasn't all. Before we left, Mr. Pitt brought to Mrs. Pole his niece, Lady Esther [sic] Stanhope, and begged her to be her chaperone, as she was only just coming out. But it was not easy; Lady Esther was in a bad temper; she did not like her uncle's suggestion; however, there was nothing she could do but join us.

"Her fancy dress had nothing feminine about it, except the mask. This was the first time I had seen her. She was very tall, very thin, very autocratic and independent-minded. When she saw that our donkey was 'talking' while we remained silent, she remarked without the slightest compunction that we were more stupid than our donkey."

With such remarks and others like it that she left behind her, from her very first appearance in society, it is not surprising that Hester was thoroughly disliked, and even hated, by the elegant and catty society ladies of the time. They took their revenge by spreading stories about her behaviour with men, a fact that was made easier by her quite open and obvious preference for men's rather than women's company. But it would seem, at least at this time, that she contented herself with nothing more than the mild flirtations expected of young ladies.

By 1800 Hester's divided loyalties made it impossible for her to stay on at Chevening. She loved the place, and was happiest when she could ride across the Kent countryside. But she was more and more concerned about Mahon. He was nineteen and would soon be of age, but it was not just the thought of losing the title that worried her, for he was a young man utterly untrained to take any part in life, except as a blacksmith, for which he was physically unsuited. A solution must be found to give him some kind of real education.

Then there was her father. Despite everything, she loved him, perhaps the only one of his children to do so. He and she were really very alike and could understand each other. She disliked his Jacobin views, but could appreciate them. She disliked his revolutionary associations but could sympathize with the views of Tom Paine and Horne Tooke. In 1800 the 3rd Earl had returned to the House of Lords, and with his usual unco-ordinated passion had pressed for peace with France, pointing out that the misery among the British people was due to stress of war. He even used figures of George Rose, Secretary of the Treasury, to prove his point. Thus, he claimed, any dispute would be "a difference of opinion between ministers and George Rose and not between ministers and Citizen Stanhope". This motion was defeated, but instead of having his customary Minority of One, he did have one supporter this time, thus recording a hundred percent increase in his political popularity. He had also long supported Pitt in the politically unpopular subject of Catholic emancipation, and had stated his firm belief, since 1788, that every man should be allowed freedom of religious belief. He had never wavered over the years, even though this further "heresy" added to the distrust in which his views were held.

His scientific experiments were not going well either. His beloved ship the "Kent", launched so optimistically and happily in 1793, had run into all kinds of trouble. Her sea trials had been continually delayed, and it was not until four years afterwards, on 5th March, 1797, that they finally took place. Even then the special boilers Stanhope had installed were not used. Only his vibrators, or oars, were tested and they were hand-operated and employed only to ferry the ship downstream from Deptford.

The Navy Board was opposed to the use of steam as a means of propelling ships, and stated categorically in its report of 6th May 1797, that "an invention of this kind could never be applied to any advantageous purpose in His Majesty's Navy". It was useless for Stanhope for prophesy, as he frequently did, that one day in the near future steamships would sail across the Atlantic to America. His "wild" pronouncements merely caused immense hilarity. In January 1798, the Admiralty curtly informed him that he must

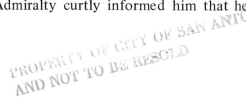

discontinue his experiments, and in November of the same year the unused boilers were removed from the ship. She was rigged with sails, armed with fourteen twelve-pounders, and became a gunboat.

The blow seems, at least temporarily, to have deprived the 3rd Earl of much of his inventiveness, although he returned to the steamship idea, equally unsuccessfully, later in his life. He had spent twenty years dreaming, planning and actually building a steam-propelled ship. Now, at the age of forty-seven, all his work had come to nothing. Nor had he succeeded in his political or private life. No wonder he brooded and flew into unaccountable rages. With all his intelligence, and even genius, he was reduced to pacing impatiently the corridors of Chevening.

To Hester, trying to find a way of releasing Mahon from his "prison" and knowing that if she succeeded, her father would be even further hurt, the tension became unendurable. It was with gratitude that she accepted the invitation of her Chatham grandmother to make her home with her at Burton Pynsent, near Curry Rivel, Langport, Somerset.

Burton Pynsent had come into the possession of the Pitt family in a curious way. Sir William Pynsent was a wealthy West Country baronet, and had been a Member of Parliament during Queen Anne's reign. He had, however, been utterly disgusted when the government agreed to the Treaty of Utrecht in 1713. He had promptly resigned from Parliament, and retired to his estate at Burton Pynsent. There he had lived, as something of a recluse, for the next fifty years. Then his admiration for Chatham, who as "Mr. Secretary Pitt" had resigned in 1761 when the Cabinet refused to go to war with France and Spain, made him will his whole property to the statesman; this despite the fact that, as far as is known, the two men never met. After Sir William died on 12th January 1765, Chatham found himself the possessor of a large estate in Somerset and an income of £3,000 a year. The will was contested, and it was six years before Chatham could be sure the property was his. After his death Lady Chatham had retired there, and it was from here that the answers to those many letters written by Grizel Stanhope about the happenings at Chevening had come.

It was a large rambling house, built at different periods and in different styles. Chatham himself had added a magnificent library.

Lady Chatham had a special "bird-room" built where she could sit listening to the twittering of the brightly coloured birds as they flew about the room from branch to artificial branch. "Capability" Brown was engaged to remodel the gardens and to open up the vistas that overlooked Sedgemoor, with distant views to the Quantocks, the Bristol Channel and the Welsh Hills. It was "Capability" Brown who ordered the planting of a hundred cedars that were to last longer than the house — with the exception of Chatham's library.

It was here that Hester now came to live, riding her black mare across the country and planning the escape from Chevening of her "incomparable" Mahon. She enrolled everybody she could. Lady Chatham, who adored her and would do anything for her, backed her full-heartedly, as did Pitt and the Grenville side of the family. The only members of the family who were kept unaware of the plans were Grizel, her Stanhope grandmother, who would never countenance any act of "treason" against her beloved son Charles; and, for their own sakes, the Mahon's two younger brothers, Charles and James.

After much careful thought, Hester decided that the only solution was to smuggle Mahon out of the country and send him, under an assumed name, to a foreign university where he could make up for some of his lost education. No sooner had she thought up this odd, romantic and impractical-sounding scheme, than she began to implement it.

"Money", she wrote later to Lord Glastonbury, "you know, was a very essential article; that has been liberally supplied by Sir Francis Burdett, though he chose to be ignorant of the plan it was to be adopted for, and gave it into the hands of a third person."

She decided to send Mahon to Erlanger University, Germany. Jackson, who had visited the place, had provided letters of introduction to Professor Beyer, "a man of great ability and most extensive knowledge", and to the Margravine of Brandenburg — Baireuth, who held court there. Jackson also provided Mahon with a passport. The escape was planned to take place early in 1801, and owing to Mahon's complete ignorance of the world, everything had to be explained to him in detail; with a change of name he finally escaped.

Hester, in a letter to Lord Glastonbury, tells what happened then:

"Mahon has a man with him, in capacity of a servant, whose fidelity I can rely on; this man, with directions from me, accomplished Mahon's escape from Chevening most astonishingly, for, though he was persued a few hours, no tidings could be had, and till this moment they have never been able to trace him one step."

The escape was completely successful. The family, including Pitt, were delighted. To Jackson, she wrote:

"This evening's post has not only brought me your letter, but a volume from Mr. Pitt. I did not tell you, but I had written to him a few days ago being rather tired of *suspense*, and he says he received my letter and Mahon's at the same time. Mr. Pitt speaks in the highest terms of approbation of all that has been done, which pleases one mightily and gives me every assurance that both now and hereafter he will do everything in his power for dear Mahon. . . ."

She also wrote to her uncle Charles, 8th Earl of Haddington, justifying her conduct. This was necessary since she had reason to believe that her grandmother, Grizel, Charles's aunt, would not approve of any action that upset the 3rd Earl. He was, after all, Grizel's sole surviving son. She wrote:

"It was impossible that anything legal should be done for Mahon while under age, yet it was of great importance he should be fitted by a liberal education for some public life against that point arrived. Had he been sent to College, he could have been brought back by his father, by going abroad he will be able to evade any researches made after him . . . A foreign University was then the only medium through which Mahon could receive education."

Haddington's reception of the news of Mahon's escape was cool. While stating that he was "truly happy" that Mahon was "in all probability comfortably and advantageously settled", he did, however, add:

"Your dear mother, of whom you can have but a faint remembrance, if at all . . . was a woman rarely to be met with, wise, temperate, and prudent, by nature cheerful and without levity, a warm friend, and free from all the petty vices that attend little minds. I am sure if she could now communicate her ideas, her advice to you would be to act steadily, without fear, when you had well considered what was to be done; to do all the good within your reach in the present circumstances of your family, and when it should seem helpless and out of reach, to preserve as much as possible a prudent silence to all but tried friends. . . ."

Hester duly thanked Haddington for his advice, adding that Lady Chatham had asked if she might keep the letter because "of the character it contains of my dear Mother", Lady Chatham's daughter. To Jackson, she wrote that she had received "the prettiest and most sensible letter in the world from Lord Haddington" and added that she thought her uncle's advice was "vastly good".

She received ecstatic letters from Mahon. In a letter to Lord Glastonbury she wrote:

"His astonishment, his happiness, and gratitude to his friends, is expressed so naturally and with so much feeling, it is quite delightful. Dear fellow! if he had been ten times my own brother I could not have been more anxious, more interested about him. . . . Charming, charming, incomparable Mahon!"

Her only real concern now was for the well-being of Mahon's two brothers, Charles and James; for, she wrote: ". . . if some precautions are not taken they will be flogged to death to make them confess what they are really ignorant". She had experienced her father's fury before. "The Logician", as she called him, had once put a knife to her throat. But she had felt no fear; "only pity for the arm that held it". However, ". . . this was a sort of feeling I should rather not again experience".

Her father's reaction, however, was less violent than expected, for she adds; ". . . therefore the understanding that he remains quiet, and employs others, is a great satisfaction to me. Otherwise I should be in some *dread* of seeing him here and going through some of those scenes which I have unfortunately so often before witnessed."

Mahon very quickly took to his new life. In April 1801 Hester wrote to Jackson:

"Mahon writes in high spirits. Says he is much pleased with the Professor (who in fact is an excellent creature, and having travelled a good deal is more a man of the world than the generality of Professors) that he was entered at the University and was forthwith to begin his studies. He had been introduced to the Margravine, and had dined with her. . . .

"The Margravine writes me a long letter, and begins with her benediction for having saved a young plant (as she calls Mahon) from the *infernal* principles of Jacobinism. She expresses herself in the highest terms of approbation of him, and her surprise (she is an admirable judge on this point) at the ease and manliness of his address and manners. This surprise originates, of course, in what I had told her of his style of life at home. He seems to be quite familiar in French, and promises a rapid progress in German. The old lady concludes, 'Enfin, je vous promets que nous en ferons un sujet utile et honnête."

Mahon wrote to Hester from Germany on 6th April 1801:

"I send you, my dearest sister, a miniature which I beg that you will have the goodness to accept, as a small but sincere token of my unspeakable affection. I am sorry that it is not better executed and more worthy of your acceptance, but such as it is, I thought that you would wish to have my picture and I therefore send it as a mark of gratitude which I owe to you for your many kindnesses, and which I should wish to evince as well in small matters as in the greatest.

"It shall ever be the study of my life to act in such a manner as to give you reason to be satisfied with my conduct and to show the world that I am worthy of being your brother, an honour which those who have the pleasure of being personally acquainted with you will not deem inconsiderable. You know how happy and overjoyed I am at having obtained my liberty. . . ."

This was her first real exercise in the use of power; and the whole affair had gone right. She had discovered that she could influence people and get them to do things for her; that she had organizing ability and the necessary courage to take risks. Not only had she saved "incomparable Mahon" but she had struck a blow for the aristocracy. "I am an aristocrat, and I make a boast of it", she was to tell Dr. Meryon years later. Pride in her name, and the need to help others were to be two of the main driving forces of her life from now onwards.

With the successful escape of their eldest brother, Charles, now sixteen, and the youngest, James, thirteen, longed to get away from Chevening; and, like Mahon, turned to Hester for help. She promised to do what she could. But she was preoccupied for the time being with a completely different matter: at the age of twenty-four she was deep in her first real love affair – with her cousin, the second Lord Camelford.

Camelford was also a Pitt, coming from the older branch of the family. His father, a gentle and erudite man, had been made a peer in 1784, shortly after William Pitt had become Prime Minister. George III was so grateful to Pitt for taking on the burden of the premiership, that he had handed out no less than four peerages that year at Pitt's suggestion. Not that the 1st Lord Camelford was all that interested in politics. He spent his time studying, travelling and looking after his health which was not very good.

By a strange freak of fortune the second Lord Camelford was the exact opposite. Also called Thomas, after his father, he had always been big and strong. "The Cornish Hercules", Lady Chatham had called him when he was three years old, and as he grew up he developed a dare-devil streak, in complete contrast both to his parents and to his gentle sister, Anne.

He was sent to Berne and to Charterhouse, in the hope that some kind of education could be instilled into him; but he rebelled against all school work, and at the age of fourteen joined the Royal Navy and sailed as a midshipman in the frigate "Guardian" commanded by Captain Riou, bound for Botany Bay in Australia with stores for the newly established convict settlement.

The first of those adventures that were to be such a feature in young Tom's life now took place. The ship was holed by an iceberg and for months nothing was heard of the Captain and those volunteers, including Tom, who had stayed on board. Then the frigate miraculously turned up at the Cape of Good Hope. Tom was something of a hero.

But the crisis in his life occurred eight years later, on 13th

January 1798. Camelford was by now in acting charge of the sloop "Favourite" based on Antigua. When enemy ships were reported approaching the island, Camelford automatically took over command of both his ship and a frigate called the "Perdrix", despite the fact that the ship's Captain, Charles Petersen, was senior of the two. When Petersen objected, Camelford coolly shot and killed him. Although Camelford was duly court-martialled, he was acquitted, the Court accepting his contention that he acted as he did in order to put down a mutiny.

The following year, on 18th January 1799, he set off for Dover, on an incredible mission. Despite the fact that France and England were at war, he had decided to cross the Channel and make for Paris. His object was to steal charts and bring them back with him. He managed to hire a boat for twelve guineas; but the boatman took fright because it was a capital offence to embark for France. He reported the matter to the authorities and Camelford was arrested and arraigned before the Privy Council. But once again he convinced his judges that his motives were honourable.

The Admiralty, however, did not take so lenient a view. This, on top of the Antigua affair, was too much for them. He was promptly relieved of the command of his ship, a fact that put him into such a rage that he immediately resigned from the Navy altogether, no doubt much to the relief of the Sea Lords. With his chosen career at an end, Camelford set himself up in London and led the life of a rake and debauché. He soon built up a reputation for drunken wildness and unpredictability. He would think nothing of attacking complete strangers, of beating up the watch at night, and of making London talk of his escapades.

Hester was now seen a great deal with him, but whether she ever had any intention of marrying him seems doubtful. The names of many young men were linked romantically with her. Jackson had written to her early that year, from London, about the rumours of various intended marriages, ". . . and the last, not the least, Lady Hester Stanhope to Mr. Methuen, junior, of Corsham. You shall have my congratulations, but, upon Lord Lyttelton's plan, when they become due". Hester promptly replied:

> "Thank you for your news. I have been going to be married fifty times in my life; said to have been married half as often, and run away with once. But provided I have my own way, the world may have theirs and welcome. . . ."

To the recognition of her own power, and the knowledge of her
efficiency, she now added an increasing independence of mind. As
she told Jackson, she did not care what her world thought of her.
This was a bold announcement at a time when a woman's
reputation was considered vitally important, particularly if she
happened to be unmarried. Unwittingly, no doubt, she was
striking a blow for that woman's freedom that was not to occur
for over a hundred years.

So, she was seen about quite openly with her disreputable
cousin, Camelford, for the fact was that she admired him. To
begin with, he was taller than she, "tall and bony" she described
him later, "rather pale — with his head hanging generally a little on
one side". He was also adventurous, had been all over the world,
seen everything, done everything. He was courageous and not
afraid of consequences. She even defended his action in Antigua
when he killed Petersen: "He did it", she said ". . . from a quick
perception of what was right to be done, which was a sort of
instinct with him. He saw that the ship's crew was ready to
mutiny, and he stopped it at once by his resolute conduct.
Everybody at home was open-mouthed against him, until the news
came of Captain Pigot, of the "Hermione", being thrown overboard
(by his own crew) and then all the lords and ladies began to
tremble for their sons and nephews. Then nothing was too good
for Lord Camelford, and the next mutiny which took place in our
ships showed how well he had foreseen what would happen."

He was generous too. "He used to give", she recalled, "£5,000 a
year to his lawyer to distribute among distressed persons. 'The
only condition I enjoin,' he used to say, 'is not to let them know
who it comes from.'" Sometimes he would dress up as a sailor,
and using the rough, common voice that he had learnt as a seaman,
go to a tavern or ale-house and if he saw somebody in trouble ask
for his story. "He was", she was to say, "endowed with great
penetration, and if he saw the man's story was true, he would slip
fifty or a hundred pounds into his hand. . . ."

Not all his violence was due to inconsideration. In his volatile
and touchy nature there was a "Robin Hood" streak. It would
emerge at unlikely times, as Hester recalls:

"I recollect once he was driving me out in his corricle, when,
at a turnpike-gate, I saw him pay the man himself, and take
some halfpence in exchange. He turned them over two or

three times, in his hand without his glove. Well, thought I, if you like to handle dirty copper, it is a strange taste.

" 'Take the reins a moment', said he, giving them to me, and out he jumped; and before I could form the least suspicion of what he was going to do, he rushed upon the turnpike man, and seized him by the throat.

"Of course, there was a mob collected in a moment, and the high-spirited horses grew so restive that I expected nothing less than they would start off with me.

"In the midst of it all, a coach and four came to the gate.

" 'Ask what's the matter', said a simpering sort of gentleman, putting his head with an air out of the coach-window, to the footman behind.

" 'It's my Lord Camelford', replied the footman.

" 'You may drive on', was the instant ejaculation of the master, frightened out of his senses at the bare apprehension lest his lordship should turn on him.

"The row was soon over and Lord C. resumed his seat.

" 'I dare say you thought', he said very quietly, 'that I was going to put myself in a passion. But, the fact is, these rascals have barrels of bad half-pence and they pass them in change to the people who go through the gate. Some poor carter perhaps, has nothing but this change to pay for his supper; and, when he gets to his journey's end, finds he can't get his bread and cheese. The law, 'tis true, will fine them; but how is a poor devil to go to law? Where can he find time? To you and me it would not signify, but to the poor it does; and I merely wanted to teach these blackguards a lesson, by way of showing them that they cannot always play such tricks with impunity.' "

Though she claimed that she admired Camelford because he was "a true Pitt, and, like me, his blood fired at a fraud or a bad action", she liked to be seen with him precisely because of the sensation that being with him caused. She particularly enjoyed the look of anguish on the faces of William Pitt's brother and his wife. This elder brother had inherited the Chatham title and hoped that when Camelford finally got himself killed — as his endless duels and fights would inevitably bring about, even if he did not die of drink — the Pitt fortune, originally built up by "Diamond" Pitt, would come to them. The idea that it might go to Hester made them so upset that they did everything they could to dissuade her from marrying him.

But it is unlikely that she ever really seriously thought of marrying him. Certainly he had no such thoughts. He preferred simple, warm hearted girls from a lower class than his own. His life was too erratic even for a "Marriage de convenance" and with Hester, it could not have been that at all. After a brief few months, he drifted off into other affairs, and Hester was left to ask his friends how he was getting on.

Travelling fairly extensively between Burton Pynsent, Bath for her health, London and Kent, she had not much time to worry about Camelford, and moreover was again busy with her brothers' affairs. Once more she began the intrigues and made arrangements for their escape from Chevening, and in 1802 was as successful with them as she had been the year before with Mahon. Indeed so secret had the arrangements been that she had not even told her sisters about the plan. Charles and James even visited Griselda the day before their flight, and said nothing about it. Charles joined the Army, and James, young though he was, joined the Navy.

So, the last of the children had now left Chevening; and the 3rd Earl continued with his political activities and his inventions as if his children had never existed. Louisa now spent more time at Chevening than before. She had grown tired of the social life in London, and had turned, with some passion, to music. She persuaded a Bohemian music teacher called Mrs. Walburga Laekner to give up teaching and live at Chevening instead.

Towards the end of 1801 Hester began to make plans to go abroad hoping to see her "incomparable Mahon". On 18th October 1801, she wrote to Jackson:

"I shall not at this moment take a retrospective view of Mahon's concerns, or of my own peregrinations, but give you the piece of information I longed to communicate, viz: that I may perhaps see Mahon *before you*. Mr. and Mrs. Egerton have only been waiting till peace was made good to go abroad, which they now intend to do next May."

Later, in the same letter, anticipating a possible query from Jackson why she chose the Egertons (who were not the most exciting people in the world) as companions, she wrote:

> "You will, perhaps, wonder at my not having fixed upon
> more dashing persons for companions. In that case we must
> all have dashed away together; in the present case I shall have
> perfect liberty to act in all respects as is most pleasing to
> myself, and in so doing be certain of pleasing them. They
> want a companion, and I want a nominal chaperone."

The important word is "nominal". Despite her independence,
self-assurance, and alleged indifference to the opinions of Society,
she was still, at this stage of her life at least, sufficiently
concerned with her reputation to need a chaperone. By choosing
the Egertons — "She is very sensible", she wrote to Jackson, "and
he vastly good-natured, but vastly shy, and not brilliant . . ." — she
kept to Society's rules, but yet allowed herself maximum freedom.

But she was worried about her grandmother Chatham's health.
On 13th June 1802, she again wrote to Jackson:

> "Dear Grandmama's health having undergone so great a
> change since I arrived in the Winter, has been at times the
> source not only of uneasiness, but of melancholy reflection,
> as when I once part with her, I have little chance of ever
> seeing her again."

It was not until September 1802 that she was finally able to leave
Burton Pynsent. She stopped for a few days on her way to join the
Egertons at Dover, at Walmer Castle, Kent, where her uncle,
William Pitt, was living in semi-retirement.

He had resigned from the Government on 5th February 1800
after a disagreement with George III on the question of Catholic
emancipation. Addington had formed a Ministry instead, and Pitt,
after seventeen years of public service, had gone to the square but
comfortable fortress on the Kent coast just south of Deal, to
struggle with the private problems of health, debts and the
demands of his numerous relatives and hangers-on.

Pitt was pleased to see his niece, and wrote to Mrs. Stapleton, a
friend of Lady Chatham:

> "Hester arrived here yesterday on her way to join her

travelling friends at Dover. I hope to enjoy the pleasure of her Society, at all events till Monday, and perhaps if the winds are contrary, some days longer."

Hester was equally pleased — writing to Francis Jackson on 21st September 1802, she remarked ironically: "I am enchanted with everything here. I have never seen the face of a woman till today. Charming! — nothing but pleasant men." Then she added: "I am to meet Mahon in three weeks, and he is to travel some time with me and return by sea."

Travel to France had become once again possible after the signing of the Treaty of Amiens, on 1st October 1801. The balance of advantage lay with Bonaparte, now First Consul, but England was war-weary, and Addington's Ministry was determined to make peace.

The cautious, accommodating Egertons and the determined Hester travelled first to Lyons where they were met by Mahon. The reunion between brother and sister was ecstatic. After crossing the Alps they left the unhappy Egertons, who considered all foreigners cannibals, and hiring mules and muleteers followed unknown footpaths down through the Italian foothills. But once in Italy proper, trouble began. Mahon was no longer the gauche half-educated boy Hester had rescued from Chevening. Two years at Erlanger University and, particularly, at the court of the Margravine had changed him into a fashionable young man. Writing to Jackson from Turin on 25th October 1802 Hester had this to say about her brother:

"As far as I can judge, Mahon appears to have made great progress in every branch of learning, and to be remarkably well versed in the politics of Europe. He has the same good heart as ever, but, visibly, has been flattered about his abilities, and converses not pleasantly — too much like a Frenchman out of humour. An immense quiz in his dress; but that I have already reformed in part. He speaks likewise in his usual hurried manner, which he most positively must get the better of; indeed, I have no doubt he will, if he only takes pains, as he can speak extremely well when he likes. This is one of the things *most likely* to annoy Mr. Pitt, and therefore you may imagine how he is teazed about it."

She was worried not only by the change in Mahon, but because of the possible effect it might have on Pitt. She was beginning to realize that in Pitt lay her best ally, not only for herself but for her brothers and even her father. As she told Dr. Meryon years later, on explaining why she had left Chevening, ". . . it was better to be where I should have Mr. Pitt by my side to help me . . ."

They travelled on together to Florence, then she and the Egertons went on to Naples, while he went to Leghorn. The rift between brother and sister was partially healed, when, as she wrote to Jackson from Naples on 16th December, she received a letter from him:

> "His letter, dated the 7th of December (his birthday, you know) is a remarkably kind one, in which he begs me to give him my opinion of his conduct without reserve, and send him every instruction to think necessary. I am pleased with this, as it proves to me he is rather changed since we parted, for he then thought no person's judgement equal to his own; in short to say the truth, his conduct disgusted me extremely, and I am quite happy to discover that the Society of a few English at Leghorn has taught him he is not the prodigy he thought he was."

She spent the whole winter in Italy, and was in Venice the following May when news that the uneasy truce between England and France was broken. Now Bonaparte, who had latterly taken to calling himself by his christian name, Napoleon, as if he were on a level with the Louis of France, was ready to start the complete conquest of Europe.

Hester had originally planned to end the Grand Tour in Paris, but that had to be abandoned now. Instead, her party found its way back through Germany, spending a short time at the Court of the Electress at Stuttgart, where the down-trodden Egertons tried to improve their position in Hester's eyes by claiming, on one earlier meeting, friendship with the Electress. Alas, the Electress did not even remember the name. They were the first, but not the last, of the non-aristocratic people to be caught up in Hester's whirlwind movements. Her judgement of the patient and long-suffering couple was "a fidget married to a fool".

Bad news met her when she finally reached England. Her

Chatham grandmother had died in April. Apart from losing one who loved her, she also lost her home. Burton Pynsent now belonged to William Pitt's elder brother, Lord Chatham, and there was no love between them. In any event, the Chathams had adopted another niece, the gentle, orphaned Harriet Eliot. She could not return to Chevening, nor even to her Stanhope grandmother at Ovenden, who had still not forgiven her for arranging Mahon's escape. Nor could she turn to either of her sisters, for they were both "poor relations", dependent upon William Pitt for their existence. Nor were her three half-brothers in any position to help her.

In desperation, she turned to William himself.

CHAPTER SIX

INVASION SCARE

Pitt once said "under no circumstances could I offer her a home in my house", when discussing Hester's future; but now he relented. She was, after all, the child of his only sister, who had died so young. And then, he was already more or less responsible for her brothers and sisters. He had helped Griselda and Lucy when they left home. Recently, he had arranged for Mahon, shortly back from Italy, to be given the Lieutenancy of Dover Castle. Both Charles and James had been virtually told to look upon Walmer as their home, and could come and go as they pleased. Indeed, this forty-four-year-old bachelor was much more of a father to Stanhope's children than the 3rd Earl himself. It was rumoured that the irascible peer had already cut them out of his will, and was far too busy playing around with Mrs. Walburga Laekner, whom his wife had mistakenly brought to Chevening, to worry about them.

On the other hand, though out of office Pitt had hopes of returning to power one day; and Hester, with her lack of tact, her directness and caustic wit, might not be the ideal companion for a politician. Nor was he in good health; he suffered badly from gout and had to go frequently to Bath for the waters. The strain of his seventeen-year ministry and indulgencies had weakened his body. And what, with feminine cunning, might she not do to his comfortable bachelor establishment?

Nevertheless Hester came to Walmer. She was twenty-seven, a fine, attractive woman, with a whip-like sarcasm. She liked to make fun of her stiff prim Grenville relatives by referring to them as "broad-bottomed". But she loved Walmer, and the company that came there. She wrote to Francis Jackson:

"Here then am I, happy to a degree, exactly in the sort of society I most like. There are generally three or four men staying in the house; we dine nine or ten almost every other day. Military and naval characters are constantly *welcome* here; women are not, I *suppose*, because they do not form any part of our Society. You may guess, then what a pretty fuss they make of me."

But, if she received much from Pitt, she gave him much in return. This large, exuberant young woman had, beneath her bravado exterior, a very maternal heart. She had already "mothered" her two sisters and three half-brothers, now she set about "mothering" Pitt. There was a farm near Walmer where hay and corn were kept for the horses. She and Pitt would go there together. He had arranged to have a room set aside there, where he could write letters. After a while a woman would come in with some simple food. He would sit there eating slices of bread and butter, and hunks of cheese, and declare them much better than the elaborate meals he often had to take.

They also shared an interest in the Army. With the renewed outbreak of war, Bonaparte had decided to invade England. Britain was once again, as in 1797, fighting alone against France, and Bonaparte, now First Consul for life, had a wide strategic plan. He began assembling a huge army at Boulogne, with the hope of slipping it across the Channel during a fog. England awoke to the fact that for the first time since the Armada there was real danger of invasion, and patriotic calls immediately went out. Martello towers were constructed along the southern coast to act as lookout and defence posts, an intricate signalling system was introduced, and volunteers raised.

An interlinking military canal was dug, forts, first, second and third lines of defence were worked out; regiments were hurriedly put together, and as hurriedly sent to south-eastern England to repel the invaders. A scare campaign depicted Bonaparte as a monster. Small children were warned that if they did not behave, "Boney" would get them. Ribald verses poked fun at the French

First Consul, inexperienced but enthusiastic yokels paraded with pitch-forks on village greens and there was a great deal of patriotic drunkenness. In fact the British thoroughly enjoyed the scare.

Pitt threw himself into these military activities with the same energy as he had put into politics. As warden of the Cinque Ports, he was nominally in charge of much of the defences along the coast. He also raised and commanded a volunteer regiment. Hester persuaded Pitt to get her the command of another regiment. Together, they would ride off to inspections.

In a letter to T. J. Jackson, dated 19th November 1802, she wrote:

> "It is parade after parade, at fifteen or twenty miles distant from each other. I often attend him, and it is quite as much (I can assure you) as I am equal to, although I am *remarkably* well just now. The hard riding I do not mind, but to remain almost *still* so many hours on horseback is an incomprehensible bore, and requires more patience than you can easily imagine."

Sometimes the weather was so appalling that they would get wet through during these long rides. Hester later recalled: " — I have been so drenched, that as I stood, my boots made two spouting fountains above my knees."

The rough treatment did not have an adverse effect on Pitt's health. Writing in 1803 to Sir Walter Farquhar, Pitt's personal physician, Hester noted:

> "I had the pleasure of seeing Mr. Pitt today, and am happy to see him looking so well. The choicest blessing this country can boast of (his health I mean) we owe to your care. How unlimited then ought to be our thanks to you!"

Pitt was proud of the progress he made, and began to feel that this part of the country, the nearest to Bonaparte's army, was ready for whatever might threaten. Writing to Rose, one of his political assistants, on 18th October 1803, he declared:

> "I wish the arrangements for defence were as forward everywhere else as they are in Hythe Bay under General

The Port of Alexandria, where Captain Henry ''Chivalry'' Pope, who commanded the frigate *Salsette,* conveyed Hester in February 1812, after the shipwreck off the island of Rhodes. Though Hester was grateful to Captain Pope, she found Alexandria ''quite hideous''.

This is how Hester's servants and slaves would load up her camels before one of her expeditions, such as the one to Ascalon in search of lost treasure.

(above) Hester's house at Therapia on the Bosporus was very like these. Therapia was ten miles from Constantinople. Many of the more prosperous people lived here during the summer, when a cool breeze from the Black Sea to the north made the heat bearable. Hester particularly disliked the intense heat.

(below) The court and fountain of Santa Sophia, the most famous and opulent of the churches in Constantinople.

The gardens along the Bosporus were famous for their beauty. It was in such surroundings as these that Hester plotted with Latour Mauborg, the French Chargé d'Affaires at Constantinople, her personal "invasion" of Napoleon's empire.

The approach to Constantinople at the time that Hester and her companions visited the city. She was held up for five days sixty miles from the town by storms and the cowardice of the crew.

(above) A view of Constantinople and the church of Santa Sophia.

(centre) Hester's costume was a magnificent creation and consisted of red-and-white pantaloons, a bright dark damask red kaftan, a blue and orange silk overcoat and a dark green shift. Her turban was decorated with feathers. *(top left)* The Ladder of Tyrus, a steep defile on the seacoast near Tyre. *(bottom left)* Tyre. It was near here that another caravan set up its tents and turned out to belong to a slave trader. *(top right)* Hester on her horse crossing a river near Damascus. She was often taken for a young Turkish nobleman. *(bottom right)* A slave market at Aurut Bazaar, Constantinople.

Jerusalem. The high walls which gave the city a sombre appearance to travellers can be clearly seen. Years earlier a fortune-teller prophesied that Hester would visit Jerusalem and become ''Queen of the Jews''.

Sidon was the nearest landing stage to Hester's first house in the Lebanon, the ex-convent Mar Elias.

(above) Hester's house at Djoun. These fortress-like domains were often convents or farms. In times of turbulence, the inhabitants could, and did, lock themselves in and wait for more peaceful days to return.

(below) Tyre, showing a falucca. Hester travelled in this type of vessel, unchanged since Biblical days, on many occasions.

The port of Beirout. This was the main port in the area. Turkish government officials as well as merchants from many countries lived here.

The Cedars of Lebanon were famous as tourist attractions even at the time Hester and her companions were travelling in the area.

Walmer. Hester stayed with her uncle, William Pitt, after her grandmother had died at Walmer in 1802. She was happy here. During the time of the invasion scare, Pitt commanded a volunteer regiment, as did Hester. (*Frank Hemel*)

Moore. We begin now to have no other fear in that quarter than that the enemy will not give us the opportunity of putting our preparations to the proof and select some other point which we should not be in reach of in the first instance."

Hester was delighted to have her own "army"; writing to the faithful Jackson, on 14th January 1804, she noted:

"We are in almost daily expectation of the coming of the French and Mr. Pitt's regiment is now nearly *perfect* enough to receive them. We have the famous 15th Light Dragoons in our barracks; also the Northampton and Berkshire Militia. The first and last of these I command and have an orderly dragoon whenever I please from the former, and the band of the latter."

She loved being often the only woman among so many men. After dinner, she would, even when alone, be expected to retire to the withdrawing room, and leave the men to their wine. But, as she later told her doctor:

> ". . . When I went to the drawing-room, I had to give the secret word for spies, to see the sergeant of the guard, and then the gentlemen would come in from the dining-room. But, if they were late, oh, how sleepy I got, and would have given the world to go to bed!"

Not that she did not treat them very cavalierly at times; as for example when she changed the dress of her regiment, the Berkshire Militia. She described how this happened:

> "Somebody asked me, before a great many officers, what I thought of them, and I said they looked like so many tinned harlequins. One day, soon after, I was riding through Walmer Village, when who should pop out upon me but the colonel, dressed in entirely new regimentals, with different facings, and more like a regiment of the line.
>
> 'Pray, pardon me, Lady Hester' — so I stopped, as he addressed me — 'pray, pardon me', said the colonel, 'but I wish to know if you approve of our new uniform'.
>
> "Of course I made him turn about, till I inspected him round and round — pointed with my whip, as I sat on horseback, first here and then there — told him the waist was too short, and wanted half a button more — the collar was a little too high — and so on; and, in a short time, the whole regiment turned out with new clothes."

Nor was she afraid of behaving even more high-handedly where colonels were concerned. Something of that imperiousness that was to make her later exclaim to Dr. Meryon ". . . people of my rank and spirit are incapable of insults towards their friends: it is only the vulgar who are always fancying themselves insulted" appeared even when she was at Walmer. Dr. Meryon recounts:

"Once at Walmer Castle, the colonel of the regiment stationed there thought himself privileged to take his wife occasionally to walk on the ramparts of the Castle. I do not know the localities, and am ignorant how far, in so doing, these two persons might infringe on the privacy of Mr. Pitt and Lady Hester Stanhope; but, without intimating by a note or a message that such a thing was disagreeable, she gave orders to the sentry to stop them when they came, and tell them they were not to walk there. Let any one put himself in the place of Colonel W., and fancy how such an affront must have wounded his pride."

Nor was she any less gentle with the younger cavalry officers, even though she might adore them as dinner companions. As she later reminisced:

"I recollect once at Ramsgate five of the Blues, half drunk, not knowing who I was, walked after me, and persued me to my door. They had the impertinence to follow me upstairs and one of them took hold of my gown. The maid came out, frightened out of her senses; but, just at the moment, with my arm I gave the foremost of them such a push, that I sent him rolling over the others downstairs, with their swords rattling against the balusters.

"Next day, he appeared with a black patch as big as a saucer over his face; and, when I went out, there were the glasses [quizzing-glasses] looking at me, and the footmen pointing me out — quite a sensation!"

Yet she could be tender and considerate, especially where Pitt was concerned, as the following anecdote she liked to recount shows:

"I remember once what an improvement I made at Walmer, which arose from a conversation with some friends, in which Mr. Pitt agreed with them that Walmer was not certainly a beautiful residence, but that it only wanted trees to make it so. I was present, but did not seem to hear what was passing.

"Mr. Pitt soon after went to town. Mindful of what he had

let drop, I immediately resolved to set about executing the improvements which he seemed to imply as wanting.

"I got (I know not how) all the regiments that were in quarters in Dover, and employed them in levelling, fetching turf, transplanting shrubs, flowers, etc.

"As I possess, in some degree, the art of ingratiating myself where I want to do it I would go out of an evening among the workmen, and say to one, 'You are a Warwickshire man, I know by your face' (although I had known it by his brogue). How much I esteem Lord Warwick; he is my best friend.'

" 'Were you in Holland, my good fellow?', to another.

" 'Yes, my lady, in the Blues.'

" 'A fine regiment; there is not a better soldier in the army than Colonel So-and-So.'

" He was my colonel, my lady.'

"Thus, a few civil words, and occasionally a present, made the work go on rapidly, and it was finished before Mr. Pitt's return.

"When Mr. Pitt came down, he dismounted from his horse, and, ascending the staircase, saw through a window, which commanded a view of the grounds, the improvements that had been made.

'Dear me, Hester, why this is a miracle! I know 'tis you, so do not deny it: well, I declare it is quite admirable; I could not have done it half so well myself.' "

There were times when the relationship between Pitt and Hester were misconstrued by those who did not know they were uncle and niece. She recounted to her doctor one such episode with much glee:

"When first I went to live with Mr. Pitt, one day he and I were taking a walk in the park, when we were met by Lord G, having Lady —— and Lady —— , two old demireps, under his arm.

"Mr. Pitt and I passed them, and Mr. Pitt pulled off his hat. Lord G turned his head away, without acknowledging his bow.

"The fact was, he thought Mr. Pitt was escorting some mistress he had got.

"Well', said I, 'there goes Falstaff with the Merry wives of Windsor.' " 'Yes', rejoined Mr. Pitt, 'and I think, whatever he may take you to be, he need not be so prim, with those two painted and patched ladies under his arm.' "

Hester's appreciation for soldiers did not consist solely of a love of uniforms and the men who wore them. She was concerned with their well-being. Pitt's elder brother, now Lord Chatham, "never", she told Dr. Meryon, "travelled without a mistress. He was a man of no merit, but of great sâad (luck). He used to keep people waiting and waiting whilst he was talking and breakfasting with her. One occasion when he was due to review the artillery, he kept them waiting from daylight until three o'clock." As Hester recalled, she could stand it no longer:

"At last" I agreed with the aide-de-camps to go off together and settle matters as well as we could: so, getting Lord Chatham's leave, off we went.

"Colonel Ford, the commanding officer, was a cross man; and that day he had enough to make him so. But I managed it all very well: I told him that pressing business detained Lord C; that he had commissioned us to apologize; and that I should have pleasure in saying the men looked admirably: then I added that Mr. Pitt hoped to see him in the course of a few days at the Castle, and so on.

"The colonel looked dreadfully out of temper, however, and Bradford and I rode back at a furious rate. It was one of those dark, wet days that are so peculiar to England.

"A day or two after, the colonel and some of the officers were invited to Walmer, and I behaved very civily to them; so that Lord Chatham's laziness was forgotten."

She was pleased about the progress of her two younger half-brothers. In her letter to T. J. Jackson of 4th January 1804, she wrote from Walmer Castle: "I am at this moment alone here with my little brother James, who has left the Navy for the Army. He is too clever for a sailor — too refined, I mean." Of Charles, she wrote: "Charles is a great favourite of General Moore's, and indeed he deserves it, for he is a most excellent fellow . . ." But of Mahon, now stationed at Dover Castle, she had only this to say: "Mahon is very idle about his duty as a soldier; it vexes me extremely."

But life seemed very pleasant to Hester at this period. There was plenty of movement, and whether she was at Walmer or in London, there was always something to do. On March 8th 1804, she wrote to Jackson from York Place:

"I have been in town some weeks, and am as comfortable as possible. I live with all Mr. Pitt's friends in the pleasantest way that can be. Lady Stafford I think is my leading female acquaintance, and perhaps the one I go out with most. It is uncertain how long we remain in Town, and it is really a matter of indiffernce to me, as I cannot but be happy anywhere in Mr. Pitt's Society."

She was watching over Pitt's health as zealously as ever, and worried about the irregularities of his bachelor-trained habits. In a letter to his doctor, Sir Walter Farquhar, she wrote:

Walmer Castle,
April 5 (1804).

"... I hope soon to have the pleasure of seeing you but in the meantime must first state to you what I think about Mr. Pitt's health, not omitting to say how very uneasy his constant cough has latterly made me; which ill within these last six days he would take no care of, exposing himself to these Easterly winds late in the evening, mending his duty not as a soldier & Colonel of a Regiment but more like a Drill Sergeant. This, however, is I trust at an end for the present at least; I wish also as were another custom which I fear a prejudicial one; drinking wine & water in considerable quantities at night, although he does not sup, only eats a crust of bread. I wish it were possible to forbid totally even the appearance of wine & water, & that you would desire him to take some harmless mess instead of a nature which would little matter whether he took it or left it if he disliked it. He drinks, I fear, occasionally a good deal too much wine at dinner but lately he has been, I am told, very moderate. I can assure you I have suffered more than I can express at every glass of wine I have seen [him] drink at night, as I know from experience how hard the cough would be the next day. As to bile, gout, etc., I shall say nothing about: I only wish to confine myself to naming those things which do him harm & which he will not in all probability name to himself."

In the meantime, news of Camelford came in March 1804. He, believing, on the unreliable evidence of a past mistress, that a certain Mr. Best had insulted him, immediately challenged the man to a duel. Best denied all knowledge of having even mentioned Camelford's name to the woman. But Camelford would not believe him, and the duel took place. Camelford was fatally wounded, and died a few days later. Just before he died Hester wrote to Francis Jackson: "You know my opinion of him, I believe, therefore you can judge if I am not likely to lament his untimely end. He had vices, but also great virtues, but they were not known to the world at large."

By now, the country had become really concerned about Bonaparte's huge army that stretched all away along the northern coast of France. The regiments might be ready, the Martello towers manned and the local volunteers prepared to die, however inefficiently, but the cause of the country's worry was doubt about its leadership. George III was entering yet another period of mental instability and Addington was still Prime Minister. He was a well-meaning and industrious man, but not of the calibre the situation required; and, certainly, measured against Pitt, his predecessor, fell down completely. As George Canning cruelly wrote:

"Pitt is to Addington
As London to Paddington!"

Addington increased his own problems by putting forward his brother, Hiley Addington, and brother-in-law Charles Bragge, for membership of the Privy Council — eliciting a second ditty!

"When the faltering periods lag,
Cheer, oh cheer, him, brother Bragge!
When his speeches hobble vilely,
Or the House receives them drily,
Cheer, oh cheer, him, brother Hiley!"

Addington had no illusions about his abilities, being content to be Speaker. He had only become Prime Minister because Pitt had refused to abandon his stand on Catholic emancipation. He had tried to get Pitt back into the Government in March 1803, by proposing that Pitt's brother, Chatham, should be made Prime Minister and that he and Pitt should both serve under him. But for the time being Pitt would not consider this or any other proposal.

On 15th March 1804 Pitt made the first move against the Government. He attacked the Board of Admiralty, accusing it of unpreparedness. In the subsequent debate Fox and Wilberforce supported Pitt, while Sheridan and the rest of the Prince of Wales' supporters opposed him, resulting in the following division:

For Pitt's motion:	130
Against:	201
Government majority:	71

This was enough to convince the Chancellor, Lord Eldon, that the time had come to put country before party, and he sent his eldest son, Member of Parliament for Boroughbridge, with a private letter to Pitt suggesting a meeting. Pitt replied immediately, and showed by his letter that he was aware of the situation and prepared to accept whatever responsibilities might come of it:

> York Place,
> Tuesday night, March 20, 1804.
>
> My dear Lord,
>   Mr. Scott was so good as to give me your note this evening in the House of Commons. I am very glad to accept your invitation for Saturday, as whatever may be the result of our conversation, I think the sooner we held it the better. The state of public affairs makes it impossible that the public suspense should last very long, and nothing can give me more satisfaction than to put you confidently in possession of all the sentiments and opinions by which my conduct will be regulated. Believe me, my dear Lord,
>
> Yours very sincerely,
> W. Pitt.

The King's health was the main problem. His manic depressive attacks came with greater frequency than ever. He could not stand the slightest contradiction and became violent if his wishes were frustrated. On a number of occasions his doctors had to strap him down in bed. It seemed unlikely that he would be of sufficiently sound mind to make any decisions and that a regency might be the only alternative.

But the Prince of Wales was a known opponent of Pitt. The Earl of Moira, Commander of the forces in Scotland stationed at Edinburgh, was the man the Prince of Wales wanted as head of a government under a regency. Moira attempted to persuade the Prince that Pitt would have to be included in any government, but the Prince parried, by saying that Pitt would never serve under anybody, and that since Moira was to be head of the government, the question was academic. Moira nevertheless continued to press the Prince of Wales on the principle of including Pitt in any future government and the Prince finally agreed, somewhat sulkily, but repeated that he was certain Pitt would never act in a subordinate position. Moira replied: "Whatever situation your Royal Highness may intend for me, Mr. Pitt shall not feel himself subordinate in any Cabinet; and on the footing of the broad union which I propose, I shall consider my business in the Cabinet to be to moderate between Mr. Pitt and Mr. Fox."

Moira thus saw the need for a government of all parties and was prepared to form such a government, despite the opposition of the very man, the Prince of Wales, who, as Regent, was to put him in power. Pitt, however, did not trust the Prince of Wales's word, nor did he believe that the King's health was as bad as Moira made out — there was a tendency to exaggerate the moments of crisis. There might well have to be, in time, a regency, but Pitt did not feel that the time had come. It not right to form an administration without the King's consent, while there was still a chance of his recovery.

"My present notion", he wrote to Lord Melville on 29th March 1804, "therefore is to take the first moment after the present recess, at which the state of the King's health will admit of such a step, to write a letter of His Majesty stating to him the grounds of my opinion, explaining the dangers which I think threaten his Crown and his people from the continuance of his present Government, and representing to him the urgent necessity of a speedy change."

The trouble, Pitt could see, was that, in the King's delicate mental state, any frustration could send him into a complete mental breakdown. This had to be avoided at all costs, even if it meant the exclusion of politicians, such as Fox and Grenville, or their followers, who were anathema to the King. "I should, therefore, at the same time", he wrote, "let His Majesty understand distinctly, that if, after considering the subject, he resolved to exclude the friends of both Mr. Fox and Lord Grenville, but wished to call upon me to form a Government without them, I should be ready to do so as well as I could from among my own immediate friends, united with the most capable and unexceptionable persons of the present Government; but of course excluding many of them, and above all, Addington, and Lord St. Vincent."

It was not until Monday, 7th May 1804 that Pitt finally had an audience with the King. It was more than three years since they had met at a private audience lasting three hours. The Lord Chancellor, who had brought Pitt to Buckingham House (after rebuilding called Buckingham Palace), remained in the antechamber. Pitt probably knew more about the King's state of health than anyone in the country, including his doctors. For seventeen years he had served him as Prime Minister, carefully watching his changes of mood, ever alert for signs of petulance, exaggerated attention to detail, hurried speech and trepidation — indications of yet another mental crisis. But this time he could come to no firm conclusion. When he re-joined the waiting Lord Chancellor he said: "Never in any conversation I've had with him in my life, has he so baffled me."

With all the eloquence and power at his command Pitt attempted to convince the King of the need to form a strong, truly national government, which would mean the inclusion of Fox. But the King was adamant; it was hard enough for him to accept the return of Pitt, but to agree to Fox's participation was altogether too much. Seeing that persuasion would have no effect, and afraid that further argument would destroy the King's uneasy mental balance, Pitt agreed to form a government without Fox.

As soon as he left the King, Pitt sent Lord Granville Leveson-Gower to Fox to tell him the position. Fox, then living in retirement at Ann's Hill, immediately renounced all claims to a post in the Government. He had made his position clear the day before in a note left at Thomas Grenville's house, in which he stated that he wished it "should appear as a record, and be known, that he stood in the way of no arrangement; that he was sure the King would exclude him; but that this ought not, on any account, to prevent the Grenvilles from coming in, and that as far as his influence went, it should not prevent his own friends".

To Granville Leveson-Gower, he added: "I am, myself, too old to care now about office, but I have many friends who for years have followed me. I shall advise them now to join Government, and I trust Pitt can give them places."

Grenville, on the other hand, was not so accommodating. Pitt had sent George Canning to him with the news that the King specifically excluded Fox from the Government, and Grenville replied that he would not take office if Fox were excluded. This attitude was subsequently confirmed at a meeting of his supporters.

Pitt was both furious and upset. He had hoped that his close family ties with Grenville would guarantee the latter's co-operation. According to the Lord Chancellor, Pitt said: "I'll teach that proud man that, in the service and with the confidence of the King, I can do without him, though my health is such that it may cost me my life."

At the same time, Fox's supporters had not shown the same magnanimity as their leader. Despite his exhortations they refused to serve in any capacity under Pitt, and thus deprived of the support of Grenville and Fox, and their respective followers, Pitt was obliged to fall back upon his own friends and those followers of the recently fallen Addington who could be accepted. It was inevitably a weak government, but at least it was a government.

On Wednesday, 9th May 1804 Pitt had another audience with the King. That evening he wrote to the Lord Chancellor:

> "I have had another interview to-day, not quite, I am sorry to say, so satisfactory as that of Monday. I do not think there was anything particularly wrong, but there was a hurry of spirits, and an excessive love of talking, which showed that either the airing of this morning, or the seeing of so many persons, and conversing so much during these three days, has rather tended to disturb."

However, despite his concern for the King's stability, Pitt concluded that it was safe enough, as long as care was taken not to overtax the monarch's strength, to go ahead with the formation of the new government. Next day, 10th May 1804, the seals of office were formally brought to the King by Addington, and as formally handed over to Pitt. The awkward question of Catholic emancipation, which had been the cause of Pitt's resignation three years earlier, was carefully ignored in order to spare the King's equilibrium. With the French Army about to descend upon southern England, this was hardly the time to indulge in theological disputations.

For Napoleon, as he now firmly called himself, had not been idle. Real (and imaginary) plots against his life were discovered, and these were enough to give him the excuse he needed to consolidate his position in France. A decree was issued by the Senate on 18th May 1804, a week after Pitt had become Prime Minister, announcing that "the Government of the Republic is entrusted to an Emperor", and astonishing *non sequitur* that did not appear at all unusual to the French people who in a plebiscite approved the appointment of the new head of state by 3,572,329 votes to 2,569.

Hester's circumstances changed with Pitt's return to active political life. There were still visits to Walmer, where Pitt was always able to regain some of the strength he was fast losing in the strain of carrying, almost single-handed, the burden of war with Napoleon. Although attempting to renew a great European coalition against Napoleon, counteracting France's strategic plans, rallying the country, and holding together his weak Government, he still held on to his local command, and rushed from the serious debates of Parliament to his duties as a field commander.

The estranged Grenville wrote scathingly: "Can anything equal the ridicule of Pitt, riding about from Downing Street to Wimbledon, and from Wimbledon to Coxheath to inspect military carriages, impregnable batteries and Lord Chatham's reviews?"

Hester, so much closer to him, followed wherever he went, looking after him like a mother, for she could see the real Pitt and the strain events were having on him. Like her, he showed the world an impassive and almost indifferent face. He did not frown or pout. His voice was usually quiet. At times, his eyes seemed to be colourless, almost lifeless. Then suddenly they would light up with passion. "It was", said Hester, years later to Dr. Meryon, "something that seemed to dart from within his head, and you might see sparks coming from them." Only she knew of the terrible strain under which he lived:

> "Up at eight in the morning", [she later recalled] "with people enough to see for a week, obliged to talk all the time he was at breakfast, and receiving first one, then another, until four o'clock; then eating a mutton chop, hurrying off to the House, and there badgered and compelled to speak and waste his lungs until two or three in the morning! — Who could stand it? After this, heated as he was, and having eaten nothing, in a manner of speaking, all day, he would sup with Dundas, Huskisson, Rose, Mr. Long, and such persons, and then go to bed to get three or four hours' sleep, and to renew the same thing the next day, and the next and the next."

Sometimes he would be able to take a hot supper after the House had risen at three or four in the morning; but even as he ate and drank the wine he loved too much, for despite the pressure of work and responsibility, he did not give up his long habit of drinking well into the night, a fact that Hester did not really approve of, for she told Meryon — "then home to a hot supper for two or three hours, to talk over what was to be done next day: — and wine, and wine! — Scarcely up next morning, when tat-tat-tat — twenty or thirty people one after another, and the horses walking before the door from two till sunset, waiting for him. It was enough to kill a man — it was murder!"

She tried in all sorts of ways to alleviate the strain and make life easier for him, both at Putney and Walmer. He suffered a great deal from the cold in the House of Commons, complaining that the wind cut through his silk stockings. Once she was wearing a large tippet and muff of very fine fur; the tippet covered her shoulders, coming down to a point behind. "What is this, Hester?" asked Pitt, "something Siberian? Can't you command some of your slaves to introduce the fashion of wearing muffs and tippets into the House of Commons? I could then put my feet on the muff, and throw the tippet over my knees and round my legs."

Pitt's finances were always in a terrible state. Hester recalled when a hackney coach drew up and four businessmen got down carrying a gold box containing £100,000 in bank notes. Finding him alone for once, they offered him the money, but he turned it down. He had long impressed on Hester that he would not receive gifts or bribes, wherever they might come from, or for whatever cause. She would often act, in these and in other cases, as a buffer between him and the world.

Politicians and others used to come and ask her questions, in order to learn about his state secrets. One questioner was particularly keen to find out who would be the next ambassador to Russia. Hester pretended to consider the question seriously. She put forward three ficticious names, and immediately hinted that two of them could not accept the appointment. That was enough for her correspondent. Next day the name of the third man appeared in the paper "The Oracle", which Pitt never read, as the future ambassador to Russia. When the real choice came out, which was none of the three mentioned, her questioner upbraided her for giving him false information. "But", she recalled later when recounting the episode, "I did not deceive him: I only told him what was true, that if I had the choice I would choose such and such persons."

She could be extremely rude at times and on one occasion at a Cabinet dinner she completely cut one of the guests, a certain Earl. When Pitt asked her whether she hadn't seen the man, she replied: "No, I saw a great chameleon as I came in, all in pigeon breasted colours. . . ." The Earl was wearing over-coloured court dress, an act of foppishness that Hester found despicable, and she was not one to hide her disapproval.

But sometimes her sharpness was in defence of Pitt. She had been friends for some time with Lord Abercorn, but Abercorn had earlier deserted Pitt for Addington, and in so doing had managed to secure for himself the Order of the Garter. Hester never forgave him. One day at Court she was complaining to the Duke of Cumberland about Abercorn's treachery when Abercorn presented himself: "Now, little bulldog", said the Duke (who liked a good row) "have at him". Hester, seeing the Garter round Abercorn's leg, riposted, "What's that you have got there, my Lord?", and before he could answer, she continued, "I suppose it is a bandage for your broken legs." The sally had a double significance. Abercorn had, in fact, once had both his legs broken, and Addington's father's profession was bandaging broken legs.

Although outspokenness of this kind often made Pitt warn her to be more careful, he, nevertheless, had a very high opinion of her abilities. One day, he said to her: "I have plenty of good diplomatists, but they are none of them military men; and I have plenty of good officers, but not one of them is worth sixpence in the cabinet. If you were a man, Hester, I would send you on the Continent with 60,000 men, and give you *Carte Blanche*; and I am sure that not one of my plans would fail. . . ."

On another occasion, when discussing the alleged unreliability of George Canning, Hester defending Canning, suggested that the young man was perhaps disguising his true opinions in order to help Pitt. "I have lived," replied Pitt, "twenty-five years in the midst of men of all sorts, and I have never yet found but one human being capable of such a sacrifice." "Who can that be?" asked Hester. "Is it the Duke of Richmond?" She named two or three other possibles, but Pitt interrupted her — "No", he said, "it is *you*".

There were those who thought that Pitt allowed his high-spirited niece too much say in political matters. But, in truth, their relative positions were carefully defined: when he was asked — "What will Lady Hester say to that?" he retorted very quickly: "Lady Hester and I have made a bargain together, we each give advice on condition that neither ever takes it."

She could amuse him, protect him, look after him, but there was never any doubt that, where politics were concerned, he alone made the decisions. This was how it had always been and he wasn't likely to change. Though Hester might perhaps have liked to believe that she had some influence over him her admiration for him was too great to allow such ideas to remain.

Moreover she was seriously and deeply in love for the first time, and that was occupying her whole attention; for the object of her passion, Lord Granville Leveson-Gower, Pitt's colleague, was not the easiest man to catch.

CHAPTER SEVEN

GAINS AND LOSSES

Lord Granville Leveson-Gower (pronounced Loosen-Gore) was thirty when Hester fell in love with him. He was born on 12th October 1773; his mother, Lady Stafford, and his sisters spoilt him. He was a pretty and effeminate looking child. In a mezzotint after Romney, where he is shown, as a young boy, dancing with his sisters, it is difficult to believe that he isn't a girl. He grew up to be a cherubic-looking man, with the kind of effeminate handsomeness that was popular at the time.

Whilst on the Grand Tour, at Naples, when he was twenty, he met Henrietta, Lady Bessborough, who was twelve years older than he. The love affair lasted, at least as far as she was concerned, for the rest of her life. She and her sister, the Duchess of Devonshire, were among the greatest hostesses of the day. Beautiful, daring and accomplished, the Spencer sisters, as they were before their marriages, made their salons the meeting places of the great, the wealthy, the witty and the aristocratic.

Lady Bessborough knew, and was known by, "everybody" in the small enclosed circle of princes, landed gentry, politicians, artists and writers who between them effectively ran the country. Like many attractive women of the time, she combined social duties with her care for her husband and children. She was, in fact, devoted to her family, and for all her love for Leveson-Gower would never sacrifice them for him. A compulsive letter writer, her letters were filled with details of political and artistic activities, as well as social gossip and long extracts from books that had particularly pleased her. In a letter written from Chatsworth in mid-winter 1802, she wrote:

> "How I miss you every hour! Every moment makes me feel your loss more. I have not power left even to repel impertinence, and I have met with it. Think of that fool Jules [Prince Jules de Polignac] saying to me to-day, Allons donc ne soyez pas si triste il reviendra . . . . Do not break your neck skaiting [*sic*] or hunting, do not drink, and do not flirt."

Not that she had any illusions about him. She knew that he was the most sought after man of his time, and that he was incapable of resisting a woman who wanted him. At the same time, his many affairs tended to cancel each other out, so that despite a surface unfaithfulness to Henrietta, she remained the woman in his life.

Hester must have first met him with Pitt. Indeed after Pitt's return as Prime Minister, Leveson-Gower, like Canning, served him in various political undertakings, after spending the night at the house in Putney where Pitt stayed when Parliament was in session. She threw herself into the affair with all the uncaring zest that had marked her game with Camelford. But conditions now were very different. Then, she had merely been the daughter of the eccentric 3rd Earl Stanhope, whereas now she was the niece of the Prime Minister, accepted by him as a trustworthy recipient of news of the highest order, and meeting everyday ministers and members of Parliament. Worse still, the affair was with one of Pitt's most devoted admirers and trusted servants, which was embarrassing for Pitt.

It was embarrassing, too, for Leveson-Gower. He undoubtedly wished to marry, but his idea of a wife was somebody much less imperious and "difficult" than this twenty-eight-year-old Amazon of a woman, who would soon put an end to his charming "alliance" with Henrietta Bessborough if she could. Besides, he needed a wife with money, and Hester had none.

Pitt had said that his niece would never marry, since she would never find a man as clever as herself. But Hester was as determined to marry Leveson-Gower as he was to avoid it. Falling really deeply in love for the first time, at twenty-eight, was a dangerous business. Leveson-Gower could see that the scandal that was linking his name to hers could do him immense political harm.

The gossip papers began to speak openly of an engagement between them, a fact that led Lady Bessborough to write warningly to Leveson-Gower:

". . . You have, I conclude, read the Paragraph announcing your marriage to Lady Hester l'on ne va pas si souvent chez une Demoiselle impunément; everybody is talking of it."

Meanwhile Pitt was trying to get together a third coalition against Napoleon. This meant the sending of a trusted ambassador to the Court of St. Petersburg. Partly because of Leveson-Gower's diplomatic qualifications, and partly in order to allay the gossip that was forming around his niece, he offered Leveson-Gower the ambassadorship. Although it would mean separation from his beloved Henrietta, it would also mean safety from Hester. Granville Leveson-Gower accepted the offer with alacrity.

Henrietta Bessborough viewed Leveson-Gower's approaching departure with mixed feelings. First there was the anguish of separation: on hearing that he was dining with Pitt and Hester, she hoped that he would go along afterwards to see her: ". . . considering how soon I must quite lose you, and how little of the time that remains I can spend with you . . ." But she also took a practical view of the intention of spending the night at Pitt's house, rather than with her. "Is it quite honourable, Dear G", she continued, "to encourage a passion you do not mean seriously to return? and which, if you do not, must make the owner of it miserable? And how can you be certain of what lengths you or she may be drawn into? We know she has strong passions and indulges them with great latitude: may you not, both of you, be hurried further than you intend? If Mr. Pitt knew even what has passed already, do you think he would like it? and without intending blame to Ly H, is it possible not to recollect the stories of C. Lennox and the D. of Manchester, etc? In short, do not be angry, G . . . I hope I see en noir."

Whether it was because of Henrietta's advice or in order to keep the record straight with Pitt, Leveson-Gower probably told Hester that there could be no possibility of marriage between them.

(left) William Pitt. His political career was extraordinary. He became a Member of Parliament at the age of 21, was Prime Minister by the time he was 24, and remained so for the greater part of his life. (*Frank Hemel*)

There is no exact record that this was so, but it is more than likely. He was, anyhow, more concerned with the sadness of leaving Lady Bessborough, and of having to abandon his exciting life in London for the reported dreariness of the Russian Court. Before leaving they arranged a code between them, for letters were often opened, and even the Foreign Office messengers were sometimes intercepted. As Lady Bessborough always wrote with great detail and frankness about all kinds of people in the political and social worlds, her letters were designed to hide to all but Leveson-Gower the identity of the people she was writing about. Thus Pitt became "My Uncle"; Canning, "The Pope"; the King, "Mr. Wyatt"; and Hester, "My Niece" — sometimes "Hetty".

On 11th October 1804 Leveson-Gower sailed to Russia via Whitstable, Yarmouth and Elsinore (Denmark). Before leaving he wrote a short letter to Henrietta:

> Whitstable
> Thursday 11th October, 1804
> 5 o'clock:

> "You must have seen how I suffered in parting from you last night — I know not that I have ever passed so heartrending a moment . . . I shall endeavour to write from Elsineur as I pass the Sound. You will of course hear from me from Yarmouth. Canning has been with me above an hour, and stays until my departure, which will be about 6 o'clock . . . I shall go about 40 miles to-night, and get to Yarmouth tomorrow . . .
> You cannot conceive the anxiety I feel about your health . . . By Canning's advice I have sent no trinket to Hetty, though I bought one for that Purpose. I have just sent a note to inquire after her, but have as yet got no answer . . . God bless you — adieu."

Lady Bessborough, who was at Hastings at the time, told him of her concern for him on his journey. "How I shall watch the wind", she wrote. She also mentioned Hester's strange behaviour, and the possibility (which she immediately dismissed) that Hester might kill herself. For though Lady Bessborough continually advised Leveson-Gower to be careful, she and Hester were on the best of terms. "I shall always be kind to her", she added in her letter, "from a strange reason — she belongs in some manner to you."

Lady Bessborough was not the only one to be alarmed by Hester's behaviour. When Hester realized that Leveson-Gower had escaped she felt a terrible blow to her pride. For her, of all people, to have been jilted — for that, she knew, was how her world viewed the matter — was unbearable. She sped hectically from place to place, abusing people and trying, somehow, to rid herself of the pain. She clung to Lady Bessborough, until friends, including the Queen and the Princess of Wales, advised her to break off relationships with the woman Leveson-Gower really loved. But, even so, Hester had to make the break in person. Honesty, even at this delicate moment, was to her, imperative. She called on Henrietta, and naively blurted everything out.

Lady Bessborough wrote that same day to Leveson-Gower, now safely, if unhappily, installed at St. Petersburg:

"Hetty is this moment gone — her visit has been a very nervous one to me, as you will see it must when I tell you our conversation. Alas! I am but too conscious of deserving what has happened, but deserving a thing does not often lessen the pain of it. I have not spirits just now to give you an account of a violent and entertaining argument she had with Ld Abercorn who was here. I can only tell you what pass'd when he went. She seem'd very much distress'd, and I could not for a long time make out what she meant in begging me with the greatest earnestness not to attribute to caprice or any change in opinion or *affection* towards me if I remark'd a change in her manner and if she saw less of me. On pressing her to explain, she at length told me she had been advis'd, almost *order'd*, to break off all acquaintance with me. . . . At the moment that pride but too natural to me revolted, from thinking she sought me while it was useful to her and wish'd to cut me when it ceased to be so. I only answer'd gravely she had better follow the advice. She burst into tears, and kissing me passionately, said: "I see you impute to me what arises from the ill nature of others and originates chiefly with the Queen and the Princess of Wales." After a moment's reflection . . . I determined to advise her as I would have done my child, and told her, however hard it might seem to

Facsimile of a letter written by Hester. (*Frank Hemel*)

me or groundless it might be . . . that her friends could only have the motive of her good, and that she ought by all means to comply with them. . . ."

Next day, she wrote again, elaborating on Hester's behaviour: "Hetty talked a great deal of you — for the *last time*, she said, for she told me she meant to avoid everything that could remind her of you, never to mention you; never to enquire after you, and if possible never to think of you more."

So the friendship between the two women, a lop-sided one from the beginning, came to an end. Hester, unable to face the barely concealed laughter of "friends" in London, rushed to Walmer, and there shut herself up in complete solitude. Strange tales were told about her. She tried to kill herself, she had had a baby, she had gone mad. In fact, she was nursing a broken heart, and could only recover her spirits in the grandeur of Walmer and the sea.

She started work again remodelling the gardens at Walmer, as she had done before. She looked up old army acquaintances. She even made it up with Mahon and his new wife, but her preferences, where the family was concerned, were now for Charles and James. Charles was so gentle, James so faithful. She wrote sadly to Francis Jackson, still a diplomat in Berlin, wishing she were a bird, and could visit him, and told him that she had lost her looks, as she always did when she was unwell. While Lady Stafford reported in December 1804 that Hester had "A dingey complexion, no Rouge, a broad face and an unbecoming fur cap". A mother's prejudice perhaps.

The long hard winter of isolation passed and in the spring she returned once more to Pitt and the world of politics and international tension. Napoleon was still waiting with his great army for an opportunity to cross the Channel. His plan was to send Villeneuve, his admiral in charge of the main French fleet, to the West Indies, knowing that Nelson, who was shadowing him, would follow. Once in the West Indies, Villeneuve was to shake off Nelson, and return secretly to European waters, join up with the Spanish fleet, and together sail for the Channel. With Nelson cruising aimlessly around the West Indies, there would not be sufficient ships in home waters to prevent the Franco-Spanish fleet from gaining control of the Channel. "If we can but be master of the passage for twelve hours", Napoleon wrote in August 1805, "England will have ceased to be."

In the meantime Pitt was busy on the diplomatic scene. A treaty was signed between Britain and Russia. Austria and Sweden also joined the Treaty members, and the third Coalition against Napoleon was formed. It was hoped to raise half a million men. This formidable force, it was expected, would at last put a halt to Napoleon's ambitions in Europe. But Nelson soon divined what Villeneuve planned to do and sent a fast brig back to England to warn the Government, then followed immediately himself. He was back on guard in the Channel before the French and Spanish fleet had even met.

General Maek, who commanded the Austrian forces, was convinced that Napoleon was only interested in invading England. This was, he felt, his chance to move against the French Emperor. He passed the river Inn and moved into Bavaria, then took up a strong position at Ulm. From there he could control the Danube. But Napoleon, though still intent on invading England, moved his army in September with astonishing speed, encircled Maek at Ulm, and defeated the Austrians. He then pushed on into Austria.

On the other side of Europe, off the Spanish coast, a different kind of battle was about to be fought. The French and Spanish had at last met and formed a combined force. Nelson swooped down upon them. On 21st October 1805, he completely destroyed them off Cape Trafalgar, and thus put an end to any hope Napoleon might still have had, of shifting his army over the Channel. At the moment of victory Nelson was killed.

"Good heavens!", wrote Lady Bessborough to Leveson-Gower, "What news! How glorious if it was not so cruelly damp'd by Nelson's death. How truly he has accomplished his prediction that when they meet it must be extermination."

Nelson had to be back in England by Christmas, but instead he had achieved what he had set out to do and died in the effort. People in the streets walked about with black arm-bands, the name Nelson printed on them. It was said that he lived to hear of his victory and many wished that they could die as he had done, in the moment of glory. Pitt was so saddened that he could not sleep the night he was told the news.

On 9th November Pitt attended the Lord Mayor's annual banquet. He was hailed as "the Saviour of Europe". Upon rising to reply to the toast he seemed utterly exhausted, hardly able to speak at all. It was almost in a tired whisper that he began: "I return you many thanks for the honour you have done me; but Europe is not saved by a single man." Suddenly his strength returned and his voice became once more resonant and vibrant: "England has saved herself by her exertions, and will, I trust, save Europe by her example." Then he sat down; it was perhaps the shortest but certainly one of the most telling speeches of his career.

But he was desperately ill. Only Hester, who watched over him, and perhaps Charles and James Stanhope, who visited him frequently, knew, apart from Pitt's doctor, exactly how ill he was. Hester tried to get him to rest, to put aside each day, at least for a while, his self-imposed task, but he drove himself on and on, interspersing work at Parliament with visits to Bath, in an attempt to repair his health and gain new strength. It was during a visit to Bath, that Hester suggested he should take her eiderdown quilt with him. "Instead of being too hot one day under a thick counterpane", she pointed out sensibly, "and the next day shivering under a thin one, you will have an equable warmth." Charles and James, who were there, ridiculed the whole idea. It was such a "bundling effeminate thing". Hester was piqued: "Big as it looks", she replied, "you may put it in a pocket handkerchief." When Charles and James said it was impossible, Hester, who disliked being contradicted, immediately flew into a rage and ordered the eiderdown to be brought. Pitt, trying to calm her, said: "I am sure the boys do not mean to say you tell falsehoods: they suppose you said it would go into a handkerchief merely as a *façon de parler.* "Eventually even Hester had to laugh when a footman arrived carrying the eiderdown over his shoulder, and was almost completely obscured by it. It was, she claimed, the only quarrel she ever had with Charles and James. It is not recorded whether Pitt took the eiderdown with him to Bath or not.

On 2nd December 1805, Napoleon, moving eastwards into the Austrian Empire, met the combined armies of the Emperors of Russia and Austria at the little village of Austerlitz. In the ensuing battle, sometimes called "The Battle of the Three Emperors," the Russians and Austrians were utterly defeated. The Emperor of Russia withdrew from Austria, and the Emperor of Austria signed a degrading treaty. The Emperor of France was now the undisputed master of Europe and the third coalition was at an end. So decisive was the victory that its renown continued long after the event, and when it came, later in the century for a name to be chosen for a new railway station in Paris, the one selected was Austerlitz.

News of Napoleon's great victory and the terms of the subsequent Treaty of Pressburg with Austria took some time to reach England. Pitt was then at Bath, taking the waters for a new attack of gout, hoping to gain enough health and strength to face a meeting of Parliament on 21st January 1806. In a report made out a few weeks after Pitt returned to London James Stanhope recalled:

> "It was on the night of Lord Nelson's funeral that I arrived in Downing Street from conducting some French prisoners to Norman Cross. At that time I did not entertain the least idea of Mr. Pitt being ill, at least in such a manner as to justify alarm. On my arrival, however, I heard of some symptoms which I confess gave me considerable uneasiness, among others that of the voice having lost that deep-toned melody which had so often astonished and electrified the Senate, and that it had become tremulous and feeble."

Hester was also conscious of the change in him. She was at the house in Putney that he had rented when he returned. The memory of that moment stayed vividly with her all her life. Many years later she told her doctor:

> "When the carriage came to the door, he was announced, and I went out to the top of the stairs to receive him. The first thing I heard was a voice so changed, that I said to myself, 'it is all over with him'."

On Sunday, 12th January, he was well enough to write to Wellesley to invite him to Putney. On the Monday, he went for a drive in his coach; but that evening, two of his closest colleagues, Castlereagh and Hawkesbury called on him. Hester wrote to W. D. Adams from Putney at 9 p.m. on 16th January 1806:

> "Sir Walter [Sir Walter Farquhar, Pitt's physician] writes to Charles & all he can say is I believe that Mr. P. is no worse and no fresh unpleasant symptoms have appeared today. Mr. P., however, thinks himself rather better but he is so weak it is quite shocking.
>
> Not a soul has seen him today nor shall they I am determined until he is much better than we have seen him since he came here as Sir W is of opinion that L^d H and C [Lords Hawkesbury and Castlereagh] were the occasion of all this with their infernal prose...."

Hester fetched James and brought him to Putney in her carriage on 19th January. In his report, James wrote:

> "When we came to within about 300 yards from the house Mr. Rose stopped the carriage. I immediately devined the most alarming apprehensions from seeing his eyes red with tears, and his gestures those of the most poignant grief. He told us 'he was afraid that there was some danger'. These I believe were his real words, at least as far as I recollect."

On the Sunday evening Pitt took two eggs which seemed to "reanimate him" as James put it. But, by Tuesday morning he was worse. Pitt's elder brother, Lord Chatham, called, but Sir Walter Farquhar and the two extra doctors, Bailey and Reynolds, refused to let him see their patient. His pulse was 130; and by Wednesday the doctors gave him 24 hours to live. "At about 8 in the morning", wrote James, "the Bishop of Lincoln went to him and offered to administer the Sacraments, which however he declined fearing he was unworthy of receiving it." James then went on to write:

> "From Wednesday morning I didn't leave the room except for a few minutes until the time of his death. Tho' in the room, I did not allow him to see me, as I did not feel myself capable of supporting a farewell from one I loved so dearly. Hester begged to be allowed to see him, but was refused. Taking however advantage of Sir Walter being at dinner, she went into the dying man's room. Mr. Pitt tho' wandering a little, immediately recollected her, and with his usual mildness spoke to her wished for her future happiness and gave her an affecting and mournful farewell. For some minutes after she left him, he still continued to mention and several times emphatically said: 'Dear Soul, I know she loves me', and, 'Where is she?' 'Where is Hester gone?' 'Is Hester gone?' . . .
>
> "I sat up the whole of Wednesday night with Mr. Pitt. He wandered very much and spoke a great deal of Lord Harrowby, asked often how was the wind and said: 'East ah that will do, that will take him quick'. At other times he

seemed to be in conversation with a messenger, and frequently exclaimed, 'Hear, hear'. At others, he would moan much. Towards 12 the rattles began to come in his throat. Sir Walter, the Bishop, Hester, Charles overcome with fatigue laid down on their respective beds. I alternately sat by the side of Sir Walter, and in the room of Mr. Pitt. At about one, a Mr. Louth arrived from town with a phial of Heartsam and oil, a spoonful of which he insisted on Mr. Pitt taking. Sir Walter saying it could do no harm, we were willing to try and Mr. Pitt swallowed or rather had 2 table spoonfuls poured down his throat. It produced no effect except a little convulsive cough. Mr. Louth went away about half an hour. At about two, after he had been moaning saying, 'Oh dear, oh lord!', appearing in much pain and pronouncing with an almost inarticulate voice, he suddenly stopped and in his own tone said with a feeling I never, never can forget, 'Oh my country how I leave my country'.

"He never spoke or moaned again, and died at half past four on Thursday morning, 23rd January 1806."

It was exactly twenty-five years to the day since he had first entered Parliament as a young man of twenty-one. The country was stunned by his death, as it had been, a few months earlier, by Nelson's When Fox was told the news, he replied, "Impossible, impossible; one feels as if there was something missing in the world — a chasm, a blank that cannot be supplied."

To Hester it was more than a chasm. It seemed that it was the end of everything she lived for. To Sir Walter Farquhar, who wrote to her asking after her own health, she replied on 27th January 1806:

". . . All I can say of myself is that I endeavour to bear with resignation the irreparable loss. . . ."

As she told Dr. Meryon much later, she had been unable to cry when he died. It was not until about a month after Pitt's death, when she met Lord Melville, who as Henry Dundas had been a robust supporter of Pitt, and saw that his eye-brows had turned grey, that she suddenly burst into tears. Her grief at last had some outlet and the pain was eased.

Bowling Green House, Putney. This was Pitt's London house, where he stayed when up from Walmer on business as Prime Minister. It was here that Hester looked after him; and it was here that he died on 23rd January 1806; twenty-five years to the day after he had first entered Parliament. (*Radio Times Hulton Picture Library*)

But she continued with the trivialities of life and indeed took an exaggerated interest in details. There was the question of commissioning a sculptor to make a bust of Pitt. She remembered once meeting an Italian called Tomino (Mahon subsequently said his real name was Vollekins), who had asked her whether he could make a bust of her for a hundred guineas. She had refused, as she realized that he had only approached her in order to gain publicity. She remembered him now, however, and commissioned him to do the work. "The bust turned out", she subsequently told Dr. Meryon, "a very indifferent resemblance; so with my own hand, I corrected the defects, and it eventually proved a strong likeness."

Pitt's extraordinary honesty meant that he had refused gifts of money all his life. He had, time and again, been offered large sums of money by supporters or those seeking his favours, but had always turned them down. On the other hand, his extravagant way of life had run him into tremendous debt. Parliament debated what was to be done, and decided that the country, to honour his services, should pay off his debts. His last request, that his nieces should be provided for, was also met. Hester was granted a pension for life of £1,200 a year, Griselda and Lucy £600 each.

By now Hester was again homeless. Friends had offered her temporary refuge, but these were merely stop-gaps. There was no longer any member of her family to whom she could turn. Her father was becoming more and more embroiled with "Wally," as he always called his wife's music-teacher friend, and there was talk of separation. A deed was drawn up, allowing Louisa £1,500 a year on condition that she did not attempt to bring a divorce or, contrariwise, demand the restitution of conjugal rights. He also paid her debts to the value of £84 4s 6d. Then she left, taking with her besides her personal jewellery, clothes and papers "the large arm-chair from the dressing-room at Chevening, and the clock to mark musical time".

Hester's Stanhope grandmother, Grisel, was now eighty-seven. She still lived in the Dower House at Ovenden, and was still as mentally alert as ever, but it would have been impossible for her to have given Hester a home, even if either had wished it. Grisel still felt resentment for the way her grand-daughter had arranged the escape from Chevening of Mahon, Charles and James.

Hester, anyhow, was now thirty. Unmarried, and with no

money except her £1,200 pension, she was not "a catch" in the eyes of a mercenary minded society where heiresses were married off at seventeen. While Pitt was alive she might perhaps have had some political value, but after his death that value disappeared. The many enemies, particularly among women, that her sharp tongue and sarcastic wit had made, rebounded upon her.

The only two people she was really fond of were her half-brothers, Charles and James. Pitt had allowed them to make his home their home. Now that was gone, Hester decided to make them a home herself. She took a house in Montagu Square, and told them to look upon the place as their home.

So life, in a way, began again, as it had been. Charles and James, both in the Army, entertained a good deal. Among visitors were Hester's old friends, particularly George Canning, whose love—hate relationship continued unaltered by Pitt's death. Others included the Princess of Wales, but not the Prince. He and she had never liked each other. Hester thought him mean and despicable. "He was anxious enough to know me", she said, "while Mr. Pitt was alive; but the very first day of my going to court, after Mr. Pitt's death, he cut me, turning his back on me whilst I was talking to the Duke of Richmond."

Even Leveson-Gower's return from St. Petersburg in August 1806 seems not to have had any outward effect on her, and no attempt was made on either side to renew the affair.

Yet there was still talk and rumour of engagements. Lady Bessborough wrote to Leveson-Gower, now settled once more in England, that she had been told that it was "*certain* that Hetty's marriage with Mr. Hill is *declar'd* and to take place immediately: can this be so? If it is, il est bon. God bless you. I wish it may be true, for I sincerely wish poor Hetty to be well and comfortably settled".

The Hon. Noel Hill, the dangerous society wit, second son of the first Baron Berwick, had already been mentioned before Leveson-Gower's arrival as a possible suitor to Hester. During the break-up between Hester and Leveson-Gower, he had behaved with appalling bad taste, showing the eager Lady Bessborough one of the private letters "Hetty" had written. But now, it appeared, he was back in favour. But the truth was that she was as fond or not of him as she was of any of her other friends. Society gossip had to find some romantic attachment for an unmarried woman of

Sir John Moore, killed at Corunna in January 1809, at the same time as Hester's favourite brother, Charles. She was reputed to have been engaged to Moore. The death of these two men was largely responsible for her decision to travel abroad. (*Frank Hemel*)

thirty, seen about with first one man and then another. At all events, nothing came of the so-called engagement with Noel Hill, as with the other men whose names from time to time were linked with hers. She was, in truth, attracted to one man, a man who had been much admired by Pitt, and whom Hester had seen quite frequently at Walmer – General Moore.

Moore was the only general, apart from Wellesley, in whom Pitt had had any confidence. During the 1804–5 invasion scare, Moore had been in command of the troops in south-east England nearest to Napoleon's great army encamped around Boulogne. He was a strict disciplinarian, who believed in the value of hard training. He could also accept the suggestions of others. When Pitt put forward the idea that the troops should be trained to fight in the sea, so as to engage the invaders before they had even landed, Moore immediately issued orders that they should be trained to fight breast high in water. He even managed to bring some sort of cohesion to the undisciplined, if enthusiastic, bands of volunteers, raised by towns and villages along the coast.

After the invasion scare had passed, he had fought with distinction in Sicily. Now he was back in London and at forty-seven was a man's man, handsome, straightforward and honest. He began to visit the house in Montagu Square more and more frequently and was the complete antithesis of Leveson-Gower. The more Hester saw of him, the more she appreciated him, until she even began to wonder how she could have felt so deeply for Leveson-Gower's long eyelashes, cupid face, pouting mouth and simpering, effeminate ways.

But changing over from the one to the other was a slow process. She could see that Moore was the better man in every way, but she could not get rid of the love she had for Leveson-Gower. She was neither the first nor the last woman to acknowledge that a man was no good for her, yet still go on loving him. But, given time, the passion she still felt for Leveson-Gower would fade and be replaced, she hoped, by the sincere affection she felt for Moore; and, she hoped, he for her.

To Charles and James, Moore was a hero. Sometimes, they would discuss between the three of them this or that aspect of the general. When comparing his looks, one day, with another man, Charles asked Hester whether she did not think General Moore was the better of the two. "He is certainly very handsome", she

replied. "Oh! but", said Charles, "Hester, if you were only to see him when he is bathing, his body is as perfect as his face." Hester did not even smile, though inwardly she was smiling at Charles's naïvety.

Napoleon had continued on his triumphant way, defeating the Prussians at Jena and entering Berlin in 1806. Whilst there, he had issued the Berlin Decree. Next year, he added a supplementary edict at Milan. These decrees were the basis of the Continental System. Unable to invade Britain, he decided to blockade her. He forbade France, or any of the countries he had conquered, or that were allied to France, to trade with Britain. Although most of the countries of Europe obeyed Napoleon's orders, either willingly or by force majeure, Portugal refused. She defied Napoleon and continued to trade with Britain. Napoleon reacted with his usual swiftness. He made a treaty with Spain partitioning Portugal, deposed the Spanish, and gave the throne instead to his own brother Joseph. He then sent one of his best generals, Junot, at the head of a combined Franco-Spanish army into Portugal.

But, despite all his brilliant deviousness, Napoleon had forgotten to take into account the intense national feeling of the Spanish people. Incensed by having their King arbitrarily removed by a foreigner, they rose in revolt. Napoleon, believing that this was nothing but a local disturbance, sent an army of untrained recruits under Dupont to restore order. They were unsuccessful, and in the event the general and 18,000 men surrendered to the Spanish at Baylen. It was an unpleasant shock for Napoleon, but it had an invigorating effect on the British Government. Morally bound to come to Portugal's assistance, Britain now saw that there might be, in Spain and Portugal, the one area in Europe where she could still fight Napoleon on land.

Sir Arthur Wellesley, as he now was, was sent to Portugal with an army of 10,000 men in July 1808. He landed at Oporto, forced the heights of Rorica, and, reinforced, met Junot at Vimiera, where, on 21st August 1808, he defeated the French general. The effect in Britain was electrifying. For the first time for years the English had defeated the French in a land, rather than a sea battle. Lady Bessborough summed up the general feeling when she wrote: "... We shall no more be told, I hope, that whatever we may do by sea, our land troops are inferior to every other Nation;

that we are always worsted, and that it is ridiculous to cope with ye French".

The euphoria did not last long. Wellesley was superseded while the battle was still being fought by Sir Harry Burrard ("Betty" Burrard as Wellesley scathingly called him) and then by Sir Hew "Dowager" Dalrymple. Wellesley believed that if the British Army followed up its advantage – the reserve corps had not even been engaged – the whole French Army could be taken. But while the two senior officers dithered, the French began to retreat in good order. When Dalrymple signed the Convention of Cintra with Junot, the French Army was allowed to get away intact. Wellesley, to his disgust, was ordered to put his name to the Convention or be accused of insubordination.

In the recriminations that followed, Sir John Moore was given command of the Army in Spain, and Charles went with him. Moore wrote to Hester on 16th October 1808 from Lisbon:

"Private.

I had the pleasure to receive a very few days ago your very kind letter of 26th September from S. Wales. The same conveyance brought me the appointment to command the Army destined to serve in Spain . . . Charles's regiment was in the number of those, named to remain in Portugal – and this was breaking his heart and so was it mine – but I have at last contrived an arrangement in concert with Sir Henry [Burrard], who is the most liberal of men, to take the 50th with me, and now all is well – the Regts are already marching – his will move in a few days, and as soon as I have seen everything in train here, I shall push on, to get to their head.

Pray for good weather; if it rains, the torrents will swell and be impassable, and I shall be accounted as a mere bungler . . . I had given Charles a message to you, not thinking that I should have had time to write, but I have found a spare half hour, and I was unwilling to let an opportunity pass without acknowledging your letter, and thanking you, as I do, a thousand times for your kindness to me. I am quite glad at the account you give me of your health. I wish you were with us the climate now is charming – we should give you riding enough, and in your red habit, à l'amazone, you would animate and do us all much good.

> I have the honour to remain,
> Always my dearest Hester,
> Yours sincerely and Faithfully,
> John Moore.

> Do remember me kindly to James.

So the English general and his army marched north-east into Spain; while Soult, the French commander turned, after Napoleon and his brother had captured Madrid, towards him. Moore was not at all confident of the outcome. From Salamanca, he wrote to Hester on 20th November:

"I received some time ago your letter of the 24th October. I shall be very glad to receive James if he wishes to come to me as an extra aide-de-camp, though I have already too many, and am, or shall be obliged to take a young Fitzclarence. But I have a sincere regard for James, and besides can refuse you nothing, but to follow your advice. He must get the Commander-in-Chief's leave to come to Spain. He may then join me. He will, however, come too late; I shall already be beaten. I am within four marches of the French, with only a third of my force, and as the Spaniards have been dispersed in all quarters, my junction with the other two-thirds is very precarious, and when we do join we shall be very inferior to the enemy."

On 23rd November he wrote again to Hester from Salamanca:

"We are in a scrape, but I hope we shall have spirit to get out of it; you must, however, be prepared to hear very bad news. The troops are in as good spirits as if things were better; their appearance and good conduct surprises the grave Spaniard, who had never before seen any but their own or French soldiers.

"Farewell, my dear Lady Hester. If I extricate myself and those with me from our present difficulties, and if I can beat the French, I shall return to you with satisfaction; but if not, it will better I shall never quit Spain."

He was unable to beat the French in central Spain, and had to fall back towards Corunna where ships waited to evacuate him and his army. It was at Corunna that in January 1809 he turned on Soult and defeated him, thus giving time for the embarkment of his army to be carried out; James Stanhope had just come out from England to join him as aide-de-camp. Sir John Moore was mortally wounded, and, as with Pitt a few years earlier, James was at his side when he lay dying from the wound in his side. "Stanhope", he said in a low voice, "remember me to your sister." They were his last words.

But Moore was not the only one to die. Unknown at the time to James, Charles Stanhope lay among the hills, shot through the heart. Captain John Paterson, who was there at the time, described what happened in a book "The Adventures of Captain John Paterson", which was published in 1873:

> "About this period [when Major Napier was in command, the Colonel of the 50th Regiment being wounded] the right centre forcing through the enclosures and lanes beyond the village [Elvina] came exposed to a raking fire and in consequence was most severely handled, several officers and men being killed — Among the former was the Honourable Major Stanhope, who received a musket ball in the chest and expired without a struggle. He was a man of dignified appearance, reserved in his deportment, but withal a zealous officer. Having joined the regiment at the outset of this campaign, his career was brief though splendid."

Later again in the same account, Paterson recalls:

> "The remains of Major Stanhope were lowered to the grave by his brother officers and comrades, with their sashes. He had worn this day a suit of new uniform and a pair of light silver epaulets, in which, with his military cloak around him, upon the same hour as his lamented chief, he was consigned to an honourable tomb.
>
> "While we were engaged in the performance of this melancholy duty, the Honourable Captain Stanhope of the Guards, aide-de-camp to Sir John Moore, rode up, directed

by the torch light, to the mournful group. It was the first intimation which he received of his brave relative's fate.

"Dismounting, and overcome with grief, he took a last farewell, and have obtained his ring, together with a lock of hair he tore himself hastily away from the heart-rending scene."

PART TWO

A WANDERER IN ARABY

CHAPTER EIGHT

DEPARTURE

It was a terrible blow for Hester. Ever since her mother's early death she had been searching for a protector, for herself and her sisters and brothers. They had found it all, along with a genuine affection and family closeness with Pitt, but now he was dead. Since Mahon's "ingratitude" Charles had become her favourite; since Leveson-Gower's defection, Moore had become her hoped-for husband: now both were dead. It must surely have seemed to her that it was only necessary for her to grow fond of somebody for them to be immediately whisked away. It seemed to her that she would never recover from the double shock.

In a letter, dated 1809, its pages thickly black-edged for mourning, but so torn that some of it is now illegible, she wrote, probably to T. J. Jackson, but again the name is indistinct:

"You are very kind to me my dear friend. I would have written before but really I have been unable to do a thing. To have lost by one fatal blow the best and kindest of brothers and the dearest of friends is a misfortune so cruel I never can recover it. I try to resign myself to the will of God & reap what consolation I can from the idea that my beloved brother fell in the proud execution of his duty adored by all who accompanied him to the field. The last observation the dear and lamented gen[1] [. . . portion torn . . .] was upon the furious [. . . torn . . .] for had then given under [. . . torn . . .] must have been cut [to] pieces. He rode up on seeing

their wonder [*sic*] exertions & called out, "Well done the
50th Well done my majors" (my brother and his friend
Napier commanded the Regt the Lt Col being absent) Moore
rec^d his death blow shortly after and my poor brother fell
nearly at the same time. Thank heaven the latter did not
suffer one instant or had time to reflect on the me[mory] of
those who remain to deplore his loss. The gallant gen^l lived 3
hours but the agony he was in never deranged his ideas — he
was perfectly collected — [... portion torn ...] if what he
must have [... torn ...] if last words he was [... torn ...]
remember me to y^r sister."

She spoke of Colonel Anderson whom Charles admired, and
who was also present at Moore's death, and gave Hester details of
the scene. Then she said of James who found his brother and
friend both killed:

". . . I often consider him with astonishment & wonder how
it is possible that he is alive. His cloak buckled upon his horse
was shot thro, and the spent ball hit but did not wound
him."

Towards the end of the letter, she wrote:

"I have written you a sad confused letter, but I feel as if I
had just waked up from a horried dream, so you must forgive
it. My father has behaved like a beast. So has Mahon."

She had to do something. Just as, after Leveson-Gower had left,
she had hurried to Walmer, so now, once again, she fled to the
country. The previous summer, she had spent touring South
Wales. (Moore's 'red habit, a l'amazone' letter had been in answer
to one she had written then.) She decided to spend a longer time
there, and her choice fell on "Glen Irfon", a small farmhouse
situated in the Black Mountains, near Builth Wells.
Although this was to be a withdrawal from life, she travelled in
a certain style, taking with her Miss Elizabeth Williams as her
personal companion, as well as maids, grooms, horses, carriages,
endless trunks and full-size portraits of Pitt and her favourite
Royal Prince, the Duke of York. She had written to the local

vicar, the Rev. Rice Price, before leaving London, giving him precise instructions concerning the arrangements to be made:

> "I shall want the parlour; the little room over it for my bedroom, a door to be made to communicate with the bedroom. The room over the kitchen for my maids, and a bed, in the loft or elsewhere, for a boy. The parlour must have two rush chairs or wooden ones, and be carpeted all over with green baize, or the coarse grey cloth like soldiers' great-coats. A table to dine on, a fly-table [a table let down from the wall] and shelves for books. The bedroom must have two chairs and a table; no bed, as I shall bring down a camp bed and furniture complete. Bedside-carpets I shall expect to find, and a chest of drawers. The dressing-room must have two chairs, a table with a looking-glass, two wash-hand basins, two water jugs, one large stone pitcher for water, two large tumbler glasses, two large cups for soap, a tin kettle for warm water, and a little strip of carpet before the table."

It was almost as if she were the quartermaster of a regiment making arrangements for the arrival of a new unit; and like a good regimental officer she brought, or sent on in advance, all the stores she needed. She forgot nothing: special pale green paint to repaint the rooms, white paint for the shutters; even the vegetable and flower seeds to be sewn in the garden. She trusted nobody in these arrangements, but made them all herself. The vicar's wife was inundated with letters giving precise details for the minutest of arrangements; and when, at last, the great lady arrived, a regimental tour of inspection was carried out to see that she had been obeyed.

Once installed Hester threw herself wholeheartedly into the county and local life. It was almost as if she dared not let herself stand still, for fear of what her thoughts might do to her; that only by a febrile and continuous attention to the daily events of life could she keep from her mind the recollection of her losses. Besides riding across the bleak, boulder-strewn mountains, or visiting distant farmsteads bringing with her bales of locally weaved flannel for the cottagers, she developed a passion for dairy farming. She had her favourite cow called Prettyface, and learnt how to make butter. She even took to studying medicine, and produced some home-made medicaments which she tried out on the local population.

Discovering that Thomas Price, the Vicar's son, had ideas of becoming a writer, she encouraged him in this ambition. Though the young man had little real talent, he had a considerable eye for journalistic detail and left a description of her which was probably quite accurate. "She was", he wrote, "neither handsome. nor beautiful in any degree, for her visage was long, very full and fat about the lower part and quite pale, bearing altogether a strong resemblance to the portraits and busts of Mr. Pitt."

Like many other women, she improved with love. Her attractiveness lay in her sparkle, in that feeling of energy and vitality that she showed, particularly in the presence of officers. Men were dazzled by her. But when there were no men around, or when she was mourning the loss or disappearance of a favourite man, her personality changed and she seemed to onlookers to be a rather plain woman of thirty-three.

Not that she entirely gave up the business of attracting men. James Stanhope came to stay during the summer, bringing with him a certain Nassau Sutton. Sutton had been one of the young officers stationed on the coast when she and Pitt had raised and inspected the regiments, from Pitt's Wall at St. Margaret's Bay to Deal Castle. Now unwell, Nassau needed comforting and caring for. All of Hester's maternal instincts, mixed too with her need for male admiration, came to the fore. In a short while she had made a new "conquest" and it was noted that she was no longer dull and dowdy, but "beautiful" again.

When the summer was over, she packed up "Glen Irfon", the Prices, the cottagers, cows, horses and flannel weaving, and returned once more to the house in Montagu Square. But with the coming of Winter it seemed sadder and more desolate than ever. Full of ghosts and memories of Charles' gentle personality and Sir John Moore's handsome gallantry, it became more and more unbearable.

And then there was news of Leveson-Gower. On his return from St. Petersburg, he married Harriet Cavendish, Lady Bessborough's niece, at Chiswick on Sunday, 24th December 1809. Three days later, Leveson-Gower wrote to Lady Bessborough:

"Every hour I passed with Harriet convinced me more and more of the justice and liberality of her way of thinking, and of her claim upon me for unlimited confidence. She is indeed a perfect angel."

For Hester, the news, no doubt gleefully conveyed to her, must have been painfully hard to bear. Within the small aristocratic circle she moved in all news was carried almost simultaneously from one side to the other. Lady Bessborough had won all the way along the line. It would have been hard for any woman to take, and was impossible for one with so much pride as Hester.

There were other causes for distress. Canning, whose hate–love relationship she had always treasured, started, mainly in self-defence, to denigrate Sir John Moore's achievements, and to praise those of Wellesley instead. To Hester, whose sense of loyalty to friends was as great as her pride, this was unpardonable. It was not only an insult to the General she hoped to marry, but, in some way, it made less noble Charles' death. She would, she swore, have no more to do with Canning, or any other false friends, including the Prince of Wales, "that immense, grotesque figure flouncing about half on the couch, half on the ground" as Lady Bessborough once described him.

Then there was the question of her finances. While Pitt was alive, credit was endless. Now that he was dead, and the country knew that she existed on a state pension – a difficult enough thought for a proud woman like her to entertain – of £1,200 a year, matters were very different. Cash payment was demanded. The house in Montagu Square was expensive to run. She could not afford, whilst in London, to keep a carriage, and would not accept charity. Perversely, although she complained of the meanness of the rich Grenville side of the family, she would not accept any favour of them.

Finally, her health, shaken by the shocks she had suffered, had deteriorated so much that her doctor, the same Sir Walter Farquhar who had tended Pitt, advised her to get away for a while, preferably on a sea journey. This coincided with plans she, James and Nassau Sutton had been discussing. James was due to return to his regiment in the Peninsula and Sutton needed fresh air for his health. Why did not the three of them travel together to Gibraltar? Once there, further plans could be made. There was vague talk that Hester and Nassau might spend as much as a year perhaps in Sicily, one of the dwindling number of places in the Mediterranean not occupied by the French. But all that could be decided in the future.

The essential matter now was to get out of England. But how? It was not easy to secure a passage in war-time. Hester, however, solved the matter in her usual imperious way. She wrote to her relative, General Richard Grenville, demanding that the Navy put a vessel at her disposal, adding: "If after Mr. P [Pitt] has added during his administration, 600 ships (line of B and frigate) to the Naval force of this country, a relation or even a friend of his cannot be accommodated with a passage in one of them it is rather hard, and if they do not chuse to do the thing handsomely they may let it alone. I am much too ill to be worried."

The illness prompted Farquhar to advise Hester to take a personal doctor with her. She enquired of Cline, reputedly the finest surgeon of the time, whether he could recommend anyone. Cline asked his son, Henry, and Henry remembered his friend, Charles Meryon.

Charles Meryon was due to spend some years at Oxford taking his degree, but he started badly. Missing the coach, he ran after it as far as the Oxford-road turnpike, and when he finally overtook it, and climbed aboard, he was sweating profusely. It was extremely cold, and perched on the "box" outside he caught a chill. However, "the merriment of a college life" as he later put it, gave him little time to do anything about it, so that the chill turned into a nasty cough. Within a fortnight he was back in London, in bed, with catarrh. It was here that Henry Cline found him, and put the proposal to him.

Charles Meryon was small, rather timid and had a slight impediment in his speech. He had no money of his own, no degree as yet and no wealthy or influential patrons to help him in his career. Henry Cline explained to his sick friend that although the salary would be small, the prospects were excellent. After all, Lady Hester Stanhope was Pitt's niece, and anyone who had been her physician would undoubtedly benefit from that fact. It was hinted, too, that if all went well Hester herself would not be ungenerous.

It sounded like the answer to a prayer. To get away from the damp London climate to the warm Mediterranean was heaven enough; to do so as the personal physician of "une grande dame" like Lady Hester Stanhope was almost more than an impecunious and unqualified medical man could hope for. Charles Meryon accepted the offer, which Cline reported to his father; four days later Charles Meryon had an interview with Hester. Despite the fact that he was only half qualified, she decided that this shy and impressionable young man was the sort of person she wanted as her travelling physician. She appointed him immediately and asked him to dine that same evening — the first of many such dinners.

Although no exact time limit was placed on the duration of the journey, there was no question of this being a final flight from England. In a Codicil, dated 30th December 1809, to the will she had made in 1807, Hester wrote:

"... And whereas he [James Stanhope] and myself are about to take a voyage to Sicily in the same ship and shall probably return to England together consequently we may both be lost in the course of our voyage either out or at home in which case it may be uncertain whether he survived me or not against both which events I am desirous of providing and supplying by this my codicil ... etc."

She packed her belongings and arranged for the house in Montagu Square to be let — it might yet be needed on her return from Sicily. Then, on 10th February 1810, she embarked at Portsmouth on board the frigate "Jason", which was to escort a convoy of merchant ships to Gibraltar.

Her party consisted of her devoted companion, Elizabeth Williams, who had accompanied her to Wales the year before. As Hester was travelling light, she only took one man-servant to carry her voluminous luggage. There were also her two favourite men — her brother, James, and her admirer, Nassau. Situated somewhere in the social ladder between the servants and the personal friends, was her newly appointed physician, Charles Meryon. Thus the great adventure had begun.

Turner's painting of Gibraltar; where Hester first stopped on her journey of 1810. She travelled with her youngest brother, whose regiment was stationed at Cadiz. She left him there and travelled on to Malta.

CHAPTER NINE

MALTA AND GREECE

The journey started badly owing to delays. It took the "Jason"
and her convoy a week to reach Land's End, and a further week to
cross the Bay of Biscay. A week later they were still at sea, off the
coast of Spain. Then, on 6th March, they were struck by such a
violent storm that the convoy was completely dispersed. The
"Jason" was driven so much off course that it seemed likely that
she would founder on the shoals of Cape Trafalgar. Only by fine
seamanship and a good deal of luck did the travellers avoid ending
their odyssey then and there.

At last they rounded the Cape, and making for the African
shore, were able to shelter in the Bay of Tetuán, near Ceuta.
Gibraltar lay across the other side of the Straits. But it was the
sight of Mount Atlas that surprised Meryon. It was not, as his
reading of the classics had led him to believe, a single peak, but a
chain of mountains.

Further surprises awaited the party when they eventually
reached Gibraltar. The flowers were in bloom, the water was warm
enough to bathe in. On the other hand the mosquitoes were
intolerable, and excursions to the mainland were limited by the
fact that French Cavalry units were operating within three miles of
the "Rock".

Hester, because of her name and social position was reluctantly
dragged into the small, cramped round of garrison activities. She
hated them all. She disliked the food, meat was scraggy and
vegetables scarce. She hated the Spanish, who were usually drunk

on bad wine. There was nowhere to ride except on the flat isthmus of sand joining the "Rock" to the mainland. Then James was recalled to his regiment, the 1st Foot Guards, which was stationed at Cadiz. For brother and sister (for though only half-related, they always regarded each other as of full kinship) it meant a sad farewell.

With James' departure, Nassau Sutton seemed no longer interesting. His attraction to her had anyhow been somewhat muted. It had been a question of "faute de mieux". Now, suddenly, she found him tiresome and boorish. With little trouble they agreed to go their separate ways, Nassau to Minorca, Hester and her now reduced party to Malta, aboard the frigate "Cerberus". They visited Fort Mahon (where the 1st Earl Stanhope had won his battle and taken the name for the Stanhope heirs), and finally reached Malta on Easter Day, 21st April 1810, so that their arrival was inadvertently greeted by the ringing of bells, firing of guns and crackers.

The Governor, General Hildebrand Oakes, offered to put her up, but she preferred to stay in the rather gloomy palace, where Elizabeth Williams' sister and her husband, Fernandez, lived. The Williams sisters had been befriended by Pitt, who took a close interest in their welfare. Hester had known them both for some years so it was therefore natural that, on arriving in Malta, she should look up the married sister. The Fernandez couple lived in a large palace that was once used as a hostel for visiting French knights of St. John.

Though Hester had disliked the narrow military world of Gibraltar, she found the more sophisticated one of Malta much more to her liking. With Europe almost entirely under French control, the English and Neapolitan nobility had taken to the Mediterranean. Hildebrand Oakes was a highly civilized man who lived up to his position. His palace was like the court of a king where banquets and festivities followed one upon another; dinners for fifty or sixty people were not uncommon.

As Meryon recounts, with naïve pride:

"On one occasion, it fell to my lot to hand a lady of rank into the supper-room, and, taking a seat by her side, I found myself directly opposite to the Governor, separated by the breadth and not the length of the table, with the Duchess of

Pienne on his right hand, Lady Hester on his left, and a string
of Lords and Ladies and Counts and Countesses on either
hand."

The poor young man, who had lain so low with nasal catarrh in
London, had landed in a society beyond any normal expectation.
Despite his awkwardness and the impediment in his speech, he was
well received by these, to him, superior people. With a certain
charming modesty he recorded that Hester "had not yet begun her
tirades against 'doctors and tutors' " so that she was "delighted to
see me enjoy myself and pleased at the attention which the
General showed me, in common with his other guests". However,
for his own pleasure, he preferred the Maltese girls because they
were smaller than he, and had "beautiful hands and feet".

In May 1810, Lord Sligo, a somewhat erratic and wealthy
young man, arrived at Malta in his spendid yacht. On board was a
twenty-two-year-old friend of his called Michael Bruce. Bruce had
been born in Bombay, his father, Craufurd Bruce, being a member
of the East India Company. Craufurd Bruce was a wealthy man
and a generous if somewhat awe-inspiring father. He had a country
house, "Taplow Lodge", near Maidenhead, a town house, and an
estate in Scotland. He sent Michael to Eton and Cambridge.
Michael, like his father, seems to have been a somewhat didactic
person. Even at the age of twenty-two, when he visited Spain, he
liked to criticize the British and Spanish generals. He had no time
for Arthur Wellesley, and of the poor Spanish general, Venega, all
he could say was that he was "the object of contempt and ridicule
even of his own officers and men".

From Spain he had gone to Palermo in Sicily. When it became
evident that the French were amassing a large army at Calabria
under the command of Murat, recently created King of Naples by
Napoleon, in order to invade the island, he prudently left for
Malta, where he stayed with the Governor.

It was during this stay that he became friends with Hester. He
and Sligo had, it is true, called at Gibraltar on their way from
Spain to Sicily, when Hester was also there; but there is no
positive record that they met, or if they did, that they felt
anything for each other. It was at Malta that the casual meeting
developed into something quite different.

In a letter to his father, he wrote:

Michael Bruce, Hester's great love.
She thought he had a brilliant
career in politics before him and
wanted to teach him all that she,
the grand-daughter of the great
Chatham, could teach. But he
never lived up to her expectations.
(*Frank Hemel*)

"When my arrival here I found Lady H. Stanhope and as I find her much more agreeable much cleverer and better informed than my companions, I have left them and ascribed myself to her party."

It was, once again, Hester's aura and wit that had drawn this man, twelve years younger than she, into her circle. Nor was the fact that she was a Pitt overlooked. In the same letter, Michael reports:

"Lady H. Stanhope who is now my Compagnon de voyage is a woman of very extraordinary talent. She inherits all the great and splendid qualities of her illustrious grandfather."

On 28th May 1810 General Oakes told Hester that the Palace of St. Antonio, his country house some five miles from La Valetta, was now free, as Lord and Lady Bute who had been staying there had gone back to England. Would she like it?

A 250-yard avenue of orange trees led into the courtyard of the palace. It was a large, irregular building, made from the soft island stone. Vines grew in profusion over the walls, square belfry-like towers dominated the palace. Inside, the rooms were cool and dark. The floors, also of stone, were free of carpets. The garden was magnificent, full of orange, pomegranate and lemon trees. The walks were lined with ten-feet-high myrtle trees and oleanders.

It was to this romantic place that Hester and her party moved on 1st June 1810, Michael Bruce following shortly afterwards. The handsome and, on the surface, effete young man, concealed an almost boring seriousness. His father wanted him to go into Parliament, believing that his talents would undoubtedly lead him to the highest position in the land. Michael shared his father's views, but wanted first to travel, so that when the call to office came he would be properly equipped to meet the challenge. He already had very fixed and unusually critical opinions of the state of politics in England. All this he undoubtedly expounded to Hester — to whom it must have seemed like Mahon all over again.

It was, too, all those other people she had mothered since she was a child: Lucy, Griselda, Charles, James, Pitt himself, even Thomas Price from Wales. But this time they were all concentrated in a young, handsome, wealthy man who seemed as infatuated with her as she was with him. It was not long before she became his mistress, not secretly but openly.

Meryon was shocked, writing of Hester, "not hesitating to fix in a large chateau, herself a single lady, with two single men". He did not, anyhow, like St. Antonio. With his solid "middling" turn of mind, he found the orange trees along the drive far less imposing than the oaks and elms that bordered English avenues. The huge empty carpetless rooms made him feel that he was always sitting in a kitchen. He disliked being so far away from his favourite Valetta girls with their little hands and feet.

He tried to made friends with Michael Bruce, but that dashing young man had no time for the stuttering medico Hester towed around with her. Although Meryon had reluctantly to admit that Michael was doing Hester good (she really, he noted, began "to look rather winning") he was intensely jealous of Michael's ascendancy. He believed that Michael was trying to undermine his position. Worse still, Hester had fallen into the habit of taking only Michael with her when she went to dine with the Governor and members of the nobility. He missed the lords and ladies, and complained that Hester and Michael had dined out twice, and he had not been invited.

There was no one to talk to at St. Antonio, even though a new arrival, Mrs. Ann Fry, had joined the party. She was one of those archetypal English maid-servants, so often depicted in music-hall theatre and books. Although she could not give Meryon much comfort, her dislike for anything "foreign" found an echo in his own dislike for St. Antonio.

The lovers, however, had other matters to worry about. They both knew that word would soon reach England that the great Lady Hester Stanhope, and the dashing, young Michael Bruce were living in open "sin" together. Although Hester did not care what people said about her, she did care about the effect gossip would have on Michael Bruce and his career; and she cared what Michael's father thought because Michael was entirely dependent upon his father's allowance. She did not want to be the cause of him losing it, but, on a deeper level, having decided to push this young man to a successful career, she did not want her plans thwarted by an irate father. She was only too well aware of how bad the whole affair could look.

With typical Stanhope bravado she wrote directly to Craufurd Bruce (whom she had never met) one of the strangest letters ever to be written in this kind of a situation:

> Sir,
>
> If your character inspired me with less respect, I should not give you the opportunity of perhaps accusing me of impertinence, in presuming to address you upon a subject which requires all my courage to touch upon, and great liberality on your part, to do justice to those motives which induce me to expaciate [expatiate] upon it. You may have heard that I have become acquainted with your son, his elevated and statesmanlike mind, his brilliant talents to say nothing of his beautiful person, cannot be contemplated by any feeling mind with indifference; to know him is to love and admire him, & *I do both*! Should you hear this in any irregular way, it might give you uneasiness, & you might not

only mistake the nature of the sentiments I feel towards him, but my *views* altogether, & imagine that he had fallen into the hands of an artful woman who wd take him in, as far as it lay in her power. Sir, you need not be under any of these apprehensions, the affection I feel for him wd only prompt me the more to consider his advantage in every point of view, & at this very moment (while loving him to distraction) I look forward to the period when I must resign him to some thrice happy woman really worthy of him. While seeking knowledge & considering plans of future ambition, few persons are perhaps better calculated for his companion than I am, but when he has once taken his line, & become a public character, I shall then like a dethroned Empress, resign to virtue the possession of that perfection which she alone has a right to, & see whether a sacrifice demanded by principle & true feeling, cannot be made with as good a grace as one dictated by policy and interest. Sir, if you knew me, I flatter myself that it wd be unnecessary to give you any further assurance of the sincerity of my intentions, but as you do not, there is no *promise however solemn* I am not willing to make upon this subject. After what I have said I trust that no feeling of anxiety will remain as far as relates to your Son's welfare. It wd be a satisfaction to me to learn (tho' I do not wish you to write to me) that this candid confession of my sentiments, has not displeased you; do not however Sir *mistake* the tone of humility I have adopted thro' this letter, which proceeds in fact from my being one of the proudest women in the world, so proud as to despise the opinion of the world altogether, *as far* as relates *to myself*, but when I an addressing the parent of a man I so tenderly love: (& for whom he has so great an affection) a sacred sort of reverence steals upon my mind, which I hope has communicated itself to my expression, as I have intended they should convey the confidence & respect with which Sir I have the honour to remain,

Yours &c &c

Hester Lucy Stanhope

This remarkable letter was duly sent off; while Michael Bruce, although down with fever caused by a severe blow on the head, also wrote to his father, saying that he agreed with everything Hester said, but adding that if his father were angry, he was prepared to take the blame. It would, however, be some time before the letters could reach London, and Craufurd Bruce take any action.

So the lovers continued to live at St. Antonio, going to parties organized by General Oakes, visiting the Opera and taking part in any other social activity Hester felt able to accept.

Meryon was becoming more and more depressed, finding it almost impossible to be in the same room as Michael. Conditions became so strained indeed that the three of them decided not to take breakfast together anymore; and, if there were no guests at dinner, Meryon was to leave immediately the meal was over.

However, he did not have to suffer this isolation very long. Like so many people who go out to the Mediterranean for the first time, both Hester and Michael went down with a series of unpleasant disorders, enteritis, fever and boils. Meryon appears not to have been affected. Perhaps his medical knowledge helped him immunize himself. Hester suddenly realized that although she might love and admire Michael, she needed Meryon to keep alive. She was also probably extremely bored with the continual bickering between the two of them. She spoke very firmly to Michael, with a result that quarelling stopped, and Charles Meryon was once again back in favour.

John Cam Hobhouse, Byron's friend, visited Malta on 27th July. He duly met Hester but was not at all impressed with her. She was, he noted, with some surprise and a good deal of disapproval "a masculine woman, who says she would as soon live with packhorses as with women". This was at their first meeting. Their second, at dinner the next day, was no better. This time she entered into a long argument with him. "She seems to me", he wrote curtly, "a violent peremptory person."

In truth, she liked to argue like a man, and only showed feminine tenderness when she was with someone she loved. Her dislike for the company of women bordered sometimes on the paranoic. It is true that she had suffered much from the maliciousness of London gossips, particularly after Pitt had died, but many of her women acquaintances, including the Princess of Wales, had offered to help her. She had suffered more, in fact, from men.

Michael Bruce was a very ordinary person, yet to her he was a genius, and she could, in all seriousness, write to his father about his "statesmanlike mind" and "brilliant talents". It was as if the very fact that she had allowed herself to fall in love with him meant that he must be something very special, since she could only bow to a genius. It was easy enough with Pitt, Moore, and even with her own father, for others recognized their worth. But the younger men, Camelford, Leveson-Gower, Thomas Price and now Michael Bruce had not had time to prove themselves. They had, therefore, to be invested with a worthwhileness they did not possess. It must sometimes have been very hard for Michael to live up to the opinion of him held by this fascinating but imperious Amazon of his.

It became hotter and hotter in Malta. Day after day the temperature stuck at a stifling 85° F. There was no wind, and the dry-baked earth reflected back the clammy heat; it became impossible to move about during the heat of the day, even in the cooler walks of the garden. Hester was for moving on as quickly as possible. She had originally intended to settle for a while in Sicily, but Murat was still threatening the island. General Oakes strongly advised her against making any attempt at going there. But where else could she go? She did not want to return to England, particularly now that she had young Michael in tow. Apart from the compilication her love for him might cause at home, there was the purely practical financial consideration. With her £1,200 a year, and Michael's contributions, she was much better off wandering about the Mediterranean.

With Napoleon firmly in control of Europe, only the lands of the Eastern Mediterranean were still open to travellers. So it was towards this area that she now decided to move. Her eventual goal was to be Constantinople, that glittering half-European, half-Asian capital which for centuries had carried on the Roman tradition after Rome had fallen. Standing by its narrow straits it was almost the only "Mediterranean" city to be untouched by Napoleon's sombre shadow.

She had a practical reason for going there, if "practical" is the right word to describe the incredible plan that was forming in her head, and which she discussed quite openly with Meryon and Michael Bruce. In a letter home, Meryon wrote, on 10th June 1810:

"You must have heard Lady Hester talk as I have done to believe that she can entertain any such project as what I am going to mention. She intends at Constantinople, to make friends with the French ambassador, and through this means to obtain a passport to travel through France. Protected by this, she will set off from Turkey, proceed through Hungary, Germany, and arrive at Paris. When there, she means to get into Buonaparte's good graces, study his character, and then sail for England to plot schemes for the subversion of his plans."

There is in this wild scheme a hint of that equally impossible plan of Camelford's earlier in the war, when he had tried to set out from Dover to remove charts from Paris. There, Camelford too, had been armed with a piece of paper that was to be the magic means of getting him through enemy country. Hester, who had always admired Camelford, considered that had he not been "betrayed" by the boatmen, he might well have been successful. What is strange is that her two male companions appeared to encourage her; but then Michael Bruce had, beneath his trim exterior, a certain wildness that was to become evident later, and Charles Meryon was so impressed by Hester, that he believed her capable of anything.

It was not so easy to get away from Malta, especially on board a Navy ship. They were all needed to patrol the Straits of Messina, and to keep the Mediterranean generally open, so that, amongst other things, wealthy young men like Sligo could sail their yachts peacefully from one island to another. It looked at one moment as if Hester would have to hire one, in this case an American brig, bound for Smyrna. Luckily however, Captain C. Brisbane, in command of the 38-gun frigate "Belle Poule", called in at Malta from Corfu. As he was returning immediately to Corfu, the gallant Captain offered to take Hester and her party as far as the Ionian Islands.

The party set off on 2nd August 1810. Elizabeth Williams was left behind to spend a little more time with her sister. Michael Bruce and Meryon travelled with Hester, as did the unhappy Mrs. Fry and two German servants, one a valet from Coblenz called François. By 8th August, they had reached the island of Zante, off the West coast of Greece, where a British regiment, the 35th of

Foot, was stationed. The "Belle Poule" went on to Corfu, but Hester and her party stayed a fortnight on the island, the guests of the Governor, and watched the drying of the recently harvested currants.

The next move was the relatively short journey to Patros on the Peloponnese mainland. They left Zante on 23rd August. Hester's party was again given government transport. But there was a problem. Greece was under Turkish control, and it was not at all certain that the Turkish Governor holding the fortress at the narrow entrance of the Gulf of Lepanto (Gulf of Corinth) would allow an English ship to pass. Thus a felucca, a small coasting vessel driven by oars, was provided so that the passengers could disembark at Patras.

They reached Patras the following day, which was a considerable emotional experience for Meryon, as this was the first time he had set foot in Greece, a country he had studied through the classics for fifteen years. It also gave the two German servants an opportunity to come to blows.

The Marquis of Sligo had been staying with the Pasha of Morea at Tripolizza, in Central Peloponnese. On hearing that Hester and his old friend Michael Bruce had arrived at Patras, he hurried over, and jointed the party. They all now made their way by felucca along the Gulf of Lepanto, sleeping on board at night, and landing among oleander, laurel and arbutus bushes for their meals during the day.

They arrived at Corinth on 7th September. The wind was blowing strongly and they had difficulty in landing. Corinth was a small, miserable town, there being then no canal through the isthmus to give it importance. It was so hot that both Sligo and Meryon slung their hammocks in an arbour of vines in the hope of getting relief.

After three days, the whole party set off across the eight miles of isthmus that separated Corinth from Kenkri on the Athens side. They travelled on post-horses that Sligo managed to procure, presenting a splendid sight as they made their way across the isthmus. Sligo's entourage consisted of a Tartar, two Albanians (armed, much to Mrs. Fry's terror, with silver-stocked pistols and silver-hilted Mohammedan swords that had neither guard nor cross-piece), an interpreter, a Turkish cook, an artist to paint views and costumes, and four English servants. With Hester's equally large

Athens. Here, on arrival, Hester met Byron. They did not like each other. Byron soon found an excuse to get himself invited elsewhere. Hester found the Greek ruins rather boring and wanted to move eastwards as soon as possible.

party they formed a cavalcade of no less than twenty-five people.

It took them four days to find a two-masted ship to take them on to Athens. The Captain wore a red skull-cap and had his twelve-year-old-son with him. Hester very much wanted to hire the young boy as her personal attendant, but the Captain refused to let him go. The journey did not take long, and just as they passed the Molehead at the Piraeus, one of those improbable historical meetings occurred: a man jumped from the Molehead into the sea. Sligo recognized him immediately as a Cambridge contemporary. It was Byron.

Byron had not yet published "Childe Harold" and attained the overpowering popularity that was to be his. Indeed, at this stage, he was mainly known for his exploit of swimming, like Leander, across the Hellespont. He had, whilst at Cambridge, published, in 1807, his "Hours of Idleness" but these had been torn to pieces by the reviewers in the "Edinburgh Review". He had replied, in 1809, with a scathing attack on reviewers in "English Bards and Scotch Reviewers"; but although this had brought him local fame, it had not made him generally known. To Sligo and Bruce, however, he was an exciting, talented person, one they were happy to meet on their leisurely journey. Sligo called out to him to dress and join them at the port as soon as possible.

They moored at the far end of the port, in front of the Custom House. Sligo's Tartar immediately seized a dozen local horses, and loading them with the party's baggage, set off for Athens six miles away. Sligo followed on one of Byron's horses to look for carriages for the main party.

It took them some time to settle down in Athens. Hester had a house to herself, Michael Bruce and Meryon were lodged in another. The meticulous and somewhat finicky medical man hid the crevices in the floor with a mat, then his servant put up his camp-bed and mosquito net. Bruce and Sligo, however, were content to lie on the floor. The servants slept outdoors.

Byron called every day for the first four days after their arrival. He and Hester, however, quarrelled from the very first day. She had entered into an argument with him over the equality of men and women, a subject in which he was not interested. So he agreed with her for the sake of peace and quiet, but to Hobhouse he wrote, "I have seen too little of the lady to form any decisive opinion, but I have discovered nothing different from other she-things, except a great disregard of received notions in her conversation as well as conduct. I don't know whether this will recommend her to our sex, but I'm sure it won't to her own."

To Hester, he was just a "well-bred man like many others". Her opinion of his work showed what little she knew of poetry, for she declared that it was easy enough to write verse. As for his renowned looks, only his cheek and forehead appealed to her.

After four days, he was mysteriously called away "on pressing business" at Patras, and did not return until a few days before they left. It was perhaps Meryon, observant but little regarded, who was the most perspicacious, for later he wrote, "what struck me as singular in his behaviour was his mode of entering a room; he would wheel round from chair to chair, until he reached the one where he proposed sitting, as if anxious to conceal his lameness as much as possible".

Sligo was not just a wealthy young man travelling about the Mediterranean. He, like Michael Bruce, was keenly interested in archaeology. He had, on a previous visit to Athens, carried out excavations. Now he continued them, employing gangs at different points of the Acropolis and other sites. He dug up a great number of ancient Greek ornaments. He and Michael Bruce visited Delphos and Thebes.

Hester remained indifferent to all this archaeological excitement. Ruins bored her; she had, perhaps because of her culture starved upbringing, no interest in the past, even the past of ancient Greece. She could not understand, and did not like, the long discussions the young men had about Greek history. To her, accustomed to being with Pitt, history was the present. She wanted to go to Constantinople, not to see architectural beauties, past or present, but to put into operation her plan to visit France and study Napoleon at close quarters. While her companions eagerly talked over the glories of the past, she was busy working out action for the present.

Of them all, however, it was the despised Meryon who found the greatest fulfilment in Athens. As soon as it became known that he was a medical man, he became beset, as he put it, "with the sick, maimed, halt and blind, importuning me for advice and medicine". Most of these belonged to the foreign colony in Athens, but he also had Greek and Turkish patients. It did not take him long to realize that here in these foreign cities there was plenty of scope for a young man such as himself.

But Hester was all for getting on to Constantinople and eventually, after a month and four days, it was learnt that a 200-ton Greek ship was due to sail from the Piraeus for Constantinople. Not the most prepossessing of vessels, it was loaded to within two-and-a-half feet of the deck with wheat, payment from the people of Athens to their Turkish overlord. It had only one cabin – hurriedly white-washed to kill the vermin. The crew were slovenly-looking, mainly drunk and mostly mutinous. However, it was better than nothing, and for £25 the

Constantinople – the Golden Horn. Hester and her party arrived here at 11 o'clock at night on 3rd November 1810. Her arrival was greeted by the ferocious barking of Cerberus-looking hounds.

party secured a passage to Constantinople. The servants slept on top of the wheat, in the two-and-a-half-feet space below the deck. Sligo, Michael Bruce and Meryon slept on deck although the nights were beginning to be cold. Hester and Mrs Fry were allocated the white-washed cabin.

They sailed on 16th October, were delayed at Sunion for two days by a storm, and then sailed slowly on, stopping here and there. At one place, the avaricious Captain tried, despite the already overcrowded state of the ship, to take on, unsuccessfully, another twenty passengers. Then the weather cleared and "Dolphins gambolled round our prow", noted the observant Meryon, "and light airs filled our cotton sails". Finally, on the evening of the 24th October they passed Gallipoli and entered the Sea of Marmora, where they became becalmed.

But the calm was followed suddenly by a tremendous storm. Panic immediately seized the crew. Instead of fighting the storm, they dashed about collecting money from the passengers. When they had got enough, they tied it in a handkerchief, and fastened the bundle to the tiller, swearing that if they reached a port, any port, safely they would give it to St. George's shrine. The saint must have been listening, for the ship ran before the wind and eventually made Erakli [now Eregli], on the north-west shore of the Gulf of Rhodosto, some sixty miles from Constantinople. The travellers were by now so disgusted by the filth, dishonesty and incompetence of the ship, that they decided to leave it. They were lodged in a Greek monastery, and that same evening, Michael Bruce and Sligo set off for Constantinople.

Five days later, they returned, having arranged accommodation in Constantinople, and bringing with them a Turkish officer armed with a firman or permit to visit Constantinople. They also brought two open boats to take the party to Constantinople, as the roads were dangerous.

On 3rd November 1810, at eleven at night, they landed at Topkhana, one of the principal stairs leading to the Pera district of Constantinople, where a house had been hurriedly made ready for Hester. Preceded by a huge lantern, the party wearily climbed the steep rise. On each side, Cerberus-looking dogs slunk and filled the air with incessant barking, much to the fright of Mrs. Fry. Only Hester was comfortable, since she had a sedan. Most of the luggage had been sent on by mistake to Smyrna, but at least they had finally reached Constantinople.

CHAPTER TEN

CONSTANTINOPLE

Hester took an instant dislike to the house in Pera. It was too small, like the street in which it was situated. There was no view, and she was used to the vistas around Chevening, Walmer and Burton Pynsent. Even St. Antonio had its feeling of expanse. She soon set about looking for a palace (they were quite cheap at the time) outside Constantinople. On Fridays, when the Sultan travelled in state to the Mosque, she contented herself by riding side-saddle through the streets of Constantinople – the only woman to do so.

Meanwhile the men were busy growing moustaches and buying horses, Meryon buying fine Persian one, of great endurance. The silent open-air appearance of the place surprised them, as did the fact that all the shops of a certain trade would be together, so that there would be a tailors' bazaar, a furriers' bazaar, and so on. Only the jewellery shops were enclosed.

It was while they were here that an answer to Hester's June letter came at last from Craufurd Bruce. For although he had duly written both to Hester and Michael, on 20th August, the letters had taken three months to catch up with them.

It was with relief that they read that he accepted the situation between them, and that there would, therefore, be no fear that the funds the kept Michael going would be stopped. No doubt, to Craufurd Bruce's solid banker's mind, his son, whom he continually saw as a future statesman of the stature of Pitt, would benefit more by being taken up by Chatham's grand-daughter than harmed by the gossip his liaison was bound to create.

Hester soon found a house, ten miles from Constantinople in the village of Therapia on the Bosphorus. It was situated on the harbour and had three storeys, each consisting of one large room with four smaller ones leading off it. The furniture was somewhat sparse, consisting mainly of sofas fixed to the walls, which in turn were decorated with frescos on a white background. It would have been a pleasant place in summer, but deadly draughty and cold in the winter. Hester rented it for six months at £25 a month, and moved into it by stages towards the middle of December 1810.

During the move a very disturbing and curious letter was received from Craufurd Bruce. It was addressed to Michael, but was enclosed in one sent to Hester. In it, Craufurd Bruce was utterly outspoken even extremely offensive. He asked Michael whether a temporary infatuation was worth the loss of social position that might be entailed. It was all right for Hester to do what she liked, but while he, Craufurd, admired her in many ways, he felt that in any woman who behaved so brazenly as she did "there must of necessity be something fallacious (*something unsafe and unsound*) in the mind when a woman can depart from the circumspect proprieties of her sex and yield her reputation in society for the temporary gratification of any passion".

This unexpected *volte-face* on the part of Craufurd Bruce may have been due to an anonymous letter he received soon after he had sent off his first two conciliatory letters. It was posted from Dover on 20th August 1810, written in handwriting that was quite obviously disguised, and came immediately to the point:

> "Your son is gone to Constantinople with an artful woman as his *mistress* Lady Hester Stanhope. She means to make him marry her, he knew her first criminally at Malta."

It went on to beg Craufurd Bruce to do all in his power to rescue his son, and concluded by asking Bruce senior to put an advertisement in the "Courier" or the "Globe" newspaper saying: "C.B. has received his friend's letter", so that the writer would know that he had "done his duty".

Although the letter by itself may not have been the complete reason for Craufurd Bruce's change of view, it must undoubtedly have increased the fears he already had. If this letter was an example of the kind of reaction that his son's liaison with Hester could produce, then the advantage of being associated with

Chatham's grand-daughter would vanish. However, Craufurd seems to have wanted to have it both ways; for he did not hesitate to enclose his appeal in a letter to Hester (perhaps he thought Michael would show it to her anyhow); more important, there was no talk of cutting Michael off.

Realizing, probably, that Craufurd Bruce's change of view was due to gossip or worse, Hester wrote back that he should "never believe any *report* you may have about me" and pointed out, sensibly enough, that if Michael had picked up a woman in the streets, it would have done him no more and no less harm than being associated with her. Michael also wrote, under Hester's control, a letter to his father; and so, for the moment, the matter rested.

Hester seems to have had an absolute desire, amounting almost to an obsession, to broadcast her affair to as many people as possible. Perhaps it was that this being her first openly acknowledged unmarried liaison with a man, she needed to parade the fact for her self satisfaction, a form of "look-what-a-clever-girl-I-am" pride; or, possibly knowing the gossipy nature of those around her, she wanted to get the news in first. She wrote, therefore, to Hildebrand Oakes, in Malta, hinting at this and telling him that Sligo would soon be visiting Malta and would convey interesting news. She also wrote to James telling him what had happened.

No sooner had Hester moved to Therapia than she fell ill. The cold, draughty rooms, the bitter Black Sea wind that swept down from the north, and the lack of fire-places gave her a chill which rapidly turned into a fever accompanied by a terrible cough. Never strong, and always threatened through heredity with consumption, her attack looked dangerously like the dreaded illness. Meryon was very alarmed and treated her with all the skill he had at his disposal. Mrs. Fry, despite hating Therapia even more than Pera and St. Antonio, looked after Hester with unchanging devotion and care. Michael and Lord Sligo went off on an excursion to Smyrna. They bought fourteen horses especially for the journey.

The weather at Therapia was unpredictable. One day it might be mild, even in December and January, then snow-storms would envelope them until as late as March. While the two young men made interesting finds on their long expedition, Hester was slowly recovering from her illness and making friends with the inhabitants.

She was rather proud of her success with the Turks, who were

reputed to be the most intractable and stand-offish of all people. In a letter, she wrote: "I have made my own way with the Turks, and I have contrived to get upon so intimate a footing, that the Pasha's brother, brother-in-law, and captain of the fleet, dined with us, accompanied by the confidential physician".

She went on to say that this might not sound a very high achievement, but in fact it was a considerable success since the Turks had very little contact with foreigners. However she rather overstepped the mark when she decided to visit the Turkish fleet in men's clothes, "a pair of overalls, a military great-coat and cocked hat". The Captain Pasha (Admiral of the Fleet) insisted that she changed her dress.

Her success, anyhow, was due to Meryon. He had, quite unexpectedly, cured the Danish minister. As a result his reputation rose to an extraordinary height. Everybody wanted him, including Hafiz Aly (the Captain Pasha) who was married to a woman from the harem of the Sultan himself (a fact that accounted for his rise to power). She was consumptive, and he himself suffered from an excess of red corpuscles in the blood (plethora). Meryon was unable to save the woman but he cured the Captain Pasha.

Some time later, the Captain Pasha, who lived at Buyukdereh, a village on the Bosphorous, in order to be near his fleet which was anchored at the mouth of the Black Sea, called Meryon to him again. Since his wife's death, he had purchased a white girl as his concubine. The girl had become pregnant, and the Pasha, fearing that childbirth would spoil the perfect symmetry of her body, asked Meryon to perform an abortion. This was a perfectly normal Mohammedan custom. However, Meryon explained that, in his country, such action was forbidden, and so he declined the offer. The Pasha, though thinking Meryon a little odd on this particular matter, had so high an opinion of him, that he continued to patronize him, and through him, Hester and her friends.

Towards the end of March, Michael Bruce and Lord Sligo returned at last from their three-month expedition to Smyrna. They brought back with them yet another of their wandering Cambridge friends, Henry Pearce, whom they found travelling the usual Asia Minor route. He joined Hester's party, just at the time

(left) The Sultan of the Turks.

when Sligo was called to Malta to be invested with the Order of St. Patrick by Hildebrand Oakes, at the command of George III in England.

More important perhaps from Hester's point of view the dashing young man was entrusted with the task of telling General Oakes, with whom she had now become great friends, the great news she had hinted to the General — her liaison with Michael Bruce. She was particularly anxious to get the General's blessing as she had just received a furious letter from James Stanhope, berating her for her treason to the family's fine name. He declared, quite frankly, that he would like to shoot Michael.

Sligo, impractical and impetuous as ever, offered to go to Cadiz to bring James round to a better understanding of the situation. He was also given the task of convincing Craufurd Bruce, as well as General Oakes, of the honourable nature of the Hester—Michael affair. He left within a few days of his return on his delicate missions.

Although Hester had recovered from the fever that had attacked her during the winter she still had an unpleasant cough and was very weak. It was decided that she should recuperate at some salubrious place. Michael, who had visited Brusa — capital of the province of Brusa, in central Asia Minor — during his Smyrna expedition, suggested this place, as it was famous for its sulphur baths. Acquaintances of theirs also recommended the place. Hester, though still wishing to put into practice her Napoleon plan, abandoned because of her illness, realized that a complete cure was necessary and agreed to go.

As usual it was the long suffering Meryon who had to make all the arrangements. He set off at midnight on 1st May 1811 (in order to avoid the heat) in an open four-oared barge, equipped with a protective awning. He was accompanied by Aly, a janissary (Turkish soldier), and his servant. They covered the sixty to eighty miles to Mudania, the nearest landing place to Brusa, in twelve hours. They set off immediately for Brusa, eighteen miles inland, and travelling through a luxuriously fertile countryside, reached Brusa that same evening. Next morning he hired three cottages just outside the city.

It was a beautiful and romantic place. Snow-covered Mount Olympus, the highest mountain in Asia Minor, stood in the background. Two streams, formed by its melting snow, ran down

Philadelphia, near Smyrna (now Ismir) in Turkey, visited by Hester on her visit to Brusa in 1811.

the Vale of Brusa. Springs of fresh mountain water seeped from the slopes and cascaded in gentle streams towards the fields and vineyards lower down. The roads were bordered by all kinds of trees — walnut, chestnut, cherry, fig and mulberry, while the hedges were full of apple trees and pear trees, alternating with peach and apricot.

There were, however, snags in this paradise. The main one (added to the presence of thousands of beggars) was the complete refusal of the Turks to have anything to do with "Christian dogs", even such distinguished and wealthy Christian dogs as Hester and her party. However, the ever resourceful Meryon, despite the fact that he could not speak a word of Turkish (not from indolence, but because nobody would teach him) broke the reserve. His reputation as a healer had reached Brusa, and the Governor called him in to look after his young son. As a result, Hester and her party were invited to the Governor's house and through him to the houses of other notable people in the locality. Mademoiselle Arles, daughter of a French silk merchant in Brusa, acted as interpreter.

Had it not been for Meryon it is unlikely that Hester would ever have been accepted, for the somewhat odd reason that nobody knew whether she was a woman or a boy. This was because she rode side-saddle, her face uncovered, whereas Eastern women rode astride with their faces covered. Then again, her English riding-habits looked remarkably like the costumes worn by pages in the Sultan's Palace. So deep was the conviction that she was a man, that when she visited the women's public baths, the ladies were panic stricken and, dressing hurriedly, hid themselves until she had left.

But she was happy there and her health improved. She regained her exuberance and her attractiveness, for, as ever, it was her personality rather than her looks that made her seem desirable.

Hester's reception room in her house at Bebec on the Bosphorous, which she hired for £50 furnished for six months. The divans around the walls served as resting places for guests, who were treated to green sherbet.

Michael Bruce was at the very height of his passion for her. The simple rural life, though set in so different a countryside, recalled her time at Chevening and Wales. She was always happier in the country living a country life, for although she could be scathing and sarcastic in the presence of rulers and wits, she was gentle and compassionate with the poor and simple.

But the time came to return to Constantinople and set in motion her great Napoleonic plan, for the lease on the house at Therapia had ended. Moreover she had little desire to return (without Michael Bruce) to a place where she had been ill. Once more the indefatigable Meryon was told to find yet a new home for one whom he always referred to as "Lady Hester".

On 1st June 1811 Meryon set off for Constantinople, and by the 4th had found a typically Turkish-style house three or four miles out of Constantinople, at Bebec on the Bosphorus. He immediately hired it, furnished, for six months for £50. It was a large weather-boarded house painted red (only the Turks were allowed to paint their houses red). It had a harem with barred and latticed windows, an extensive garden and a marble swimming-pool. Constant northerly winds kept it moderately cool and habitable in the summer.

Meryon returned to Brusa with news of his find, and soon they were all packing up and saying good-bye to the temporary friends made at Brusa. On 1st July 1811 they made their way down to Mudania on the coast and embarked the same evening. Two days later they were safely installed in their new home at Bebec.

They were hardly settled in when General Oakes's much awaited letter arrived. It was dated 22nd June and it left no doubt that the General, broadminded and sophisticated though he might be, considered that her liaison could do Michael Bruce nothing but harm. Like almost everybody else he was convinced the Bruce was some kind of political genius that England could hardly spare away from her shores.

He added somewhat wryly, on learning that Sligo intended to visit Cadiz in order to placate James Stanhope, that he wished Sligo were "a little older, and had a greater knowledge of mankind & of the World". Their enthusiastic champion might be full of worthy intentions, but was somewhat lacking in tact.

Hester replied briefly to the General, telling him that she now had the whole-hearted support of Michael's father. Craufurd

Mosque of the Sultan Achmet in Constantinople.

Bruce had written yet another letter, changing his stance again, and virtually abandoning his son to her. She would, she said, write more fully in a week or ten days. The fact was that she was now well and truly launched on her Napoleonic venture.

Michael had gone to Adrianople, and Hester had at last made contact with Monsieur Latour Maubourg, French Chargé d'Affaires at Constantinople. Owing to the war between England and France, no contact whatsoever was allowed between British and French subjects in neutral countries, and Hester was aware of this. On several occasions she had met young Stratford Canning, the somewhat stiff cousin of George Canning. Twenty-four-year-old Stratford Canning was British Minister (there was no Ambassador) at Constantinople, and he and Hester got on moderately well. Nevertheless when one of his spies, poking around Bebec on quite another matter, came back with the astounding news that Lady Hester Stanhope, niece of the great William Pitt himself, was seen at Bebec in secret and animated conversation with Latour Maubourg, Stratford Canning could hardly believe what he was told. He decided to visit her at once.

The trouble was that Canning, although approximately the same age as Michael Bruce, was too young and too didactic. He treated her as though she were an inferior, demanding an immediate explanation for her behaviour. Never one to take easily to a command, she told him, in effect, to mind his own business, and refused to promise not to see Maubourg any more. Canning was furious, and perhaps worried. As minister he was responsible for the behaviour of British subjects in his area. Their misdemeanours, when reported to London, would adversely affect his career. He knew, too, that Sligo was a friend of Hester and that wealthy and debonair though he might be was very unpopular with the Navy.

It was the affair of the "Brig" or (as Hester preferred to call it) "Sligo's scrape" that worried his friends and, in particular, the Naval authorities. The year before, Sligo had enticed two British sailors to desert their man-of-war and join the crew of his yacht. He did this because he wanted his yacht to be efficiently run, but, in time of war, this was a serious crime. While Sligo sailed gracefully from one end of the Mediterranean to the other, or sought antiquities in Athens and Smyrna, the Naval authorities had set up a Court of Inquiry, and were on his track. Canning knew this.

In a fit of temper, he forbade Hester and her party "entrée" to the British Embassy. Though Michael, on his return from Adrianople, affected to be amused in a superior way, and was careful to keep in the background, Hester wrote off immediately to Lord Wellesley, the Foreign Minister, giving her version of what had happened. It wasn't, in fact, the true version. She said nothing about her grandiose plans where Napoleon was concerned, but merely said that she wanted to go to the south of France for her health. Her request, in the middle of a bitter war when almost every European port was closed to Britons of all classes, must have seemed both odd and dubious. She ended her letter with a scathing attack on Canning's capabilities, and having sent a copy to Stratford Canning awaited developments.

At the same time she returned to the question of General Oakes's condemnation and wrote a long and dignified letter to him, defending her behaviour, adding: "If I have ever the happiness of seeing you in England, I will talk to you quite openly on this business." She confessed that her brother's harsh condemnation upset her, and ended her letter with another attack on Canning, declaring that he was "a bigot and an idiot" adding, "to say the truth, I believe he is jealous".

But her letters and machinations had no effect and the Embassy remained closed to her. Wellesley took no action; he merely wrote on the back of her letter the cryptic comment: "Received 18th October. Answer: None required". Worse, she was informed that, despite her work on Maubourg, no passport to France was forthcoming. Her plan for defeating Napoleon had, therefore, to be abandoned.

It would soon be winter. She had no intention of staying on in Constantinople where her reception was as cold as the northerly winds that came down from the Black Sea. She decided, instead, to spend the winter in Egypt.

Meryon, as usual, set about making the arrangements. He hired a Greek vessel with an all-Greek crew for £65. Then he sold his horses, dismissed his Albanian groom, forwarded some of his belongings to England, and sadly said farewell to the many friends, both professional and private, he had made there. His susceptible heart was much touched by the gifts of embroidery that some of the proud and aloof Turkish ladies gave him. He was particularly happy when he was told that a cerain high-born Turkish lady, "began to think, since she had known me, there might be some good sort of people among the infidel barbarians of the West and North".

The travelling party consisted of Hester, Meryon, Michael Bruce, Henry Pearce (who had more or less taken Sligo's place in her entourage) and Mrs. Fry, who though she dreaded the idea of Egyptians was happy to get away from the infidel Turks. They took with them seven Greek servants, a maître d'hôtel, four men-servants, a cook and scullery-boy and a stray dog. The holds were full of wine and each traveller had a separate cabin. Thus fortified, they left Constantinople on 23rd October 1811.

Sea of Marmora. When Hester set off from Constantinople on her journey south to Egypt in October 1811, her ship had to shelter for five days near the Princes Islands at the northern end of the Sea because of adverse winds.

CHAPTER ELEVEN

SHIPWRECK

Trouble started almost at once. No sooner had they left the Bosphorus than the wind turned against them and they had to wait five days in the Princes Islands, at the northern end of the Sea of Marmora. When the wind changed to the north they were able to make progress again, and, passing the Dardanelles, arrived at the island of Scio where they were held up by gales for ten days.

However, they were in no hurry and were able to enjoy the sights of the island. It was while Hester was riding in the island that a drunken Turkish soldier, aboard a ship moored next to theirs, took exception to something that one of their Greek sailors said and fired off a random shot. It missed its target but neatly holed Hester's mosquito net.

The weather improved and they sailed on to Rhodes where they stopped for a few hours to take on fresh water and bread. On Saturday night, 23rd November 1811, they sailed south for Alexandria. Two days later, when they were half way there a storm hit them again. Customarily the Greek captain turned back and made a run for the nearest port, but the ship was old and unseaworthy and on the 27th she sprang a leak. Since the pumps were unserviceable Michael Bruce, Meryon, Henry Pearce and the seven servants joined the fifteen-man crew in trying to bale out the water with the inadequate buckets at hand. As quickly as they baled out, so the ship filled up with water again. They were at it from seven in the morning until twelve thirty. But the water level still mounted.

Hester, in the meantime, was not inactive. She told Mrs. Fry, who was in a state of near hysteria, to pack a small case containing essential creams and powders (Hester's cosmetics!). Having done that, she opened a cask of wine, and despite the heaving decks and waves that broke continually over the ship, gave drinks to the crew.

Soon after noon the water-logged ship began to list until the sea was level with her gunwales. This was enough for three of the Greek servants to lose their heads completely, and, abandoning all efforts to bale out the ship, fell to their knees imploring the Virgin Mary to save them.

Courage returned when, in the early afternoon, the island of Rhodes came into sight. The captain tried to make for the island, but the ship would not answer to the helm and she could make little headway against the wind. He tried to lower the anchor but the ship merely pulled at it. The water was rising steadily and it was obvious she would never right herself. It was more than probable that she would soon sink.

The order was given to abandon ship and take to the longboat. In order to give the impression that they expected the ship to survive, the passengers left all their clothes on board. The crew took with them what they could. Meryon, at the last minute went down to his cabin and calmly removed what he considered most useful to them in their predicament: some money, a sword and a pistol.

Then he came up on deck and jumped into the longboat. Hester was desperately calling to the stray dog to jump into the boat with them; but the animal, shivering with fear and sickness, refused to move. They could wait no longer and cast off. The listing ship with its lone dog passenger disappeared into the rain-blurred night.

They tried to row for the shore; but the current, the swell and the wind made this impossible, so they decided to make for a rock standing a couple of miles off-shore. Waves broke continually over them and they were pitched and tossed on the sea. It was almost impossible to steer the longboat at all, but through perseverance and luck they managed to slide into a small creek on the sheltered side of the rock, where they managed to land:

It was a bleak place. There was but one small cave sheltered from the flying spray. This was assigned to Hester and the half-drowned Mrs. Fry. There was no means of drying their soaked clothes. Ironically, although entirely surrounded by water, they had nothing to drink; in the hurried exodus from the sinking ship no one had remembered to bring a cask of drinking water. However, they were all so exhausted that, despite the storm and their soaking clothes, they soon fell fast asleep.

Just after midnight the sea became slightly calmer and the captain suggested that he and his crew should try to reach the mainland. When he was asked why the whole party should not make the attempt, he replied, coolly enough, that while he and his crew might succeed in reaching land, a full boatload ceratinly would not. He would, he said, send boats over to rescue them all as soon as daylight came.

In order to reassure those left on the rock, the captain said that as soon as he and his man had safely reached shore they would light a fire as a signal of success. Then they all piled into the longboat and vanished into the turbulent night. Two hours passed slowly and painfully before a light sprang up across the water. It was with a sense of relief that the stranded travellers went back to sleep.

When morning came the sea was no longer as furious as during the night, but it was still rough, and it was bitterly cold. Apart from Hester's small cave, there was no shelter. There was neither vegetation nor bird life on the bleak rock. Both hunger and thirst began to bite.

They told themselves that rescue would soon be on the way, but as dawn gave way to daylight, and there was no sign of a boat on the choppy seas, doubts and anxiety returned. Now that the captain and crew were safe, what was to prevent them leaving their erstwhile passengers stranded? For, with the ship gone, they could be of no further use. The selfish behaviour of the crew both during and after the shipwreck did not augur well. The captain's real reason for leaving last night might well have been exactly in order to abandon them and thus leave no independent witnesses to the disaster.

As the morning wore on, and there was no sign of a rescue boat, the certainty that they had been abandoned grew upon them. The Greek servants began praying to another saint to save them. Mrs. Fry, now convinced that all was lost, prepared herself stoically for the end. Hester spoke of past feasts, while Meryon calculated the risks of attempting the swim to the mainland. Only Michael Bruce and Henry Pearce, who both seemed to thrive off shipwrecks and danger, were able to take a detached, philosophical view of the possibility of death.

The afternoon came and went and there was still no sign of rescue. Their hunger and thirst was becoming really painful. The prospect of another night on that awful rock reduced them all to silence. The sea was as strong as ever. Then, just half an hour before nightfall, Meryon, who had remained on watch, saw a dark speck on the sea. He called the others. The speck grew larger and turned out to be a boat. It sailed into the creek, and was moored alongside.

To their surprise there was no sign of the captain. On their enquiring after him a very drunken sailor said the captain had not wanted to risk his life a second time, and had very sensibly decided to stay behind. It was soon quite obvious that every single member of the crew was drunk, and that it was indeed this very drunkenness that had given them the courage to face the storm again.

However, they brought with them bread, cheese, honey, chicken, water and rough distilled arrack (neat alcohol). This food, the first they had had for nearly thirty hours, was eagerly seized upon; and, when they had finished eating, they felt better.

It was now dark again, and pouring with rain. Michael Bruce was for spending another night on the rock and then leaving in the morning. In view of the drunken state of the crew, this was considered advisable, and they got themselves ready for sleep; but, as the night wore on, the crew, drinking more and more of the neat arrack, grew wilder and more uncontrollable. They announced their intention of leaving immediately, adding, perhaps wisely, that if the wind changed, as it might do, and the sea came in from another angle, they would all be washed away.

There was nothing anyone could do. The crew was determined to leave. If the passengers remained, they would be left to their fate. No other boat would come for them. It was, the Greek sailors said, for them to decide. The choice lay between starvation and drowning, for it seemed unlikely that in their drunken state the crew could possibly make land. However, it was their only chance so once more they huddled into the longboat.

It was an appalling journey, with waves coming straight at them from the shore they were trying to reach; but the sailors worked, as drunks sometimes will, with an astonishing single-mindedness. Indeed, had they not been drunk, they might have been overwhelmed by the sheer impossibility of what they were trying to do — row straight into the full force of the storm.

However, after four nightmare hours they finally neared land; and now the very direction of the off-shore wind helped them. As the sea became calmer the boat grounded on the soft sand. Then a wave engulfed the half-held boat, and it was each for himself. As the boat filled with water, and was stoved in, passengers, servants and crew jumped into the sea, and waded ashore as best they could. But even at this moment of extreme danger, courtesy reasserted itself; Hester was lifted out of the boat, and carried, exhausted but triumphant, ashore.

They had landed at a bleak place, with an empty marsh all around them. In the continuous torrents of rain, its flat surface, broken only by stones and tufts of marshland grass, looked even less inviting than the rock. But at least they were safe from the sea.

They trudged wearily inland; and, after covering three miles through the rain, finally came across an isolated windmill, the only building for miles around. They knocked up the miller, who allowed Hester and Mrs. Fry to shelter in his granary. There was no room for the rest, so they stayed out in the pouring rain, and built a huge fire with which to warm and cheer themselves.

Hester immediately settled down among the sacks of grain and fell asleep. She, like Pitt, could fall into a deep sleep almost at will. But, no sooner had poor Mrs. Fry laid herself down on the hard floor than she became aware of a feverish scrabbling all around. Looking up, in the dim light left by the miller, she saw huge rats skimming, like distorted acrobats, up and down the ropes in the mill.

That was enough for her. In the past forty-eight hours, she had nearly been drowned a dozen times, and when not being drowned, had been threatened with starvation. Now, she was expected to lie quietly down on this stinking floor, while rats swung to and fro on ropes above her head. Picking herself up, she marched out of the mill and joined the men around the fire. Hester slept peacefully on.

The morning was beautiful and fine and all trace of wind, storm and rain had disappeared. It was almost as if there had never been a gale at all. But the evidence was there in their clothes, or rather lack of them. Michael was left with nothing but a pair of breeches and a small waistcoat. The rest were similarly denuded.

It was Hester who lost most. Though she managed to take away two pelisses (ankle-length mantles with armholes), her precious dressing-box, a snuff box given to her by Sligo, a miniature of Sir John Moore and a locket containing a curl of her brother Charles's hair, she lost everything else. Michael estimated the value of her property that had gone down with the ship at between £2,000 and £3,000.

Meryon, too, lost almost everything he possessed, including his medical books and medicine chest. All those sentimental purses and pieces of embroidery given him by the ladies of Constantinople also went to the bottom. Worst of all, perhaps, was the loss of his diaries and notes; for, even at this early stage, he had seemed to see himself in the role of a Boswell to Hester's Doctor Johnson.

The miller was sent off to the nearest village to find transport, and finally returned with a number of mules and asses. These brought the shipwrecked party to the nearest village, a miserable flea-ridden place with not a single house that could keep out the rain. However, they decided to remain where they were, while Meryon (who else?) was to ride off to Rhodes; for though the money he had prudently saved would be enough for their immediate wants, they would need a great deal more.

The rest of the party followed more slowly. They stopped for a while at Lindo, a little town difficult to get at but where at least there was a clean house belonging to a Greek called Philippaki, who offered to put up the now feverish Hester for a while. Mrs. Fry, who utterly refused to learn any foreign language whatsoever, referred always to their kind host as Philip Parker.

It was from here that Michael Bruce wrote to his father, giving details of the shipwreck, and Hester continued the letter to Crawfurd Bruce that had begun at the village where they first stopped, and was headed, "From a miserable village near the extremity of the Island of Rhodes. early in Decr." It was completed later at Rhodes.

Unknown to Hester, as she lay feverishly in "Philip Parker's" house, her Stanhope grandmother, Griselda, lay dying in the Dower House at Ovenden across the park at Chevening. She was ninety-two years of age, but had retained all her faculties almost to the end of her life. In September of that year, she had written a lengthy letter to Tender, the gardener at Chevening, about the distribution of apples from the Chevening gardens.

She died on the 28th December. The 3rd Earl, now living a strangely restricted life with his "Wally" at the big house, mourned her with real sorrow. Apart from his first wife, she was perhaps the only member of his family he had truly loved.

But Hester had now moved on to Rhodes. Because it was impossible to find any kind of suitable Western European clothes, and because local taboos made it difficult to wear Turkish women's clothes, she decided, like the men in her party, to adopt Turkish men's clothes. Mrs. Fry objected strongly, but Hester overruled her. She pointed out that it would be better to wear men's clothes, than to have to wear a veil permanently. Mrs. Fry reluctantly agreed and soon the whole party were arraigned in Turkish men's clothes.

Hester found the clothes delightful. "We all mean", she wrote, "to dress in future as Turks. I can assure you that if I ever looked well in anything, it is in Asiatic dress, quite different from the European Turks."

They had anyhow recovered from the shock of the shipwreck. Hester was even able to assure General Oakes that all was well: ". . . do not fancy us dull, for we (myself included) danced the Pyrrhic dance with the peasants in the villages on our way hither."

The crew of the ship was soon paid off, rather too liberally in Meryon's view, but Hester refused to give a penny to the captain, when it was learnt that he wanted the ship destroyed; and that if it had not been for this, he might even have brought her, listing as she was, into port.

Though the seventy-five-year-old English consul at Rhodes was "a dear old fellow" and did all he could for them, there just were not the stores available on the island to replace all those they had lost, particularly from the medicine chest. There was nothing for it, but to send to Smyrna on the mainland for replacements. Naturally enough, it was to Meryon that this task was entrusted.

Meryon left, accompanied by Mustafa (whom Mrs. Fry called Master Farr), a huge piratical Turk armed with a three-foot yatagan (sword) and two pistols, and Etienne, Henry Pearce's servant, who could speak a number of languages. They rode postillion, that is to say, on horseback, changing horses at each stage, galloping over mountains and through forests as fast as they could. They left on 22nd December 1811 and were expected back within a fortnight.

But the fortnight became three weeks, then four. When five weeks had gone by, Hester, who had moved with her whole party to a cottage on the sea, three miles from Rhodes, began to be worried. It wasn't until nearly six weeks had gone by that Meryon arrived back at Rhodes, on the 29th January 1812.

There had been many reasons for the time the short journey had taken. The quality of the horses was poor; it had taken longer than expected to find the replacement stores in Smyrna; Etienne had become convinced that Mustafa was planning, with some of his friends, to waylay and rob them on the way back; and finally there had been the usual violent storms.

However, the sight of all the marvellous new Turkish costumes Meryon had brought with him filled them with pleasure. Each began to put on whatever took his or her fancy, quite unaware that, in Turkey, each item of clothing had a special social significance. After many weeks of running around looking like the cast from "Robinson Crusoe", they now resembled an assorted chorus from an inaccurate Aladdin.

There were less of them now than before. All the servants, except a Greek boy, Georgaki Dallegio, had been sacked for trying to threaten Hester into giving them new clothes immediately, when she had said that they would have to wait until they got to Alexandria. Etienne was sacked too, immediately on his return, for having, as Meryon put it "been detected in administering remedies as a doctor". So that only left Hester, Mrs. Fry, Michael Bruce, Henry Pearce, Charles Meryon and the Greek boy.

There was no longer any need for them to stay in Rhodes, and luckily Captain Henry Hope, "Chivalry" Hope as Hester called him, who commanded the frigate "Salsette", (a very much finer ship than the miserable vessel that had sunk), hearing that Hester was "marooned" at Rhodes, sailed from Smyrna to pick her up, along with her party, and take them all to Alexandria.

They sailed about a week after Meryon's return, and after an easy journey, reached Alexandria on 14th February 1812. As soon as Colonel Misset, a British resident, heard of Hester's arrival, he sent his secretary, Thurburn, to welcome her. She, Mrs. Fry and the Greek boy were soon installed in a small house, while Michael, Henry Pearce and Meryon were lodged with separate families nearby.

Arabs at the time of Hester's visit to Egypt. It was upon these men that European travellers like Hester depended for the conveyance of the considerable amount of baggage she usually took with her.

CHAPTER TWELVE

EGYPT AND THE HOLY LAND

Hester disliked Alexandria almost as much as she disliked Constantinople. In a letter to her old friend, General Oakes, she wrote: "This place, I think quite hideous, and if all Egypt is like it I shall wish to quit it as soon as possible."

However, she was determined to be received by the Pasha, the wily Albanian upstart, Mehemet Ali. Egypt, like Greece, Serbia and parts of Hungary, were all nominally under the control of the Sultan at Constantinople. So was Syria, including the Holy Land, Rhodes and all the other islands between Greece and Turkey. The Turks had set up a system of local Turkish rulers, called Pashas, who, while having complete jurisdiction in their own territories, nevertheless owed allegiance to the Sultan.

This system worked well enough as long as the Turkish central government was strong, and as long as the victorious Turkish armies were aggressive. But although they overwhelmed the civilizations they met they could not subjugate them, and as the power of the sultans declined, so nationalism reappeared among the conquered people. At the same time, local Pashas, many of whom were in fact drawn from the occupied countries themselves, became more and more independent and defied the Sultan himself.

Or, as in the case of Egypt, they were taken over by unscrupulous adventurers. Mehemet Ali was a tough Albanian of low birth who had served in the Turkish Army, and by intrigue and murder he had grabbed the Pashalik of Cairo. He was as keen

147

to meet Hester as she was to meet him, for no English woman had ever been brought to his Court, and he hoped that his proposed generosity would show her country how civilized and enlightened he was.

Although Hester would liked to have left at once for Cairo, she had to wait a fortnight while new servants were engaged. It was while she waited that Colonel Misset, with amused tactfulness, pointed out the sartorial error she had made: without realizing it, this great English aristocrat was parading about in the clothes worn by a member of the lowest order of the Turkish social hierarchy. But at last they set off, stopping at Rosetta to admire the famous gardens and to be incessantly bitten by fleas. Finally, they hired two large barges and eventually reached Cairo, on 14th March 1812.

Hester prepared for her visit to Mehemet Ali. Determined not to make the mistake of choosing an inferior form of costume again, she settled for a Barbary outfit. It cost over £300, its dominant colours being purple and gold. Her gold-embroidered pantaloons alone cost £40, her coat and waistcoat £50, her sword £20. Her turban was made of the best cashmere material and cost £50. She wound £50 worth of cashmere around her waist. Not to be outdone Michael Bruce was equally splendidly attired; he had spent £50 on his sword alone. Meryon was more modestly dressed in the clothes of a Turkish government official.

The Pasha, to show how he valued her visit, sent five horses, handsomely decorated with rich trappings, to bring her and her party to him. Palace officials led the procession. As a special favour, the guests were allowed to ride up to the inner gate, instead of customarily dismounting at the outer. He received Hester in a gilded pavilion in the garden of his harem. Again, in order to show how much he appreciated her visit, he actually rose to his feet when she entered.

They sat on scarlet velvet sofas embroidered with gold, around a central fountain. First, a green sherbet was served in beautiful cut-glass cups. This was followed by "the Pipe", which Hester declined, but which the small sharp-faced Pasha accepted. Coffee in china cups completed the refreshments. A visit to the harem, which was being redecorated, brought the audience to an end; and with the same elaborate displays of courtesy, the Pasha said good-bye to Hester. Each was as satisfied as the other with the outcome of the visit.

Rosetta, situated between Alexandria and Cairo, in Egypt, was famous for its gardens. Hester and her party found that it was also famous for its fleas, which bit them incessantly.

Hester had received a letter from James Stanhope before Sligo had had a chance to talk to the young Guards Major. He had revised his previous harsh opinion of her liaison with Michael Bruce, and this had made her feel much happier. The only minor trouble, apart from the fleas, came from Henry Pearce, whom she called Harry. She became convinced that Pearce had only joined the party because he had run out of money, and Michael was financing him. Hester had hoped that Harry would be a good influence on Michael, but in fact she considered that "the ugly little quiz" (an odd and eccentric person of ridiculous appearance) as she called him, was a toady. He was so keen to keep the peace that he would not reprimand Michael at all, a fact that Hester, who was very keen on reminding Michael of his responsibilities to the future, found disgraceful. "People I love", she told Crawfurd Bruce, "I lecture & with an earnestness as if my life depended upon their improvement . . . ."

Poor Michael must have found Hester's "lectures" very hard to bear; for he had just written to his father saying that he had decided to abandon any attempt to get into Parliament or play the role of statesman his father had planned. He gave, honestly enough, the "inadequacy of my abilities" as the main reason for his decision. His great ambition now was to join his father and help him administer his estates, for the good of those who depended upon them.

Their adventures caused amusement and even puzzlement in England. That indefatigable letter writer, Lady Bessborough, in one of her epistles at the time to Leveson-Gower, wrote: "Think of poor Ly. Hester Stanhope, Mr. Bruce and Henry Pierce [*sic*] being taken by the Arabs! If they treat them well she will rather like *an adventure*, and perhaps end with becoming a wife to an Arab Chief, I should not wonder."

The reference to "being taken by the Arabs" may be the result of a distorted version of the shipwreck on Rhodes, or may refer to the incident near Alexandria when Meryon and Henry Pearce (but neither Hester nor Michael) were detained for a short while by an over-zealous Albanian captain. As far as Lady Bessborough was

(right) Egyptian official at the time of Hester's visit to Egypt. Although Mehmet Ali had installed his own power-pattern on the country he had taken over, he relied heavily on Egyptian officials, many of whom had been trained by the French.

concerned this item of news was soon superseded by the resignation of the Duke of Northumberland from his regiment, and the troubles Lord Wellington, as Sir Arthur Wellesley had now become, faced in Spain, where her son Frederick was serving.

Hester could not leave Egypt without visiting the pyramids. It was, in those days, a somewhat hazardous business, as brigands were apt to waylay travellers. Hester, however, engaged a troop of French Mamelukes, which had remained in Egypt after the withdrawal of Napoleon's army, and joined the Pasha's service, changing at one stroke both their master and their religion.

They were magnificently uniformed and mounted, by far the most impressive horsemen in the Pasha's service. It was probably their presence rather than the pyramids that made the expedition worthwhile. With their habit of drinking and gaming, they made, while Pearce and Meryon engaged dancing girls to while away the evenings, attractive companions. At all events, when the party did reach the pyramids, Hester said that it was too hot, and while her companions visited the pyramids she remained contentedly outside, under a tent.

On the way back, Hester, Michael, Meryon, Henry Wynn (a cousin of Hester who happened to be on a brief visit to Egypt at the time), and his turbaned servant, George, all climbed into a dirty, rickety boat, rowed by one man, in order to re-cross the Nile. The river was broad and the current strong. When they were half way across, the rower, while straining at the oars, pushed a foot clean through the bottom of the boat. Rower and passengers gazed in immobile horror as the boat began to fill with water.

But help came from an unexpected quarter. The resourceful George pulled off his turban, and stuffed it into the hole, thus halting the inpouring water. Then, threatening the rower with instant death unless he pulled as hard as he could, he stood, fists doubled, over the boatman. Thus encouraged, the oarsman worked with double speed and strength. Once the shore was safely reached, George pulled his turban out of the hole, and the boat promptly sank.

The time for leaving Cairo now came. The Pasha presented Hester with a magnificent charger, which was sent off to her favourite Duke of York. A second charger, gift of one of the Pasha's noblemen, was also sent to England.

Hester was now travelling in great style. The troop of devoted

Mamelukes accompanied her. She added six green marquees, decorated with flowers, to her baggage. The cavalcade stopped at Damietta on the Nile, seven or eight miles from the sea, but the eternal fleas and the flies and mosquitoes from the nearby rice marshes drove them on. Remembering the shipwreck at Rhodes, they were careful to hire a sturdy three-masted polacca, and the party set sail for Syria, on 11th May 1812.

Five days later they landed at Jaffa, the main port for any visitors to the Holy Land, as Syria was then more frequently called. It had taken Hester two years and three months to get there. Never, at any time, had she deliberately aimed herself there; but slowly events, as if taking a part in her destiny, had, by denying her other possibilities, driven her to this historic land. Had it not been for the deaths of Sir John Moore and her brother Charles, she might never have left England at all. If Murat had not threatened Sicily she might have settled there. If Constantinople had been less unfriendly and cold, and Cairo less flea-ridden, she might have stayed in either place. Whether through fate or an inner unacknowledged urge, she was there at last.

She and Meryon were beginning to understand the language and people of this eastern part of the Mediterranean. Hester never really liked the Greeks, who seemed, she declared, to shuffle too much. She admired the Turks, and began to understand the structure of their well-bred society, and she loved their clothes.

Jaffa was full of pilgrims, some 4,000 of them, who had visited Jerusalem for Easter. Many of them were in a pathetic state, travelling long stages without rest, the women crammed into paniers slung to the sides of camels, horses, mules or asses. Nor were they all intent on religious observations. Many were out to make a good profit from bartering products from Western Europe for Damascus silks, drugs and wonderfully woven cloths. The English were conspicuous by their absence.

However, Hester decided to make that up by the magnificence of her visit to Jerusalem. She dressed herself up in her best Mameluke outfit. This consisted of a satin vest, held to the figure by a single button at the throat and waist, over which she wore a red cloth jacket. Her trousers were of the same red material, with gold-embroidered pockets. Her wide turban was made from a cashmere shawl. When she was travelling on horse-back she wore a white-hooded cloak, with tassels, which, Meryon recorded "gave

Jaffa was the main port used by pilgrims visiting Jerusalem at Easter time. Local traders charged exhorbitant prices; and there were plenty of brigands on the road to the Holy city to make a pilgrimage there memorable for more than one reason.

(right) Hester on horseback. Another of the posthumous portraits done of Hester. The costume and details are accurate enough. She was often taken for a "beardless youth" because of her habit of dressing like a man. (*Frank Hemel*)

The mosque of Omar at Mount Moriah, where the temple of Solomon stood.

Bethlehem was included in Hester's tour of the Holy Land. Meryon was not much impressed by the place and thought all the inhabitants looked like robbers.

Tyre. One of the ports along the coast that were used by coastal vessels and visitors to the Holy Land.

great elegance to her figure". She was often mistaken for a young boy whose moustachios had not yet grown, the paleness of her face being put down to the use of powder and paint, a not unusual habit among Eastern young men.

Henry Pearce, who found some much-needed money waiting for him at Jaffa, decided that it would be more tactful for him to abandon Hester's party; so they set off for Jerusalem without him. They rode through the gardens of Jaffa, saw a locust swarm covering houses and trees so thickly that they looked as though they were painted bright green, and were welcomed by a drunken monk at Ramlah, where they spent the night.

Next day they were off again, travelling along increasingly narrow and stony tracks. That evening they were guests of a "highwayman" sheik called Abu Ghosh, who usually extracted levies from struggling pilgrims, but was so impressed by Hester's magnificent cortège, that he ordered his four wives to produce the best dishes they could for his guests. The first wife arrived with mince rolled in vine leaves; the second with a marrow stuffed with mince and rice; the third with a whole roasted lamb; and the fourth with four boiled chickens covered with boiled rice. Filling though the meal might be, it did not reach any culinary heights, according to Meryon, but was the best that non-alcoholic Arabs could produce. Next day they crossed the last barren rocky mountain before Jerusalem. The city lay, sombre and imposing, behind its high walls; while only the spires of its churches could be seen.

Hester suddenly remembered an event that had taken place some years earlier, while she was still with Pitt. A fashionable fortune-teller called Brothers had got into trouble, and had been thrown into prison. Whilst there, he had asked Hester to visit him. Curious to know why he should have picked her out, she did as he requested. Instead of the favour she half expected he would ask, he told her with a strange kind of intensity that she would one day make a pilgrimage to Jerusalem, spend seven years in the desert and that she would become the Queen of the Jews and lead forth a chosen people. As she then had no intention of leaving England, she dismissed his prediction as being the ravings of a madman; but it must have stayed somewhere in her mind, for now it came back to her, and half-jokingly, half-anxiously, she said that since the first part had come true, so might the rest . . . .

Burckhardt, a Swiss explorer who, like Hester, travelled extensively around the Middle East. He invariably dressed in Eastern clothes and sometimes went by the name of Shaykh Ibrahim. (*Frank Hemel*)

The visit to Jerusalem was not particularly successful. Michael and Meryon stayed in the Franciscan monastery, but since women were not allowed Hester lodged in a house next to it. "This", Meryon scathingly commented, "consisted of a few rooms, bare of everything but fleas ..." They were pestered by beggars, both secular and religious. When they visited the Holy Sepulchre, they were mobbed by sightseers, who upon hearing that an English "Princess" was visiting the shrine became more interested in seeing her than maintaining an attitude of reverence. Even when the Turkish guards laid about them with whips and sticks the rowdy spectators continued to press around the visitors. It was hardly the right atmosphere to visit so significant a place. Even Mount Calvary was equally commercialized.

The following day they visited Bethlehem, where again sight-seers followed them, while local inhabitants nagged them into buying unwanted crosses and rosaries. To Meryon the local people looked like robbers, and he was convinced they were. They had broad stilettos stuck in their girdles, and were not slow in using them if they thought their prospective clients were not showing sufficient enthusiasm for the cheap baubles on sale.

Michael Bruce and Meryon dined with the local mufti (official head of the Mohammedan religion) but it was not much of a success. The usual chicken and boiled rice was served on a huge copper and tin tray. Instead of carving the bird, it was torn joint from joint by a servant. However, the conviviality of the company did make up, to some extent, for the unimaginative food.

They were all pleased, however, when, on 30th May 1812, the party, now augmented by ten camels and four horses, set off once again on its cavalcade. As they travelled slowly around the Holy Land they attracted more and more adherents. Friends, servants and hangers-on joined the group, until, with their tents, camels and horses, they resembled a perambulating circus. Advance publicity preceded them wherever they went. The English "Princess" who travelled with fabulous ostentation was greeted with awe and deference as much by the ruling Turkish élite as by the subjugated Christians, Jews and Arabs.

Hester's cavalcade was the continuation of an old tradition. The Kings and Queens of Europe had perambulated through their lands since mediaeval days, taking with them the whole Court, and conducting their business from whatever site they had chosen.

Fording a river near Acre. The physical difficulties of travelling around the Holy Land were often considerable. Fords could be suddenly swollen by flood water and become dangerous.

Sometimes it would be the mansion of a powerful subject, sometimes tents pitched in a convenient field. Even when the Court became more settled, wealthy families would make the Grand Tour of Europe in the same style, moving en bloc across the European countryside, and setting themselves up for a few days, weeks or months at chosen places before moving on. What was exceptional about Hester's caravanserai was that it was taking place in the Middle East, where there was almost permanent strife between Turkish overlords and their subjugated people, particularly the Arabs; and where there were also periodic waves of destructive plagues.

So, in this fashion, they returned to Ramlah, being once again regally entertained by Abu Ghosh, then on to Caesarea, Mount Carmel, Haifa and Acre. They visited Nazareth, where the famous

Swiss explorer, Burckhardt, who liked to call himself Shaykh Ibrahim, turned up, with bare legs, a turban, coarse long shirt and Eastern style slippers. Although welcomed by Michael, he was not much liked by Hester.

Most of the party were now travelling on horseback. Even poor Mrs. Fry, who distrusted Eastern horses as much as she disliked Eastern people, had to ride too. Although it was the custom for Eastern woman to ride astride, she considered this indecent; and insisted on riding side-saddle, as she would have done at home. Unfortunately, there were no side-saddles available, so that she was continually falling off her horse.

But she came to no harm, unlike Hester, who, on the day the party were leaving Nazareth, had a nasty fall. Her horse trod on a stone, slipped, threw her, and in so doing rolled over onto her. Everyone dismounted and helped to get her away from the fallen horse. Her leg was badly bruised and the trip was temporarily cancelled, everyone returning to their original lodgings. A week passed before she was able to travel again, and even then because of the poor state of her health the journey back to Acre took two days instead of one.

However, she soon recovered her health when she reached Acre again, and immediately started making plans for the continuation of her wanderings. There was little else she could do. She could not return to England even if she had wanted to, because of her promise to Craufurd Bruce; and she had found nowhere, except perhaps Brusa, where she would have liked to stay for long. Perhaps in time she would find what she was looking for – who knew?

The caravan left Acre and climbed up among the narrow precipitous paths along the coast. The camels, though secure on the flat, were not built to negotiate narrow tracks winding half way up huge precipices. Meryon, as usual, was the leader, spending his time either at the head of the column, or riding back to where the camel carrying his new and precious medicine chest stumbled and lurched. Somewhere in between, he would pass Hester with her two Egyptian grooms walking on either side of her horse's head; and Mrs. Fry who, though scared of the heights, still insisted on riding side-saddle.

In the evenings they would set up camp, then the next morning, soon after breakfast, strike tents and set off once again for the

next place to be visited. Sometimes, if the place were interesting enough, they would remain in the same location for some days.

They were not the only caravan to be travelling in this way. Near Tyre, while strolling near the campment, Meryon came across another camp. It belonged to a Turk who was sitting under a fig tree busy boiling a saucepan over a fire made between rough stones.

On a nearby carpet sat two beautiful young girls, one bronze faced, the other completely black. Neither attempted to hide their faces as Meryon and the others approached. The Turk hospitably invited them to join him, and when they had done so, asked them whether they belonged to the camp of the English princess travelling through the country. He then quite casually revealed that he was a slave trader, and that if the English lady wanted either of the girls he would be happy to oblige. Meryon and his companions hurriedly left.

They continued slowly and ponderously on their way, passing a stream where naked women were unconcernedly washing their bodies and clothes. They met six blind men, each holding on (as in the Bruegel painting) to the shirt-end of the one in front, and eventually they reached Sidon. Here the chivalrous Captain Hope of the "Salsette" appeared again for a brief reunion.

Hester then received an invitation to visit the Emir Beshir of the Druses, and set off once again, trailing her caravan behind her. The Druses were a mysterious people who lived on and around Mount Lebanon, inland from the coast. They were not like any of their neighbours, but had originally come, it was believed, from Africa. Their religion was almost incomprehensible. The men were divided into the Initiated and the Non-initiated, the latter doing all the work. The Initiated, considered holy, did the thinking, and usually wore very wide white turbans and sober black clothes. The women wore peculiar tall head-dresses, not unlike those worn by mediaeval women in Europe, but with much more voluminous folds. They were, commented Hester, "like a great tin trumpet on their heads & a veil suspended upon it, & seeming very proud of these frightful horns". The Emir who ruled this community was said to have started life as a Mohammedan and then to have been converted to Christianity. This had not, however, prevented him from having his three nephews blinded in case they might aspire to his throne.

Del-el-Kamar, or Dayr el Kamar as it was spelt, was the capital of the Druze. It had a population of 4000 and was ruled by Emir Beshyr. Typical are the tall horn-like hats of the women. Hester made a number of visits to this remote and mysterious land.

He sent down twelve camels, twenty-five mules (his own special one for Hester), four horses and seven soldiers to escort the party up to his palace. They set off on 29th July 1812. The tracks they now met made everything else seem almost flat. At times it seemed impossible that either man or beast could find a way along the dizzy, unprotected paths. Huge, ragged burnt-up mountains reared up on all sides. The villages and buildings were usually constructed at the very tops of these crazy mountains. Faint tracks could be seen meandering hair-raisingly up to them.

They climbed steadily up, peering down into endless chasms; it seemed only to need the slightest stumble on the part of their steeds to claim them as victims. But the mules and horses were used to the tracks. However terrified the travellers might be, they passed Djoun, spent a night at a village called Masbud, and then next day when it was dark reached Dayr el Kamar, the town where 4,000 Druses lived. The Emir's palace was a mile away, but he had put at their disposal the only decent house in the town. It had been built by a local politician called Girius Baz, who on orders of the Emir had been recently strangled.

The Emir, however, regally entertained Hester and her party in his rather tawdry palace – a collection of irregular rooms, just added one to the other, whenever fancy or need required. They also had time to call on Shaykh Beshyr (not to be confused with the Emir of almost the same name) and his beautiful wife, and witnessed but did not take part in a meal where a raw sheep, fat as well as lean, was eaten with apparent pleasure. Meanwhile Michael Bruce tried to penetrate the mysterious religious ceremonies of the Druses, but as soon as he approached he was driven off with curses and threats.

As there was, at least for the time being, nothing more to do in the country of the Druses, the party left on 26th August 1812, but the memory of a strange remote building at Djoun was to remain in Hester's mind for a long time.

But Hester had other matters to worry about, in particular the cost of the huge caravanserai she trailed about with her. Michael had drawn £3,700 on his father's account in the past eight months (the equivalent of £37,000 today). However generous Craufurd Bruce might be, this was not the kind of money that could be poured out endlessly. Michael's official allowance was £2,500 a year, so he was well above it. He blamed the shipwreck and the need to replenish lost stores for the bulk of his deficit.

Then the heat worried her, particularly since her horse had rolled on her at Nazareth: ". . . I am well again now, except a slight indisposition brought on by the imence [*sic*] heat which gives me such a headache I can hardly see. Sitting quite still with all the doors & windows open the perspiration runs down people's face like water. . . ."

However, when she heard that Spencer Perceval, the British Prime Minister, had been shot by a maniac called Bellingham, she had enough spirit to write, "so far from being sorry that Perceval is shot, I am extremely glad & wish a few more rascals had shared his fate, then perhaps Englishmen would open their eyes & see that they have been ruined".

Michael Bruce wanted to visit Aleppo, but Hester had had enough of ruins. She was interested in people not archaeology, and wanted to go where no woman traveller had been before. Already the idea of visiting Palmyra (which only three European men had ever seen) was like an irresistible challenge. So she declared that she would visit Damascus, in itself a hazardous business, since there was a considerable civil war going on, both there and around Aleppo. Indeed, Hester thought it unlikely that the road to Aleppo was even still open, and though she had no particular fear for Michael, for he had a strong bodyguard, she thought it unlikely he would get there.

Michael set off for Aleppo on 24th August 1812, and on the 27th Hester and her party started on the road to Damascus. They travelled cautiously because of the state of unrest. The Emir of the Druses insisted that six of his best soldiers should accompany her; while the Pasha of Damascus, who had tried to dissuade her from visiting the city, sent four soldiers and an officer to protect her when he realized that nothing would stop her. All these extra bodies had of course to be paid for by Hester. She was particularly annoyed with the officer, "a vastly fine gentleman", she wrote to Craufurd Bruce, "who throws money about right and left . . . ."

They travelled for three days (the journey normally took two) and on the morning of 30th August were within a day's march of Damascus. It was decided Meryon should go on alone and get a house ready for Hester. (The fact that Meryon might be in danger hardly entered anyone's head.) He took with him a single soldier and his groom and headed for Damascus with a courage that no one, least of all herself, seems to have noticed.

Damascus. Hester first saw the city on 1st September 1812 and rode into it at 4 pm on the same day.

The same afternoon he climbed over the last barren hill, and looked down upon the rich and beautiful city. It was Brusa, on a more lavish scale, all over again. Hurrying forwards, he called, in his dusty riding clothes, on the Governor, obtained the necessary permit to acquire a fine house in the Christian quarter, and soon had it ready for Hester.

On 1st September, he rode out to meet Hester and escort her into Damascus. It was not without trepidation that he did this, for he knew that unveiled women were not allowed to appear in public. The Turkish officer who accompanied her had often warned of the danger of riding dressed in men's clothes, unveiled, into the hostile city. Would it not be better, he suggested, if Hester took the veil just for this once? Hester refused to consider the suggestion, and at about four o'clock in the afternoon rode boldly and unveiled into the city. Some mistook her for a beardless youth, but most realized that this was a woman, riding so arrogantly into their city. Before they could recover from their surprise Hester had safely reached the Christian quarter.

CHAPTER THIRTEEN

THE GREAT EXPEDITION TO PALMYRA

Once again, Hester did not like the house Meryon had found for her. To begin with, the Christian quarter was a highly despised area, and it was too far away from the Palace and the smart area. So she went to the Pasha.

In a letter dated 12th October she told General Oakes what happened then:

> "I first was obliged to ride through a yard full of horses, then to walk through several hundred, perhaps a thousand Delibaches, and then to present myself to not less than fifty officers and grandees, the old chief in the corner, and my friend, the young bey (Youseff Pacha's son), next to him, who rose to give me his place. I remained there about an hour; the old fellow was so delighted with me that he gave me his own house upon the borders of the desert for as long a time as I chose to inhabit it; he offered me a hundred Delibaches to escort me all over Syria; he sent off an express to put, as he said, his most confidential officer under my command, that nothing I asked for was to be refused. In short, nothing could equal his civility, besides it was accompanied with a degree of *heartiness* which you seldom meet with in a Turk. The next day he sent me a very fine little two-year Arab horse to train up in my own way."

In Damascus Hester sought the help of the Pasha in her plans to visit Palmyra. Although the Turks in Damascus were reputed to be hostile to foreigners, she was able to ride alone, unveiled, without trouble.

Later in the same letter, she added:

> "What surprises me so much is the extreme civility of the Turks to a Christian, which they detest much more here than in any other part of the Sultan's dominions. A woman in man's clothes, a woman on horseback — everything directly in opposition to their strongest prejudices, and yet never even a smile of impertinence, let me go where I will."

By now her reputation had reached incredible heights. When the time came to move, the owner of the first house presented his bill. Among the items listed was: "Sherbet for the queen on her arrival,

15 piastres." Whenever she moved huge crowds assembled to watch her. Gone was all feeling of animosity. To many of the open-mouthed spectators she was a superhuman being, a goddess sent to Damascus for some divine, if inscrutable reason.

Despite Meryon's forebodings, for he well knew the fanatical hatred the people of Damascus had for Christians, she would ride out alone, accompanied only by Giorgio, her Greek page, and her janissary. But such was the magnetic hold that she had over the people (it was rumoured that besides being a goddess she was also an Ottoman, and that the whiteness of her skin was due to the paint she used) that she was never attacked or even insulted. Indeed, the women who watched her come and go would shout "Long life to her!", and pour coffee on the road before her, a high act of courtesy. Whenever she entered a bazaar everybody stood up, an honour only accorded usually to a Pasha or a Mufti. It was the same at the sumptuous sixty-room palace of the Pasha. Never before had she received such adulation. No wonder she wrote ecstatically to Craufurd Bruce: "The women treated me with the greatest kindness, how different are they from English women!" It was perhaps the first time she had said something nice about women.

However, she had more serious plans to carry out. She was now gaining an insight into the real characters of both the Turks and the Arabs. The narrow nationalistic judgement of a Mrs. Fry was far removed from hers. The Turks had a refinement and a respect for etiquette she had not expected, while the Arabs, though thieving and cruel, could be trusted.

Hester was more than ever determined to cross the long and hostile desert to Palmyra, not in order to visit the ruins, but to be the first woman to do so. But everyone, from the Pasha downwards, tried to dissuade her. It was, they said, far too dangerous. She would never come back alive. The Bedouin Arabs would mutilate, rape and kill her. Or, if they did not do that, they would at least hold her prisoner and demand a huge ransom. They further argued that even if the Bedouins, by some miracle, held off, there was sixty miles of waterless and almost trackless desert to cross. But Hester was adamant, and go to Palmyra she would. In the end the Pasha, who had now a genuine admiration, even affection for her, said that in that case he would send a strong military attachment, 800–1,000-strong, and gave orders for the troops to be alerted. The presents to be given the Bedouins were purchased and the day of departure was agreed.

Hester was not at all sure that this was a good idea. She knew that the Pasha was disliked by the Bedouins, for the hatred the Arabs felt against the Turks was greatest among the nomadic Bedouin tribes who had never been truly conquered by the Turks. She had greater confidence in herself than in any soldiers the Pasha could spare. "I am the oracle of the Arabs", she declared, "and the darling of all the troops, who seem to think that I am a deity because I can *ride*, and because I wear arms; and the fanatics all bow before me, because the Dervishes think me a wonder, and have given me a piece of Mahomet's tomb . . . ."

Even Michael tried to dissuade her from going; but when she showed him that nothing could change her mind, he wrote from Aleppo, where he had made great friends with Barker, the English consul there, suggesting that she should go by caravan. She pointed out that no caravan went the way she intended. Barker then suggested using a tartavan, a kind of Eastern sedan chair drawn by mules. Michael added that he and Barker were leaving Aleppo immediately for Damascus, and would bring the contraption with them.

Hester's reaction was scathingly contemptuous. "What an absurd idea, in case of danger, to be stuck upon a machine", she declaimed. However, fate now decided the issue. Michael was taken ill on the road from Aleppo to Damascus, and though he could still travel, Hester immediately sent Meryon off to Michael's aid. On 15th October 1812, Meryon set off on horseback, with his groom, Ibrahim, and a mule carrying his precious medicine chest, on the road where, a few weeks earlier, a caravan of a hundred people protected by fifty soldiers had been attacked, the Arabs killing sixteen men in the process.

There is considerable reason to believe that Hester was secretly pleased that Michael had had that convenient indisposition on the way back to Damascus, and that she had sent Meryon off as much to get rid of him, as to help her lover. For no sooner had the courageous little doctor left, than Nasar, son of Mahnnah, Emir of the Anizys, the tribe that roamed in the neighbourhood of Palmyra, arrived with a message from his father. If, Nasar declared, she attempted to travel to Palmyra with a body of the Pasha's troops she would be considered an enemy. "Soldiers of the city", said this earnest young man of twenty-five, dressed in a sheepskin cloak, ragged satin robe, with a green and orange silk scarf on his head, "know not the tracks and landmarks of the desert; — where the wells are — what parts are infested by hostile tribes — who is friendly and who is not; and when they have led you into difficulties, they will be the first to desert you."

His solution had a magnificent simplicity about it: "If", he said, "so distinguished a person as she was would place herself under the protection of the Bedouins, and rely upon their honour, they would pledge themselves for conducting her in safety thither and back."

It was a challenge and an appeal that Hester could not possibly resist. She immediately promised that she would trust herself to Nasar and his father's honour, and made secret arrangements to visit Mahannah as soon as possible. She then gave Nasar a suit of clothes which he distributed among his followers, and some English plum-puddings which caused a great deal of astonishment among the Bedouins, and which, brave as they were, they would not eat.

Hester immediately cancelled all the Pasha's preparations and got ready for her secret expedition. But at this moment Michael, now cured, arrived in Damascus with the indefatigable Meryon and Barker. However, fate was still on Hester's side. It was now the turn of Barker to fall ill with a fever that attacked him at regular intervals. Meryon had to stay with him, Michael also because of his friendship with Barker.

So Hester was free of them all; and told them that she was going to Hamah to arrange matters for their projected stay there during the winter. Michael hated Damascus, as he hated Aleppo. He was beginning, in fact, to yearn for the cool, green, English countryside. He had tried to persuade Hester to return too, but remembering her promise to Crawfurd Bruce she had always made some excuse.

Hester set off for Hamah, but when she reached Nebk, turned off to the right, and got a Frenchman called Lascaris, who was married to a gigantic ex-Georgian slave, to accompany her. At Tel Bysy, she was met, by arrangement, by one of Mahannah's tribe, and the three of them set off for Mahannah's camp under the guidance of the Bedouin.

It was safe enough for Lascaris to do so because he had long made friends with the Bedouins. He had been sent there by

Napoleon to find a route to India, and being plentifully supplied with money for the tribes had been accepted by them as an ally. (His wife of course was almost one of them.) But Hester was a very different matter. She was reputed to be immensely wealthy, and since the Bedouin's main source of income came from ransoms paid for the return of wealthy captives, the temptation to make off with Hester must have been enormous.

But they did not touch her. Perhaps Lascaris, who had learnt that Hester wanted him to be appointed a British agent, had something to do with it. She had written home saying, ". . . the French are sending agents in all directions (at an immense expense) into the desert, and why do not we do the same?" The idea of becoming a double agent must have appealed strongly. It must have seemed to him that Hester, as a niece of one of England's most glorious prime ministers could do exactly that. He was not to know that since the Constantinople affair she was more than suspect herself. Yet she was always genuine, and, once again, trying to help her country.

Perhaps, however, the appeal to their honour did succeed by itself to protect her. Certain it is, that she was afforded every courtesy and consideration, and spending a week in the desert, during which time she marched for three days with Mahannah and 40,000 Bedouins, she was escorted safely back to Hamah.

Writing later to General Oakes about the expedition, she described some of the sights she witnessed: ". . . horses and mares fed upon camels' milk, Arabs living upon little else, except a little rice, and sometimes a sort of bread; the space around me covered with living things, 1,000 camels coming to water from one tribe alone; the old poets from the banks of the Euphrates, singing the praises and feats of ancient heroes; children quite naked; women with lips dyed light-blue, and their nails red, and hands all over flowers and designs of different kinds . . . ."

As soon as Hester reached Hamah, she took a small house by the banks of the Orontes, and installed her new friends the Lascarises into one next door. Michael Bruce and Barker, now happily recovered, joined her on the 24th November, but Meryon was detained at Damascus by the patients he had acquired. They intended to spend the winter there and undertake Hester's much desired journey to Palmyra in the spring.

There had been some unfortunate correspondence from Craufurd Bruce. Whether Sligo's attempts to mollify the old man had, as General Oakes feared, not been made in the most tactful way, or whether perhaps Sligo had been malicious, cannot be known. But the fact was that Craufurd Bruce had changed direction once again. He was now vehemently exorting his son to break with Hester, adding, "on your return to Britain whatever may be the situation of Lady Hester Stanhope, I here must avow she cannot be made an inmate under my roof. . . ." Though he would not allow either his wife or daughters to meet Hester, he saw nothing odd in adding that he hoped himself "to be in her society most frequently and upon the most unreserved and most friendly footing".

Meryon rejoined the party in Hamah on 14th December 1812. Hester decided almost at once that he should go to Palmyra in advance to find a suitable house for her. This, despite the fact that it was now winter and that, of the three European visitors to the place, all had been severely manhandled by the Arabs during their treks. She had, anyhow, received a message from Mahannah saying that he was ill and could she send her famous doctor. A Bedouin Arab would be his guide, and Lascaris would also accompany him as interpreter. Lascaris's ostensible reason for wanting to visit Palmyra was the unusual one of wishing, so he solemnly declared, to grow tomatoes there. She had grown by now somewhat tired of him, and while she tried to get General Oakes to provide a pension for him, was glad to see him leave.

Meryon exchanged his Turkish clothes for the humbler ones of the Bedouin Arab, knowing that anything at all ostentatious would merely invite a wandering Arab to strip him, then on 2nd January 1813 he set off on his trek. Soon afterwards Mrs. Fry went down with pleurisy. With no doctor to treat her she had to battle through the illness as best she could, and for some weeks Hester had no maid to dress her, but had to rely on the attentions of an untrained local woman.

Meryon joined Mahannah's entourage, and found the great leader in the middle of a row with his third wife. Presently the whole camp moved on, the sheiks squatting near their horses while the women struck camp and packed everything up. Then the whole concourse left in search of a new spring of water.

It was bitterly cold and snow, an unusual sight in Syria, fell on the 7th, which by morning was six inches deep. Landmarks, upon which the Bedouins depended, disappeared. There was nothing to eat; Nasar, who had been out foraging for food, returned with nothing more than a few raisins. These with a few pieces of dried bread were all they had to eat, and on the 13th they moved on again.

Meryon was getting worried. He had been with Mahannah eleven days now and was virtually his prisoner. The medicines were not having any effect. Moreover he was no nearer Palmyra — indeed they were moving in the opposite direction. Mahannah's sons kept telling him that they would rob in good time, and he came to realize that Lascaris was useless.

So Meryon decided to escape and take on the desert and the Arabs on his own. For so small and despised a man, he had considerable courage. But he told Hassan of his plan, and Hassan told Mahannah, and that was that. Undaunted, however, Meryon now tried guile, telling Mahannah that the great Lady Hester Stanhope would not be at all pleased to hear what Mahannah was doing, and would certainly refuse to send the presents she had promised. This was enough for the greedy old man.

Next morning, the 14th, Meryon mounted his horse before six and, accompanied only by Hassan, carrying Meryon's gun, left the encampment in pouring rain. They had two leather bottles of water and a few raisins. Lascaris stayed behind saying that he was expecting his wife.

They were pursued by two rival Bedouins, but were saved by the rain when a gun aimed by one of them did not go off. Then at last, by moonlight, they came to Palmyra, but it was a great disappointment to Meryon. The ruins were sunk into the earth, he was hungry and thirsty after the twelve-hour ride, and was thankful enough to reach the mud cottage that Hassan had found for him. It turned out to be Hassan's own house and Meryon shared it with Hassan, his wife, four children, two high-smelling camels and a donkey. However, after a hot meal of rice he was happy enough to lie down on the hard floor and sleep, only to be disturbed by one of Hassan's children, a twelve-year-old girl, wandering about the place naked.

Meryon stayed at Palmyra until the 20th, where it rained most of the time. He found the celebrated ruins no more impressive than on the night of his arrival, but he enjoyed the sulphur baths and collected some embalming silk. He was careful not to keep any pieces of antique stone, because he knew that the Arabs believed Europeans had the power of turning them into gold (why else should they be prepared to pay for useless stones?) and would charge a high price for them. He also chose three cottages for Hester. And then set off for Hamah.

To his amazement, a little way out of Palmyra he met Giorgio, Hester's Greek page, also dressed as an Arab, and accompanied by another of Mahannah's men. It appeared that Hester had grown anxious at having no news of Meryon, and sent Giorgio to look for the lost doctor, equipping him with a case of medicine. Now, encumbered with Giorgio who had to mount behind him (the Arabs who had brought him this far going on to Palmyra), the poor doctor struggled through snow, fog and rain, and at last reached Hamah. The Orontes was in flood, but they were able to cross the bridge.

Meryon returned just in time. The exceptionally hard winter and the inadequacy of the houses at Hamah had brought a great deal of sickness with it. Indeed, Hester had probably sent Giorgio after him because she needed the doctor's medical experience more than anything else, for among others Mrs. Fry was still ill. The harsh wintry conditions had spread down from Russia, where they had come early. It was the same winter that had trapped and almost eliminated Napoleon's Grand Army on its retreat from Moscow at the end of 1812. The blizzards and snow continued throughout January and February 1813 — Syria had never seen anything like it.

But however uncomfortable the place, Hester was determined to stay there as it was conveniently placed for carrying on negotiations with the Arabs. Both Hester and Michael wrote tactful letters to Craufurd Bruce in an effort to allay the latter's fears; but as ten months or more had passed since Craufurd had written, there was nothing the old man could do. Even if he cut off Michael's funds, the travellers' credit was so high throughout the area that they could have drawn money endlessly. Hester was anyhow determined to go to Palmyra.

Michael Bruce wrote to his father on 15th January 1813 that Hamah was "very convenient for carrying on our negociations with the Arabs and for making the necessary preparations for our journey to Palmyra. In every other respect it is detestable. I have luckily procured from Aleppo Adam Smith on the Wealth of

Nations, which will afford me ample employment for the Winter."

At last the terrible winter, which destroyed nearly all the fruit trees in the area, came to an end. The snow and rain which came in through the roofs of their houses stopped, and spring arrived; but with it came news that a plague had broken out at Acre and Tyre. This worried Michael Bruce considerably. He was longing now to get back to England, but if the plague spread along the whole coast, no English frigate would put into port, and after their shipwreck they would not trust a Greek one.

A changing Hester, on the other hand, was looking forward eagerly to the future. Gone was the European traveller amiably wandering through a foreign country. She had been called Queen so often by the people around her that she was beginning to believe that she had some special status amongst them. Brothers had predicted that she would be the Queen of the Jews. Well, she wasn't that, but she was at least Queen of the Arabs. Michael, half ironically, wrote to General Oakes saying that he wouldn't be surprised if she became a second Zenobia, the ancient Queen who made Palmyra glorious and independent, until conquered by Aurelian in A.D. 272. She was led through the streets of Rome in golden chains. Hester, said Michael, might even marry one of the Arab leaders.

Michael and she were growing rapidly apart. He had seen enough of ruins, and ruins were the only reason to keep him there. He hated and despised the people and was hated in return. Mahannah had warned Hester that if Bruce went into the desert alone he could not be responsible for the consequences. Hester, on the other hand, was only interested in the people and the effect she was creating.

She wrote ecstatically to General Oakes, on 19th March 1813: "Tomorrow, my dear General, I mount my horse with seventy Arabs and am off to Palmyra at last." They set off at 10 a.m. on the 20th. It was an impressive sight and everybody, including poor Mrs. Fry, recently recovered from her pleurisy, were in male Bedouin clothes. Hester rode in front followed by the Bedouin chieftains, whose long lances were decorated with ostrich feathers. Then followed the main party, the store-carriers, the servants and followers-on. There were twenty-two camels loaded with stores, nine with corn and eight with water containers. To the rear rode Meryon and Michael Bruce.

Of the many inhabitants of Hamah who came out to see off the expedition, most thought that it was the last that would be seen of the travellers. The least that could happen would be that they would be robbed, though death would be more than likely. People fell on their knees and prayed.

Soon the cavalcade disappeared from sight and almost at once trouble began. Despite Nasar's assurances to Hester, he could not break himself of his normal robber habits. If one of the servants took off his cloak, Nasar would pick it up and put it on. When the owner asked for it back, the Arab chief would pretend to get angry and ask who dared to refuse him anything. Then, later, he would give the item of clothing to one of his own men.

The Arabs were like children out on a picnic. To wile away the time they would mount sham fights. They would take off the Keffiahs (highly coloured head-gear) and allow their long curling hair to fall loose about their faces. Then, with a war-cry and lance held horizontally, they would rush at another Bedouin. He, in turn, would swerve rapidly, and lowering his lance make a pretence run at his attacker. When they grew tired of these games, they would call for the tribe's two poets, and ask them to recite tales of the epic days.

The rest of the party, too, had a quality of childishness about them. The servants had armed themselves with every kind of strange weapon. They had sewn coins about their person. Meryon, since his lone trek, had become almost Arab-like and preferred to squat for his meals. He had shaved his head, except for a long pigtail hanging a yard down his back, and both he and Michael had let their beards grow. "It's vastly amusing indeed", wrote Hester, "I like my wandering life of all things. . . ."

Whenever they stopped for the night, a huge black slave named Guntar stood guard outside Hester's tent. He was armed with a tremendous battle-axe and looked so ferocious that Mrs. Fry felt more afraid of him than of all the Arabs put together.

It was the custom for the Arab chiefs to consult with Hester each evening at her tent, and obtain details of the following day's march. One evening, however, Nasar sent a message to say that she might be "the daughter of a Vizir, but he, too, was the son of a prince, and was not disposed at that moment to quit his tent: if she wanted him, she, or her interpreter, might come to him". Perhaps he had been laughed at for taking orders from a woman;

or, more likely, hoped by a little blackmail to up the £150 Hester had agreed to pay (a third down, two-thirds on safe return) for Nasar's protection. Hester acted with her usual decisiveness. She ignored Nasar altogether, neither sending him a message, calling on him or even speaking to him.

Next day Meryon, with Hassan and another Bedouin, rode on ahead to make quite sure that the cottages he had booked were ready. It was a hazardous journey, since a rival tribe to the Anizy (Nasar's tribe), the Faydan, were reported to be in the area in large numbers. Only speed could get so small a group safely through, and though Meryon was mounted on a white horse given to Hester by the Pasha of Acre, it was not equal to the hardy Bedouin mares. Meryon was almost lost in the dark night trying to keep up with his companions. "It was only the noise of the horses before him, or the sight of them which induced him to proceed." However, they arrived safely at Palmyra, and Meryon found himself back in Hassan's hut again.

In the meantime, there was trouble in the camp. Rumours were that the Faydan were circling about and had already stolen a number of Anizy mares, and there was talk of a possible attack. Then came the shattering news that Nasar had ridden off with all his men. He had abandoned them in the dark stony desert, and the Faydan might at that very minute be preparing to attack the rich and now defenceless caravan. Hester acted immediately. She ordered all the servants to take up positions around the camp, and standing in the centre, as calmly as if she had been in a ballroom, took command.

They were tensely staring into the dark night, waiting for the sound of approaching hooves, each holding his pistol, realizing now that this might no longer be a game, but could be their deaths. After twenty minutes there was the sound of horses approaching, which proved to Nasar and his men. He airily informed them that they had just routed a small party of the enemy, but the rumour went round that he had merely ridden a hundred yards or so away from the camp, to see what effect his defection would have on Hester. Had she panicked then, he could, he reckoned, put up the price for his protection – he was evidently a classic "protection racketeer" – but when he saw that it had no effect on her, he abandoned this course of action. It may even have occurred to him that she would go on alone, or, worse

il Perspective VIEW of the RUINS of the celebrated TEMPLE of PALMIRA, in Arab

Palmyra. The object of Hester's most daring expedition. Hester put her trust in the wild Bedouin Arabs who made it impossible for visitors to see these desert ruins. Her gamble succeeded. She bacame the first woman to visit the ruined city of Queen Zenobe. (*Radio Times Hulton Picture Library*)

still, make friends with the Faydan and pay them the money still owing to him.

At about twelve o'clock the next morning, Meryon went out to bring Hester and her party into Palmyra. Crossing the Valley of the Tombs he climbed a small mountain to the south, from where he could get a good view of the desert she would be crossing. It was hot and fine. Suddenly he saw in the distance a great cloud of dust and, as it approached, could make out horsemen riding to and fro, letting off fire-arms. At first he thought they were Faydan attacking the caravan, but it turned out that they were the men from Palmyra itself who had gone out to welcome her. They were naked to the waist except for the cartridge straps crossed over their chests. Some were on horse-back, some on foot. Some fired their matchlocks into the air, others beat frenziedly on kettle-drums or waved their flags.

On arriving at the ruins, Hester was led down a mile long colonnade. As she approached the triumphal arch at the end, she was surprised to see standing on the pillar shafts to right and left beautiful girls between twelve and sixteen years of age, holding garlands in their hands. As soon as she passed these "living statues" jumped to the ground and followed her, dancing around her. More girls stood by the arch itself, carrying garlands of flowers. As Hester reached the arch, a girl, suspended there, held a wreath over her head. Thus was Hester "crowned" Queen of Palmyra.

They did not stay long at Palmyra. Hester took a quick ride round the famous ruins, but she was more concerned with convincing the Arabs that she would not collect old stones and turn them into gold as they believed. She made one of the sheiks accompany her on foot, while she rode. He was so unused to walking that he soon gave up following. Fatigue had made him indifferent to what she did.

On 30th March 1813 four Faydan Arabs were found drinking at a spring. Nasar had them marched into Palmyra and locked up, but during the night two of them escaped. When Nasar heard this he flew into a rage and threatened to kill the headman of Palmyra. Although dissuaded from taking such violent action, he went to Hester and told her that the party must return to Hamah at once. For, he explained, when the two escapees rejoined the tribe the Faydan would send a large revenge party out.

Meryon, who knew the Arabs well by now, was sceptical. He considered that this was yet another trick on Nasar's part, this time in order to get Hester back to Hamah, so that he could collect the money owing to him as soon as possible.

Hester was not so sure. She did not wish to think ill of her beloved Arabs, even though she was getting somewhat tired of Nasar's continuous changes of mood. So she visited the Faydan prisoners and was gratified to learn that her name was already known to them, and that she was respected by them and would come to no harm. "It is our enemies, the Anizys, we seek", they added grimly.

However, though reassured, Hester was happy enough to leave Palmyra. She had achieved what she had come for. The cottages, though washed out before she arrived, were still flea-ridden, and she had no wish to see the Anizys annihilated. After having her name carved in a conspicuous place on the ruins, she and her party left Palmyra early on the 4th April 1813, the fear of attack making the servants work with remarkable speed.

Nasar hurried them on by forced marches during the next two days. The countryside, even in the short time they had been away, had changed. Suddenly, grass was growing in the shallow, protected dips and, at times, there were so many blooms underfoot that it was like walking through a flower-bed. By the evening of 6th April Nasar declared they were out of reach of the Faydan. Two hundred pursuing Faydan horsemen had been stopped just in time.

However, fights broke out from time to time between the chieftains, mainly over the ownership of horses, yet the party managed to keep up a good pace. As they neared the Orantes the astonishing transformation of the desert was even more marked. The grass had grown so quickly and was so high that it could almost be cut for hay.

Meryon was busy with his pills, and was sent off to a nearby encampment to tend to the son of a sheik who had a Faydan spear wound in his back; thus he missed Hester's triumphant arrival at Hamah on 13th April 1813. The whole population, hardly able to believe that she was still alive, came out to welcome her. She was greeted with cries of "Selamet-ya meleky, selame, ya syt" ("Welcome, Queen, welcome Madame"). The man who held Nasar's money in trust, Muly Ismael, gave a huge dinner in her honour to three hundred guests. Even the horses were not forgotten — corn was provided for all the Arab mares.

She was considered to be a real heroine, for she had gone into the desert alone and returned in safety and triumph. There was not a single pasha in the whole of the Turkish Empire who could have done that, however well protected by his troops. Even sheiks could not move about with impunity. One, Sheik Ibrahim, who had consular protection, had been stripped naked on the road from Palmyra, and had wandered about some days in this state before finding enough clothes to allow him to re-enter Damascus.

Yet this incredible woman had done it without a single Turkish soldier to protect her. She had done it openly and ostentatiously, travelling with goods and treasure that many of the marauding desert tribesmen would have killed over and over again to capture.

No wonder the 10,000 people who came out to greet her, called out "El hamd Lillah" ("Thank God"), and "Allah Kerym" ("The Lord is gracious"). From that moment onwards she became a legendary figure.

CHAPTER FOURTEEN

LOVE AND THE PLAGUE

But legends have to live, and the problem was what to do next. Nasar was finally paid off and returned thankfully into his desert. Plague was spreading throughout the countryside with increasing rapidity and violence. There was only one place along the coast reported free of it, and that was to the north-west of Hamah, at Latakia, opposite Cyprus.

On 10th May 1813 Hester and Michael set off for the coast; Meryon, who was looking after a sick man, followed next day. He caught up with them while they were encamped by the Orontes and, despite his work, had time to watch the strange way certain butterflies pulled fish-like larvae out of the water, with the help of two long trailing feelers, so that they, too, could become butterflies.

Meanwhile Hester's reputation preceded her wherever she went. Sometimes she was believed to be the Queen of the Arabs, sometimes the Queen of the Jews, which led to confusion. At one camp a Jewish woman asked to see Hester, but was referred, as usual, to the busy Meryon, who asked her what she wanted. She replied that the local headman had sent lambs to the camp and she would like to kill them. Meryon, somewhat baffled, replied that their cook would kill them.

"What! Is he a Jew then?", asked the woman.

"Why", replied Meryon, "what if he is not?"

"What if he is not?", she replied. "Is not the Meleky [the Queen] one of us, and how can she eat from other hands than ours?"

183

Meryon then remembered that according to the Jewish religion a Jew can only eat meat killed by a person of the same faith. The Jewish woman had taken Hester's title, Queen of the Jews, literally. Hester's reaction on being told this tale was correctly regal: she sent her "subject" a suitable present.

The house taken at Latakia was very large but in a somewhat dilapidated condition. Its oblong courtyard was surrounded by low buildings, and a further stuccoed court on one of these was surrounded by eight or ten rooms. Where the original harem had been doors and windows opened on to the inner court. The rest of the buildings were offices and there was stabling for fifty horses — Hester had nineteen.

Yet again, she did not like the house Meryon had found for her. However, there was nothing for it but for she and Michael to settle in. Meryon, on the other hand, hired a house for himself a little way away. His reputation as a healer was as great as hers as a Queen, and wherever he travelled the sick came to him. Along with two servants, a groom and two horses, he set himself up in practice, quite happy to spend as long as need be in the pleasant town of Latakia.

Everybody wanted to be introduced to Hester, but from the very moment of her arrival she made it a firm rule that only people of note or talent were to be introduced to her; this included foreign travellers as well as local inhabitants.

But Hester and Michael were running into all kinds of difficulties, and it came as a shock one day when one of the bills he had drawn on his father's account (for £1,000) was returned. Although due to a misunderstanding it upset them, because they relied entirely on credit. Any hint that credit might not be limitless was damaging. They might even be taken for adventurers, in which event both their credit and social position could be destroyed.

They were therefore worried about Craufurd Bruce's own financial position. Until then it had been assumed that his funds were unlimited, but now it seemed there were financial problems at home as well. This just at the time when Michael had written to his father telling him that bills to the value of £2,500 were to be met, that we would like a further £500 to pay for a mare for Sligo, and that he felt that the £4,000 worth of goods lost by Hester in the shipwreck should be made up by Craufurd.

The request could not have come at a more unfortunate time

for Craufurd, who, apart from the difficulty of finding so much ready money in addition to all his other expenses, was not particularly pleased at having to find a further £500 for Sligo's mare; for Sligo had got into trouble over the two British sailors he had induced to desert their man-of-war during the summer of 1810.

Sligo had been brought to trial on 16th December 1812 and had been sentenced by the judge, Sir William Scott, to four months imprisonment in Newgate plus a fine of £5,000. One of the people who attended the trial was Sligo's mother. She was described by Michael as "what the French call une veuve fringante, a gamesome widow". So "gamesome" was she in fact that she caught the old judge's eye, and promptly married him, thus putting her son in the curious position of having a step-father who had sent him to prison!

But at Latakia, in the meantime, matters were getting more difficult. The plague was getting nearer and nearer. In June, a ship arrived from Tarsus; the bodies of seven people, who had died of the plague, had been thrown overboard. The ship was refused anchorage and had to put to sea again. But according to Meryon, there were cases of plague or near-plague inside Latakia already. Infected people were arriving there, only to die within a few days. The atmosphere was jittery, and even Meryon, usually unmoved, was affected. Every slight indisposition was believed to be the start of the plague, and when the bad south wind brought inflamation to Hester's eye, the query immediately arose — Is it the plague? Even the toothache Meryon contracted was suspect; and Michael was frankly scared of catching the terrible disease.

But what could they do? Michael was for getting back to the healthy climate of England as soon as possible. But Hester hesitated. She was certainly anxious to leave, and started trying to sell her horses. Meryon did likewise, but only got a very low price for his two. He dismissed the groom, and one of his servants.

They were ready to move but they could not decide in which direction. At times Hester wanted to return to England — she had been away three years — but difficulties there, financial and emotional, deterred her. She was still drawn to the East, and talked of mounting an even greater expedition than the one to Palmyra. She had heard of Saud, chief of the warlike Wahabys, whose desert capital was Derayah [Riyadh?] in Arabia. She had heard of his huge palaces, his 800 wives and his dromedaries who could run faster than the fastest horse. Perhaps she began dreaming of becoming Queen of Arabia as well as Queen of the Jews and Queen of the Arabs. Whatever were her dreams and thoughts, she wrote to Saud.

The summer dragged on. There were plague scares and times when it seemed to recede. There were reports of people dying in thousands in Damascus and other centres. Their servants were continually getting sick and Meryon was busy dealing with the secondary and tertiary plagues which often follow a main epidemic. Yet there were times for boating expeditions and picnics, particularly with the Barker family on holiday from Aleppo.

But behind exterior events an internal drama was being played out. Craufurd Bruce and his family were making more and more determined efforts to get Michael home, and by now neither Michael nor Hester were vehemently against the idea. They had drifted apart since their arrival at Latakia and both had changed since those idyllic days in Malta. Michael no longer wished to play courtier to Hester's Queen; with equal conviction Hester no longer had so much need of Michael in her new role.

They were soon talking about the advisability and possibility of Michael returning home. A further communication from a relative, hinting that Craufurd Bruce's health was not too good, gave the necessary excuse to a decision that both knew had already been made. Hester ordered Michael home, but as it was impossible to get a ship owing to the plague, Michael set off with his interpreter, cook, valet and groom, for Constantinople, intending to travel overland to England. Alone Meryon saw him on his way.

Hester had written to Craufurd Bruce two days before Michael had set off. In her letter she told Craufurd that Michael was at last coming home, and pointed out that she had kept the bargain she made three years earlier. She then went on to give Michael's father what can only be called some home truths about his son:

"He rides vastly ill for a man with so fine a person, & I have recommended him to go to a riding house. His seat is loose and ungraceful. . . ."

Nor did she spare his other faults:

"Don't let him make faces when he speaks it is hideous, or twirl about like a bad actor upon the stage. . . . Pray sit him down regularly to business for an hour or two every day, if he does not get the habit of it *now* he never will . . . You will probably find him acquite himself very ill at table, it proceeding from dining on the ground & eating with his fingers, & out of the dish, sometimes from custom, sometimes from necessity."

It was almost as if she were a headmistress handing over to a headmaster a troublesome boy. Admittedly, she was now thirty-seven, but he was twenty-five, and had experienced and seen more than many men twice his age. Perhaps she was afraid that Craufurd Bruce would be disgusted by the apparent uncouthness of his son. More likely, she had now realized that he would never acheive the high goal she had set for him. As she wrote the letter she must have recalled the first one she had written to Craufurd Bruce and realized that her great plans for him had come to nothing. The tutelage she had given him would not help his career, for he had decided against a career. She had failed to make him the statesman she intended. Even his charm had deserted him. He was, after all, nothing more than an idle young man with too much money.

Though unable to live with him she still loved him, and as soon as he had left, letters began to pursue him along en route: "Take care of yourself for my sake, I shall never cease to pray for you, and as loving you cannot be a sin God never will be deaf to my prayers." Even as he moved further and further away, his progress slowed by the plague, she fretted over him: "Pray pray secure yourself well against cold, and have things to change if wet . . ." and, mindful of her own danger, she asked him not to feel upset if anything should happen to her, and begged him to remember that she had "enjoyed a few moments of happiness that without *you* wd. not have fallen my lot. I shall take all the care I can of myself, & hope to embrase [*sic*] you once more."

Her own plans were still uncertain. On leaving, Michael had promised that she would have half his allowance, whatever it might be. Since he believed it could not be less than £2,000 a year it would mean that she would have a further £1,000 a year to add to her pension of £1,200. A pleasant enough sum, but nothing like the amount she and Michael had been spending together.

Besides, she had a vastly expensive and fractious staff to keep up. The ever recurring threat of the plague that prowled around Latakia like a cruel beast waiting to strike kept everyone irritable and jittery. Now that Michael was gone she wanted to get away from Latakia. But, paradoxically, it was even more difficult to return to England since it would look as though she were pursuing him. Though she loved and missed him, her pride and her promise to Craufurd, made such a move utterly impossible. The Arabian adventure could not, even if feasible, be undertaken, because, without Craufurd Bruce's money it would have been too expensive, although at one stage she thought of taking an English ship to India.

She then decided to hire a house called "Mar Elias", near Sidon in the area of Mount Lebanon. It belonged to Athanasius, a Greek patriarch; she had seen the house the previous year during her visit to Sidon. As the patriarch was away a good deal of the time he was happy to let it, and the rent was very modest. Luggage was packed and sent off in advance under the guidance of Michael's old servant who had now been transferred to Meryon's care. The rest of the party would follow on 15th November 1813.

But on 30th October the plague struck. Two of the Barkers' young children went down with a "fever", and despite all Meryon's efforts the two little girls, Harissa and Zabetta, died within twenty-four hours. Other people were dying in Latakia, dropping down in the streets and lying where they fell. The return of the plague was also confirmed at Damascus and in a village near Antioch, a few miles away. People began locking themselves in their houses, refusing to have any physical contact with anyone, for the plague was highly contagious; it was enough just to touch another person to go down with it, and death was both swift and almost inevitable — there was no defence against it. The whole Turkish Empire was in the grip of the killer plague, the worst for decades. It was killing off more people than the terrible Napoleonic wars that looked as though they were at last coming to an end in Europe.

On the day they were due to leave, Hester went down with a fever. She was followed that same evening by Meryon, and although he struggled on until the 18th November, he had to take to his bed; Mrs. Fry also became a victim. For the next twelve days, with Meryon half delirious and Mrs. Fry out of action,

Lebanon from Tripoli. Hester often went to Tripoli. Like most of the towns on this part of the coast, it served mainly as a port for the small trading vessels that sailed up and down the coast.

Hester fought the fever with the help of a French doctor and an Italian surgeon. The fever was worse at night, when the paroxysms were so violent that she lost all consciousness, although during the day they subsided for a while.

John Barker, the Consul, called on her. He was so shocked by her appearance that he was convinced she was dying. He went to Meryon and begged him, however weak he was, to come to her. Meryon agreed, but had not the strength to walk. He had to be carried to her room. He, too, was so shocked at her appearance that, despite his own weakness, he decided to stay by her side until she either recovered or died. He sealed up her private papers, and told her that she was dying.

She took the news with her usual courage and during the moments of lucidity gave instructions concerning her funeral and the disposal of her belongings. At the same time she fought the illness, bubonic, secondary or tertiary plague or whatever it was, with all her strength and with whatever medical device her doctors prescribed; the application of numerous leeches, the hourly drinking of a glass of ass's milk, the taking of a Turkish bath at the height of the fever — all local treatments believed to be efficacious.

Meryon remained by her side for fifteen days, never leaving her for more than a few minutes and never once having time to take off or change his clothes. Then at last, as he put it, "it pleased God, by the aid of a constitution naturally vigorous, to relieve her so far that I could pronounce her out of danger".

But she was weak and exhausted for a long time. Then on 15th December, just when she seemed strong enough to attempt the journey to Sidon and a boat had been hired, she went down with ague, and the departure was postponed once again. It wasn't until

The Lebanon comprised then mainly Mount Lebanon and the immediate surrounds. It was part of the Turkish empire. Its administrative centre was Acre.

1st January 1814 that she was able to get out of bed. On the 6th she was put on the back of an ass, and, with a servant on each side to hold her, led down to the quayside, where the boat still waited.

She had not been out of the house for nearly seven weeks. Huge crowds gathered to see how their Queen had survived the dreadful plague. Somebody, either to cheer people up, or, more probably, in the hope of being paid, danced in front of her playing a pipe. A few months earlier, she would have been enchanted, but now, irritable and nervy from illness, she could not stand the squeaking sound and had the man sent away. Before boarding the lantern-sailed lugger, she remembered her regal duties and distributed presents to all the people at Latakia who had helped her. Then, to the good-will shouts of the people on the quayside, they sailed at last.

The ship's hold had been specially redesigned, so as to make a comfortable suite for Hester, Mrs. Fry and the two local women who served her. The rest of the "cabins" were more like kennels, mere shelters where people could creep into to sleep. Meryon preferred the open air of the deck, for although it was January, the air was mild. They arrived five days later at Sidon. As they approached the port, the sea began to move with an ominous swell, always the sign of a coming storm. The long and terrible struggle against sickness and almost certain death had shaken Hester's self-confidence. As with somebody who has been wounded or involved in an accident, even the slightest of set-backs or threats she magnified into disasters. She could not bear the thought of going through another storm, urging everyone to hurry up and get her ashore. When an ass was found she disembarked at Sidon and was gently conveyed to a rented house, while essential repairs were being carried out at Mar Elias.

In the meantime, the plague had slowed down Michael's homeward journey. He was still only at Constantinople when he heard, in a very abrupt way, about Hester's illness. In a letter to Hester on 4th January 1814, two days before she left Latakia, he wrote:

"Upon my arrival at the English palace I was ushered into the Drawing room where a large company were assembled. Mr. Morier came suddenly in and before he gave me the Doctor's or Mr. Barker's Letters he told us that he had just received accounts of Lady Hester Stanhope being on the point of Death."

The poor young man was, however, somewhat reassured when on reading the letters he discovered that she was out of danger. He did not, despite his statements of affection and concern, hurry to her side. Instead, he said he would stay in Constantinople longer than he intended, and begged her to call him back to her should she have a relapse. A man with a stronger character would undoubtedly have acted differently, but then such a man would not have followed her so meekly for the past three years, and allowed her to dismiss him when it suited her.

The sea journey to Sidon had unsettled Hester again; the ague returned, so did the bouts of delirium. She now had a terrible hacking cough that Meryon feared would stay with her for years, perhaps for the whole of her life. He was afraid, too, for her sanity. Her personality had changed. She was harder, more autocratic, less able to make allowances for the shortcomings in others. Only to Michael could she still show warmth, softness, affection.

The convent – or monastery as it was sometimes called – of Mar Elias was situated at the foot of Mount Lebanon. It was a square, low, one storey building built on the side of a hill. The roofs were flat and the whole building was sited round a small square courtyard, where a few flowers and two orange trees grew. The white-washed rooms were small and simple. A macabre touch was provided by one of the locally engaged servants describing how the previous patriarch, on dying, had been embalmed, put into an armchair and buried in a wall by a staircase.

It was a bleak and lonely place. There were none of the famous cedars of Lebanon to be found there, only a few olive and mulberry trees. Behind were stony and barren mountains, and two miles away was the empty sea. The nearest village was Abra, a quarter of a mile away, a miserable place with no more than forty small cottages, each with a single room. At the lower end lived a few cows and asses belonging to the owner, at the high end lived the entire family; the floor was of yellow, trodden clay. There were no windows, just small square holes to let in the air. The inhabitants made a living from breeding silk-worms. It was here that Meryon looked for somewhere to live.

The Cedars of Lebanon were to be found growing at quite high altitudes. They provided shade for travellers as well as adding to the beauty of the landscape. They appealed to the romantically minded travellers of the early 19th century.

It was not until 20th February 1814 that Mar Elias was ready, and Hester was able to move into the place. She left Mrs. Fry back at Sidon, as that poor woman had now contracted dysentery. Hester wrote to Michael about her maid's illness, stating: "I cannot trust her where a kitchen is, she will eat everything she sees & therefore falls ill again."

Of Meryon, she wrote about this time:

> "The Doctor is stuck up in a village 10 minutes off from the Convent he makes *sauces* his great occupation for some time past he even made sauces and puddings for himself on bd a Ship, his belly is his favorite object, let what will happen. He now however *tries* to do better in other respects but as he has no sense, and no delicacy of feeling, he never can be made anything of, but when the continent is open I shall find plenty of persons to serve me in all capacities according to my taste."

She was now engaged on a new scheme. The Holy Land was a place of buried treasures, and maps (the faking of which was a lucrative business), charts and instructions purporting to show where treasure was buried came on to the market at regular intervals. The treasure in most cases was usually said to have belonged to wealthy Christian or Jewish familes who had hidden it, so that the Turks could not get it.

Hester had found a manuscript telling her that a vast treasure of this type was to be found at Ascalon, on the coast. She had secretly instructed Michael to contact Liston, newly appointed British Ambassador at Constantinople, and ask him to send her a ship, so that the necessary exploration of the site could be carried out. So powerful was her name, that Liston contacted the naval authorities and they in turn authorized one of His Majesty's ships to be put at her complete disposal for a fortnight. The ship chosen was the sloop "Kite", commanded by Captain Forster. It would call about the beginning of the summer.

She awaited its arrival with impatience. Now that Michael had left, she was in a bad financial position, owing Craufurd Bruce £1,000, her banker Thomas Coutts over £3,000 and being more than £1,200 overdrawn. But she was not after the treasure for herself, she only wanted the glory of finding it.

Then once again the plague struck. One of the villagers from Abra had gone into Sidon to take a hot bath, and had picked up the plague. It had not, however, showed for five or six days, during which time he had continued to work in the normal way, mixing with nearly everyone in the village, including Meryon. Then he had been taken ill, made his confession, and died.

There was immediate panic. The whole village was evacuated, people fleeing to the surrounding mountains and caves, there to live in isolated groups until either they died or the epidemic ended. They only returned to the fields during the day to feed the silk-worms. More and more people were dying, and during May so many died that there was nobody to bury the bodies.

Meryon hurried about the surrounding country doing his best for the stricken (and those who thought they had the plague, but hadn't). Hester was so terrified of catching it again that she would not let him come near Mar Elias, fearing he might be contagious. Soon there was nobody left in the village except Meryon. When it seemed as though his servant had got it, he fumigated his cottage, locked himself up in it and waited for it to strike him. He left the cottage only to fetch water from a nearby well. However, though he had been in constant contact with the villagers he had not caught it, and again began visiting the caves and grottoes where the villagers were in hiding.

As soon as a person died, the body was thrown into a common pit in the side of a mountain, its entrance blocked by a large stone. One man, on bringing his dead son to the pit, was so furious when he saw the body of the first man to die (who had thereby brought the fatal illness to the village) that he tried to drag it out to feed it to the jackals. But every time he seized a limb it broke away from the body.

Then, as suddenly as it had started, the plague left the village at the beginning of June. The villagers begn to go back to their houses, to remake their lives, and to go on looking after the silk-worms, the only creatures who had not suffered from the plague. (As it happened poor Meryon had to suffer from the silk-worms! On top of all his worries he had to face a claim for compensation from one of the village women. She said that the smell of drugs from the fumigated cottage had killed off her silk-worms.)

However, he was allowed once more back at Mar Elias, which

though not the gayest place in the world was a change from the decimated village. There was a feeling of life there, even news from abroad. On 12th June, a priest from the Druse town of Dayr el Kamar told them that Napoleon had been exiled to Elba. On 14th June there was a great deal of excitment when Captain Forster came up to Mar Elias to confer with Hester over the Ascalon treasure expedition. Hester, who had told nobody except Meryon about the projected expedition, behaved in a very conspiratorial way. Forster left, only to return on 22nd June to announce that it was quite impossible to land at Ascalon.

So Hester, rather thankfully, abandoned the plan for the time being. It had been conceived when she had been in good health, but she was still too shaken and weak from the plague and its consequences to undertake a major expedition of this sort. Perhaps she would be strong enough next year to return to the subject.

Meanwhile Hester began to miss Michael. He was an infrequent writer of letters, and still had only reached Vienna, where the Peace Congress was taking place, and where a very strongly worded letter from his father awaited him, advising him to rid himself of his "Turkish Mania". "There must surely be", added Craufurd Bruce bitterly," .... something exceedingly imposing and fascinating to enduce you to continue in this Country of Plague and Pestilence, and where you are spending to as large an amount as if you had your residence in the most brilliant Court of Europe . . . ."

Craufurd Bruce had sent a copy of this letter to Hester and it had not improved her temper. She had sent Michael home, but she expected him to return, or at least that they would meet at some convenient place. Now she began to suspect that once Michael had reached England his father would bring tremendous pressure on him to stay away from the "Country of Plague and Pestilence"; from, in fact, Hester herself. At times, as if to anticipate a possible future, she wrote to Michael saying that they should not meet again. But longed to do so all the same.

She also received news from England that little Lucy Taylor, her youngest sister, the first one to escape from Chevening by marrying her apothecary, had died at the age of thirty-four. Though Hester had cut herself off from most of her family, she had a feeling of closeness for her sisters and half-brothers. That pretty Lucy should (like Charles) die so young seemed an added blow by fate.

Finally, to add to her discomfort, she had suffered from prickly heat at the beginning of July, a very uncomfortable indisposition that was accompanied by a terrible itching. Meryon, knowing how much she disliked the heat, advised a move higher up the mountain.

Hester wrote to her "friend" the Emir of the Druses, who had entertained her so regally during her earlier visit. But the Emir was no longer so keen to have her in his area. The fact that she was regarded now as a Queen may have worried him, as he was none too secure himself. Thinking it not impossible that she might be planning to supersede him, he gave an evasive answer to her request. With something like her old spirit she wrote back: " . . . whether he gave her a house or not, she would set off next day, and would pitch her tents on the mountain, if she found nothing better". The Emir tactfully changed his mind and offered her a small well-shaded house at Meshmushy, high on Mount Lebanon, so high indeed that it was quite cool at night and mists clung to the peaks above it.

As the house was small, only a minimum number of servants were taken. Mrs. Fry was left at Mar Elias, no doubt to the relief of both mistress and maid. The small party left on 25th July, covering only three or four miles a day so that the scenery could be enjoyed to its utmost. Each evening the tents would be put up. Hester travelled on the ass the Emir had given her some time earlier. It was so hot that Meryon did not always bother to put up his tent, but slept in the open.

They arrived at Meshmushy on 29th July 1814. Hester was, for a change, delighted with the place. It was cool, romantic-looking and clean, with vegetation all around. Exhausted, she accepted its remoteness and peace gratefully. Just as in Wales, and at Walmer, she needed a period of tranquillity, so now she needed to rest again.

She was there for ten weeks and once more built up her strength and self-confidence. The plague and Michael's disappearance had almost destroyed her, but Meshmushy revitalized her. Although she would never be quite the same again, she regained much of her lost buoyancy. She often said that after leaving Malta she had never been so comfortable as she was at Meshmushy.

CHAPTER FIFTEEN

THE RICHES OF ASCALON

By autumn she had regained both health and spirits. She stopped ranting at and beating her servants, and was even quite friendly with both Meryon and Mrs. Fry. She decided to visit Baalbec, the ancient Heliopolis, about sixty miles inland from Meshmushy.

On 18th October she set off, in what was for her a very modest manner. She took only Meryon, an interpreter, eight men-servants, four women sevants and a black female slave; in all a retinue of a mere fifteen people. Her baggage was loaded on to fifteen mules; and the whole party, including Hester, rode on asses.

Her reason for doing this, despite the fact that there were plenty of thoroughbreds at Mar Elias, was to shame her relatives in England. She got the curious idea that the fact that a great lady like her was reduced, through lack of funds from England, to travel on asses, would be reported back to her home country; and her friends, relations and even the Government would be so overcome by shame that they would immediately send her large sums of money.

She was also very scared of contracting the plague, which was still virulent in a number of villages on the way. She insisted, therefore, on the complete segregation of her caravan from the surrounding countryside. Everyone was forced to sleep in tents. No fuel was to be bought from the local inhabitants for fear that it might be contaminated. The party was to rely for its firewood on trees encountered on the way. As there were practically no trees at all on their route, most nights were spent in a chilly fireless gloom.

In October 1814 Hester set off from Mar Elias on a modest (to her) expedition to Balbec. The ruins there were extremely impressive; but it rained a great deal of the time and there was danger of catching the plague. Hester, whose interest in ruins was anyhow minimal, was pleased to move on to Tripoli.

Nor would she allow any food to be bought, again for fear of contamination. A number of indigestible meat dumplings were cooked before the expedition set out, and these were eaten morosely en route. Hester, however, because of her "delicate" state of health, had a rather more varied menu, but this too was made up entirely of provisions brought from Meshmushy.

They reached Baalbec on 24th October and encamped in a field, south-west of the ruined temple. Hester's main interest was to have a good bath. After the beginning of November it became cold and began to rain heavily, flooding the tents and making life miserable. As Hester intended to travel to Tripoli on the coast, the party set off in the first week of November, in order to get over Mount Lebanon before the snows blocked the way.

They had a terrible journey through a stormy, blustery night. The mule drivers refused to unload the tents in the pouring rain, despite Hester's cursing and Meryon's threats. The tent-men unloaded Hester's tent, but each time they put it up, it blew down. The maid's candles kept blowing out. Even when all the tents were finally up, they kept blowing down. "This was", wrote Meryon laconically, "one of the most distressing nights we ever passed."

However, next day they were rewarded by passing close by the famous Cedars of Lebanon, which Meryon thought no better than those at Warwick Castle. On 11th November, during a particularly wet, cold and miserable day, they came to Ehden. This was supposed to be the site of the Eden, or Paradise, of the Bible. Although falling considerably short of a true Paradise, the cottages were well-built and clean. Hester and her party stayed there a week.

Nearby was the Catholic monastery of St. Anthony. Its anti-woman bias was so great that nothing female was allowed to enter its sacred precincts. Even the hens were cooped up outside the monastery in case one should stray into it. The cocks, on the other hand, were allowed to roam at will.

This was too much for Hester, who decided to visit this most masculine of places. She informed the Superior that she would give a dinner to the sheiks who were with her in a room in the monastery. The monks were horrified at the thought that a Protestant female heretic should penetrate where nothing feminine was ever allowed. But Hester was adamant, and if they did not allow her in she said she would inform her personal friend the Sultan of Turkey himself. The result, she hinted, would be disastrous for the monastery.

The monks, though they grumbled, had no option but to agree. Enormous precautions were taken to prevent any trick being played by the monks and their sympathizers, such as putting a bramble under the asses tail, that might throw Hester before she could reach the monastery. So the party duly set off, Hester determinedly on her she-ass. Although many of the monks and servants believed, and indeed hoped, that the very earth would open and swallow up the sacrilegious heretic on her ass, nothing in fact happened.

She reached the room where dinner was served, spent four hours there and returned without incident. It was only next day that she was thrown from her ass. Perhaps, St. Anthony was a little late in reacting. When news of her exploit spread throughout the countryside some praised her, some condemned her. When she reached Tripoli, huge crowds turned out to greet her despite the pouring rain.

Hester stayed at Tripoli until 16th January 1815. For most of the time she was busy drawing up lists and drafting letters for a new scheme. This time it was not a hunt for treasure, or an expedition to a remote part of the country, but the creation of a Literary Institute for the Ottoman Empire, like the one that Napoleon had created in Egypt.

The idea was to invite from Europe every kind of writer and artist, and to let them loose over the countryside, so that they could record every aspect of the civilization and customs of the people concerned. She proposed to raise the huge sum of money needed to finance this project by private and public subscription. Needless to say, she was to be head of the Institute.

She spent hours working out the exact amount each subscriber would give, for their contributions would vary according to their known wealth. The composition of letters to be sent caused her much thought; for, as she knew most of the people to be approached, she altered the wording accordingly. Her intensity was reminiscent of her father's singleness of mind when engaged on one of his inventions.

When not working on this particular scheme, she was busy searching for a cure for the plague, and for snake bites. Here she showed the minute attention to endless detail that she had shown in Wales when preparing a cure for the local inhabitants. It was as if she had to keep her restless Pitt mind busy, when there was no reality to occupy it. Ever since she had been toppled from her position as the Prime Minister's closest adviser (as she liked to think of herself) she had sought a replacement. Being a "Queen" was not enough; she had to be an active Queen, one continually concerned with the well-being of her "people". She also wanted to stop thinking of Michael.

Michael had not written very regularly and what letters she had received from him were not very satisfactory. He had now reached England at last, and his father had written her a triumphant letter beginning: "My dear Madam, Three weeks past I had the high gratification to fold in my Arms my long wandering Son your friend Michael." Michael had, in fact, been away for six years, of which three had been spent with Hester.

He had revised his original intention of paying her half his allowance, by ingeniously paying her enough to make their incomes equal. Thus, of the £2,500 a year his father was to give him, he proposed to pay her £600 a year. This would reduce his income to £1,900, and bring hers, with her pension and other income, to the same amount. Hester was not at all pleased at what she considered a somewhat sharp way of avoiding his obligations. Even his rider that in the event of his death his father had agreed to pay her £800 a year for life, did not improve matters. He was, after all, twelve years younger than she.

Nor did the situation improve when he invited her, somewhat half-heartedly, to meet him in Vienna; and hinted that he might even return to Syria. She turned down the Vienna meeting and was furious at his suggestion that he might return to the East. "When", she wrote imperiously, "did I give you leave to do so? When did I either expect or wish it?"

Yet she did expect and wish it, but could not bring herself to break the promise she had made to Craufurd; nor could she bear the thought that people in England, particularly her brother James and Sligo, who had become very malicious, were saying that she was pursuing her young lover. Though she longed for him, and kept herself uselessly busy to forget him, her pride would not let her fight to get him back. She, who boasted that she cared nothing for the opinions of others, cared, where Michael was concerned, so much that she could write:

> "As I wish neither to see you nor yr. father, for I cannot stand more scenes I shall not come upon the Continent at present. I am very well in the East, at least I find myself worse elsewhere. All I wish for is a little peace . . . ."

But she did not brood for long, for once again she was plunging into a new venture, or at least taking up one previously abandoned. She had never forgotten the treasure of Ascalon and was entirely convinced that the manuscript she had seen, showing where it was buried, was genuine. It was just a question of raising the cash to finance the expedition, and all would be well. With the help of John Barker she was able to find the necessary money, and believed, quite sincerely, that the British Government would finance this project which would, in her opinion, enhance British prestige throughout the Ottoman Empire.

With all the money she needed now safely behind her, she made quite certain that there would be no trouble from the Turkish authorities by promising to hand the treasure over to the Sultan. She was, she explained, not after the money, but the glory of finding it. So persuasive was she, and so great was her prestige that the Sultan, along with everybody else, believed that she really had special knowledge of the buried treasure. He therefore sent one of his top officials, known as zaym, to accompany and help her on her expedition. The Zaym, Derwish Mustafa Aga, arrived at Mar Elias on 28th January 1815. Hester had told no one in the immediate neighbourhood of her renewed plans to dig up the Ascalon treasure, so that the high Turkish official's arrival in the area caused the utmost consternation. A zaym never visited an area without some specific and usually unpleasant objective; it might be to witness a strangling, organize a beheading, proceed with the confiscation of a property, or to throw an important inhabitant into prison.

All kinds of rumours flew about the place: he was there to arrest Hester, or to arrange for her deportation. Some declared, with complete confidence, that she was in fact a highly paid spy of the Sultan, and that the official had come there to pay her money. Even Meryon was alarmed and armed himself with a freshly primed pistol.

A landscape near Jerusalem. Olives grow and travellers rest. Hester would have travelled through many such landscapes.

The Zaym ordered Hester to meet him at the Governor's house in Sidon; for such a high-up Moslem official could not demean himself by going to a Christian house. But Hester ordered him to come to her, and come to her he did. The Zaym turned out, however, to be a mild little man of fifty, who was more concerned with the difficulties of the journey from Constantinople than anything else. He arrived at Hester's house whimpering with exhaustion.

He must have been somewhat perplexed by this mission. Executions and sequestrations he could understand, but why he should give this crazy Englishwoman power to recruit labour at will, and even to overrule the will of the local Turkish overlords seemed incredible. Never had so much authority been given to a Christian. He could be forgiven for believing that the Sultan and the ruling Porte in Constantinople did not know what they were doing.

But the Sultan acted for a definite reason. The huge Turkish Empire extended as far north as Serbia, Rumania and Bulgaria, and as far south as Egypt. It was made up of a number of different races and different religions. There were Greeks, Arabs, Christians, Jews and Copts, all controlled by the Turkish overlords. Many of the component peoples of the Empire, particularly the Greeks, were agitating for freedom. The "Eastern Question", as the problem of how to deal with the subjugation of Christian people to the Mohammedan rule of the Turks was called, was raised at the 1814 Congress of Vienna. Both Western Europe and Russia felt that something must be done to prevent the periodic Turkish massacres of Christians, and general ill-treatment of the subjugated peoples; but nobody could decide what.

The Sultan was aware that in the not too distant future he might need all the support he could find to keep the peace in his restless Empire. Here, in the middle of the turbulent Holy Land, was, as far as he could make out, a strange Englishwoman, niece of the great William Pitt himself, a woman who was considered by many to be a Queen if not a goddess, a woman who could, at will, order about the ships of the greatest maritime nation in the world, and one who, for some inscrutable reason, wanted to dig up treasure and present the whole lot to him, the Sultan.

He had nothing to lose by encouraging her. If the treasure was there he stood to gain a useful addition to his treasury. If it was not there he would have nothing to pay, for he understood the British Government was meeting the cost of the expedition. In all events he would, he calculated, consolidate the affection this strange woman had for the Turks in general, an affection that might be decisive in keeping Syria quiet in case of internal trouble there, or elsewhere.

Though Hester had no firm assurance from the British Government, she felt quite certain that it would pay up. She turned Meryon into an accountant and told him to keep a careful list of all expenses. She would then, "send in my bill to government by Mr. Liston; when, if they refuse to pay me, I shall put it in the newspapers and expose them. And this I shall let them know very plainly, as I consider it my right, and not a favour: for, if Sir A. Paget put down the cost of his servants' liveries after his embassy to Vienna, and made Mr. Pitt pay him £70,000 for four years, I cannot see why I should not do the same."

The Zaym spent a few days in consultation with Hester, trying at the same time to discover whether Hester was genuine in her declaration that all the treasure would be handed over to the Turkish authorities, for nothing like this had ever happened before. Treasure seekers, whether European or local, had a habit of wanting to keep what they found. Many a "lucky" finder of coins had had to be beaten almost to death to reveal where he had hidden his find.

Hester's genuine, if, to him, incomprehensible code, was completely unshaken. After a few days she sent him off (for he too, at the Sultan's command, was officially under her orders) to Acre to prepare the way. Giorgio, Hester's Greek servant now promoted to interpreter, went with him.

They left on 1st February 1815, and Hester was to follow ten days later, since she needed time to rest after the Baalbec expedition. She also needed new horses, clothes and other stores, so she sent Meryon off to Damascus. He now seemed to spend more time as her personal secretary—housekeeper than her doctor. On the return journey he had a very trying time. Caught in a violent snow-storm, his newly purchased mare sank to its belly in a snow drift, and one of the two laden mules rolled over; the stores had to be cut from it and reassembled the next day. When he finally reached Mar Elias, he found that Beaudin, the interpreter who had also been sent on a job, had had his horse stolen. He had written to Hester telling her this, and she had scribbled laconically on his note: "Si vous avez perdu votre jument trouvez la." Find it he did.

Hester set off for Acre on the first stage of her journey to Ascalon on 15th February 1815. Meryon followed the next day, and they stayed in Acre until 17th March. Hester was treated with extraordinary courtesy usually only reserved for princes, while Meryon was rather more mundanely employed trying to cure the Pasha of Tripoli of a pulmonary complaint.

The expedition was gathering in size. To Hester's original six tents, a further twenty were added. One of them was a huge star-covered tent which consisted of an inner and outer tent. The outer tent was green in colour, and covered with yellow flowers as well as stars. Inside the inner tent, against a satin curtain, stood a Madame Recamier style sofa. Hester was delighted with it.

At last, on 18th March, the caravan finally set off. Although Hester had been supplied with a crimson palanquin decorated with six gilt spheres that glistened in the sunshine, she preferred to ride on her favourite black ass. She was accompanied by the Zaym and his party, an escort of 100 Barbary cavalrymen, various friends and camp-followers, 2 mules laden with water carriers, 12 more mules laden with luggage and 12 camels to carry and tents.

Meryon had to stay behind to look after the sick Pasha. Early the following morning, accompanied by a Barbary cavalryman, he left for Haifa, where he knew Hester intended to camp for the night. A terrible gale was blowing, but much to the annoyance of the cavalryman Meryon decided to carry on. While dust and hail stung their faces, and quicksands made fording rivers dangerous, the unhappy cavalryman cursed the English, who travelled at the wrong seasons of year instead of staying comfortably at home like sensible people.

Meryon finally reached the encampment outside Haifa and went gratefully to the dining-tent, only to find himself face to face with an apparent madman. He was about sixty years of age, with grey, uncombed hair, and looked as though he had never washed. He carried a Bible with him, and was continually referring to it to make crazy prophesies, mainly about Napoleon. His name was Loustaunau, and he had had a somewhat adventurous career, having served for a while with a Mahratta army in India against the British. He rose to be a general, but lost two fingers on his left hand. After retiring from the army he returned to France and found that the bills he had brought home with him were worthless. Married, with a number of children, he tried to establish an iron foundry in the Pyrenees where he was born, but was not successful. He was now, he said, on his way East to claim his fortune, but had in fact been encamped for two years in a shed in the orchards near Haifa. He made a living, if that was the right word, by prophesying. He was, in fact, known as "The Prophet".

On meeting Hester that night for the first time he had apparently said: "Madam, at this very moment in which I speak to you, Napoleon has escaped from Elba." This finally convinced Meryon that the man was mad; for it was well known that Napoleon was so well guarded he could not possibly escape.

Whether this story is true or apocryphal it is difficult to say. Napoleon had, in fact, escaped from Elba at the end of February, and had landed at Cannes on 1st March 1815. But news of his sensational escape had not reached the Holy Land at the time Loustanau made his startling announcement to Hester. On the other hand, word of mouth news often travelled faster than official news, and it is quite possible that the wily General, as a professional prophet, made it his business to learn facts before anybody else. It made his prophecies so much more effective.

Whatever the truth, Hester believed implicitly that the half-mad Frenchman had the power to prophesy. And now that Brothers' prophecies seemed to be coming true, she was inclined to listen more closely than before to any prophet who came along. She offered Loustaunau a home whenever he needed one, and he promised that he would be back as soon as possible.

In the meantime the storm was blowing the tents inside out, like so many umbrellas. The Zaym and every one of the 100 Barbary soldiers had abandoned the camp and taken refuge in a nearby Carmelite monastery. Hester's tent, though weighted with stones, was blown down twice. The anxious Meryon, afraid that the defenceless woman might be attacked, stayed on guard outside her tent the whole of the turbulent night.

Matters were not helped by the arrival at midnight of an Italian dressed as an English officer bringing despatches from Hester's cousin, Sir Sidney Smith, who had the weird idea of raising a Syrian regiment to fight on the Barbary coast. She immediately turned the whole idea down, as she knew it would only cause trouble with the Turks. She even went so far as to show Sir Sidney's secret letters to the Zaym, and instructed John Barker not to forward any more of his cousin's letters.

Having got that little political contretemps out of the way, she set off once again, travelling slowly with many stops, and eventually arrived at Ascalon on the inauspicious day of 1st April 1815, April Fools Day.

There had been an Ascalon ever since 1900 B.C., if not earlier. It had in turn been conquered by the Assyrians, the Persians, Alexander the Great, the Egyptians, the Saracens and the Crusaders. Unlike Palmyra, however, nothing was left of the ancient buildings since all of it had dug up in order to rebuild Jaffa and Acre. Not that this worried Hester, who was not after antique statues but gold buried by early Christians.

The tents were once again pitched, and, out of deference to Mohamedan susceptibilities, Hester and her women servants were housed in two cottages a little way away. Work began at once, and because of the Sultan's firmans, or permits, 150 local inhabitants were press-ganged each day to work on the digging. Although they received no pay, they got two free meals a day and were never beaten; so they were a good deal better off than many of their companions.

At three o'clock in the afternoon, on 4th April, "treasure" was at last found. It was a huge, headless marble statue of a deified king. It lay six or eight feet below ground and was pulled to the surface by ropes. Meryon, who in addition to his other jobs, seemed to have been in charge of the diggings as well, was delighted. He estimated that it might date from the time of Alexander the Great. Even if nothing else was found, Hester's name would go down in archaeological history with the discovery of such an important item.

By the eighth day they had reached the level at which the treasure, said to consist of no less than three million separate pieces of gold, should have been found. Great excitement occurred when a long, narrow trough was found with four grey granite slabs laid across it. This, quite obviously, was where the treasure was buried. It was decided that they should open it on the following day.

Meryon, in the meantime, had made a sketch of the headless statue, and told Hester that future generations and travellers would praise her for rescuing an antique statue while digging for gold. To his astonished dismay, she replied:

> "This may be all true; but it is my intention to break the statue, and have it thrown into the sea, precisely in order that such a report may not get abroad, and I lose with the Porte all the merit of my disinterestedness."

Meryon tried to argue with her. But she was adamant. A few years earlier, Lord Elgin had removed the famous marble statues. The Turks and many other inhabitants of those countries looked upon European archaeologists as thieves, taking away their statues for their own private gain. She was determined not to be compared to one of them. "Go this instant", she said to the unhappy Meryon, "take with you half a dozen stout fellows, and break it in a thousand pieces." Horrified though he was by this vandalism, Meryon went, and soon "the stout fellows" had broken the statue into a thousand pieces. It never seems to have occurred to Hester that she could have given it to the Sultan along with the gold.

Next day, after a great deal of heavy work, with almost every available man heaving on the ropes — horses in Syria were far too well esteemed to be put in harness — the troughs were found to be empty. The treasure, if it had ever existed, had vanished.

Hester, though disappointed, still believed in the authenticity of the original document. Writing to Lord Bathurst, Secretary of State, she declared:

> "The authenticity of the paper I do not doubt; but, as many centuries have elapsed since the Christians hid treasure there, it is not very surprising that it should have been removed."

Meryon, who had always been sceptical of the existence of treasure, nevertheless believed, or pretended to believe, in the same theory. Writing to John Barker at Aleppo, he commented:

> "This trough must have been rifled of its contents by some of the Pashas and governors who have rummaged the ruins, and ostensibly for stones, really perhaps, for something more precious".

There was nothing now for it, but to cease all excavations. On 14th April, after only a fortnight, all work on the site came to an end. Hester and her party returned to Jaffa, and Meryon was not sad to see the last of Ascalon. Apart from being upset at the destruction of the statue, he had to note sorrowfully that the peasants in the villages around Ascalon were extremely ugly. "I saw not one pretty nor even one engaging woman", he wrote, "a rare occurrence in those parts, where the human form has generally some one feature to boast of, and where all the females strove to be pleasing in their manner of speaking." Meryon could perform miracles of work and endurance, but he could not bear to miss his little Eastern women, with their small hands and feet.

Oddly enough, the failure of the Ascalon expedition did no harm to Hester's standing in the area; rather, it enhanced it. The fact that she had destroyed a 2,000-year-old statue proved that she was not a thieving European. Though people in England were horrified when they heard of this vandalism, those in her immediate surroundings praised her. They had no particular love or reverence for old stones, but didn't want foreigners to take them away and change them into gold.

The story, anyhow, soon went around that the statue had in fact been stuffed with gold coins, and that Hester, quite rightly, had kept half and, very generously, given the other half to the Sultan. But then she was so rich already, what did she care? What impressed most people, and continued to impress them, was that she, a Christian and a woman at that, had been so highly thought of by the Porte that she had been given authority over pashas, and had a dreaded zaym at her total command. No Christian, man or woman, had ever been so honoured before. She must indeed be a great queen.

Though her position was secure she was not happy. She wrote to her old friend General Oakes, from Jaffa on 25th April 1815, on her way back to Mar Elias:

"I have at last decided upon sending for James to take me away from this country, for I know so little of the state of the continent, and feel in my own mind so doubtful of its remaining quiet, or if it does, that I shall like it as formerly, that before I break up a comfortable establishment to form another at random, I wish to have the opinion of one who knows my taste, and whom I can depend upon."

She also felt completely disillusioned with Michael, writing in the same letter:

"I fear B will turn out idle though it is his ambition to be great, and I lament that his father changes his plans about him every day, and wishing him to be everything, is the sure means of making him turn out nothing at last."

CHAPTER SIXTEEN

FAREWELL, MY ONCE DEAREST B

On arriving at Mar Elias she immediately sent her expenses for the expedition to Liston at Constantinople for payment by the British Government. The Ambassador quietly but firmly informed her that the Government would not pay out a penny. Hester, desperately in debt for the first time, borrowed more money from John Barker.

She felt very depressed after her return to Mar Elias. The great effort, extending over many months, that she had put into the Ascalon expedition had exhausted her. Its complete lack of material success increased her dejection, and the financial worry and huge debts she had incurred made matters worse. She had not heard from Michael for over five months and did not even know where he was.

Having already spent her Government allowance, and having to rely entirely on John Barker's loans, there was no longer any question of moving to any part of Europe. She would not, under any circumstances, return to England. Her dislike for the English politicians who had followed her famous uncle was so great that she could not bear to be in the same country, let alone the same town as them. She reduced her staff, but with her usual generosity took on the half-mad Loustaunau and two shipwrecked Abyssinians, a woman called Miriam and her brother Elias.

All through the early summer of 1815, while the armies of Europe were being called up again to face Napoleon, despite his promise that he would from now on behave like a constitutional monarch without territorial claims (a promise that was not taken seriously by the allies), and Waterloo was fought and won, Hester remained quietly at Mar Elias, writing letters. Some of these letters were light-hearted, as for example, when she wrote from Mar Elias to General Oakes on 25th June 1815:

> "I send you by Georgio, a Greek in my service, some Tigers' skins, for I think I recollect that you liked them. Here the covering of a horse reaches to his tail, and the tigers' skins look very well when made up with crimson; but silver and gold quite spoils the effect, I think. Georgio will explain (should you like it) the fashion of Syria, for you to improve upon it. You will find the boy not stupid, but he is not all he ought to be, though honest in money matters. Don't spoil him, pray, or take his humble manner for humility; for he is at bottom *conceit itself* . . . ."

Meryon, watching her, was worried. When he had set out with her from Portsmouth over five years earlier, he had always assumed that after a year or so, she would return to England. Now, particularly since the British Government had turned down her request to pay for the Ascalon expedition, it became evident, for the first time, that she might settle in the Holy Land for life.

Though he now understood and liked the East, and probably had a better practice than he could have had in his home country, his medical studies were still uncompleted. Though everybody called him doctor, and many thought of him as a "miracle" doctor, he still lacked official recognition. It was essential that he went back to Oxford and London to complete his studies. At last he went to her, telling her that he must return, and using as an excuse the fact that his parents were getting very old. She accepted his resignation, but made him promise that he would not leave until his replacement had been found. He agreed to this, even though he knew that it might be months before this could happen. The Greek servant, Giorgio, now much promoted, was sent to England to find a replacement.

A curious period of physical stagnation now set in. When interested, Hester was always full of an extraordinary energy, but devoid of an interest she sank into a state of physical lassitude that made even the slightest movement abhorrent. When she had contracted the plague at Latakia she always had two men servants to carry her up to bed. Now, although recovered, she kept up the habit of being carried everywhere. She was very different from the Ascalon leader on her black ass.

As Meryon believed that he would be unlikely to return to the East after he had got back to London, he put into operation his long-thought-out plan for a private visit to Egypt. He set off in August and returned in November. Hester was still at Meshmushy and was, he noted laconically, "in tolerable health". They soon returned to Mar Elias, where the roofs had been repaired in the hope of keeping out the winter rain. The winter passed slowly and spring came round again, and with it, much to Hester's satisfaction, Elizabeth Williams, who, it may be recalled, had been left behind at Malta with her sister and brother-in-law nearly six years earlier.

Elizabeth Williams had, however, always wished to return to Hester's service, and had left Malta at the beginning of the year. Meryon went down to the coast to meet her at the beginning of March. He was now a seasoned traveller of the East. When he first went there he always travelled with an interpreter, a servant and a couple of mules with his bed and luggage. "Now", he recorded to his astonishment, "I was alone, a fowling piece, lying across my saddle-bows, was my only protection; I, my own interpreter; I had no bed but my cloak; and all the articles of my dressing-box were reduced to a comb for my beard, and my tooth-brushes, which generally I concealed from the view of Mahometan natives, lest the materials, being of hog's bristles, render me unclean in their eyes."

There was a cheerful reunion with Elizabeth Williams, and the return journey was enlightened by a meal at night, lit by a candle stuck in half a loaf of bread. Next day Elizabeth was safely delivered to Mar Elias, and warmly welcomed.

If Hester had very little direct news from Michael, there were plenty of rumours about him, and none made very pleasant hearing. Soon after his return to London he had gone to Paris, as so many people did when Napoleon was thought safely shut away at Elba. Here he flirted both with the Princess of Moskowa, the wife of Marshal Ney, "the bravest of the brave" as Napoleon called him, and the Duchesse de St. Lea. When Napoleon returned so unexpectedly in March 1815 most of the English visitors, including Lady Bessborough, who was on the Riviera at the time, prudently

It was in such places as this that Hester's caravan would halt for a night, a few days or sometimes a week or more. The camps were often luxurious and more comfortable than the houses in the towns.

decamped; but it was said that Michael, perhaps because of his liaison with the Princess Moskowa, managed to stay on.

At all events, he was still in Paris after Waterloo, and he was there when Marshal Ney was arrested on a charge of high treason. Behind the scenes Michael had in fact tried to help in the Marshal's defence. But on 7th December 1815 Ney was shot in the Luxembourg Gardens. There was now talk that Michael might marry the Marshal's widow, or at least live with her in Italy. No wonder Hester was annoyed.

Then Michael, like Sligo, got into "a scrape". He and two other Englishmen organized the escape from prison of a certain Count

Lavalette. Like Ney he had been condemned to death for high treason when the Bourbons came back to the throne. This Scarlet Pimpernel type of rescue operation was planned to take place the very eve of the Count's execution. Surprisingly it succeeded and the Count escaped, but his rescuers were thrown into the Prison de la Force.

As soon as Hester heard that Michael was to be tried for treason, and that the penalty could be death, she wrote to everyone she could think of who might have the slightest influence with the French. She even wrote to that large unwieldy man, Louis XVIII himself, reminding him of the days when that monarch was a simple refugee protected by the generosity of her uncle, the great William Pitt, and her cousins, the Grenvilles.

Michael in the meantime, remained in prison, writing furious letters to his father denying that he was engaged to yet another lady — this time, a Miss Crossby — and proudly declaring that as soon as he got out of prison he would adopt a profession, preferably the law, and thus not have to suffer the degradation of permanently living off his father. However, despite this, he drew a further £200 on his father's account, and reminded the old man that although this was the last year he intended to keep up paying Hester her £600, there was still a balance of £300 due to her banker, Thomas Coutts.

Craufurd Bruce's financial situation had changed with the coming of peace. Instead of being in a better position, as he had expected, he, like many other, found that peace had it disadvantages. Indeed Craufurd Bruce, that apparently endless source of munificence, was going bankrupt. The cost of living in the Holy Land had doubled since Michael had left and the whole world was in the grip of an almost uncontrollable inflation.

After a few months in prison, Michael, whether because of the Grenville intercession cannot be known for sure, was released and expelled from France. But, by then, Hester — who had acted more like a mother whose wayward son had got into trouble than a mistress whose lover was in danger — was concentrating on another matter. The previous year, a Frenchman, Colonel Boutin, a great friend of Hester, had decided to travel across the mountains that ran from Mount Lebanon to Antioch, inhabited by a war-like people called the Ansarys. He set off, shortly after visiting Hester at Mar Elias, and then disappeared.

The indolent French Consuls in the area made a few tentative enquiries, but did not press the matter. Hester was more vigorous and sent her own search party into the Ansary country. They discovered that he had been assassinated by Arabs eager to plunder him of his bag of coins. She tried to rouse the French into some kind of action, but they did nothing. She tried all through the Spring of 1816 to get the local Pasha to march into the mountains to the village where it was known that the murder had taken place, but the Pasha was afraid that his troops, who were accustomed to fighting on the plains, would be at a disadvantage in the mountains. The Pasha's troops had always been defeated whenever they went into the mountains. So the Pasha politely but firmly turned down Hester's requests, usually with the excuse that the weather was too cold.

With the coming of summer, however, there was no longer any excuse, as far as Hester could see, to delay action any longer. The Pasha, however, still hesitated but under continued pressure from Hester eventually sent one of his most blood-thirsty governors, Mustapha Aga Berber, on the expedition.

Before leaving Berber wrote to Hester, saying that as he was fighting for her it was only right that she should arm her "knight". Delighted by this romantic outlook, Hester sent Berber, two fine English pistols. But Berber, in fact, was far from romantic. He was a fanatical Mohammedan and hated the Ansarys because of their different faith. He marched through the mountain villages, killing the inhabitants and burning down the houses, quite regardless of whether or not these particular people had been responsible for Boutin's death. When he reached the village where the murder had taken place he sent back to the Pasha the heads of those who were said to be responsible for Boutin's death, but they might quite easily have been innocent. He also sent back a number of women to be sold as slaves, and had the tomb of a saintly sheik broken into, the much revered bones of whom were burnt. When he had finished he returned in triumph to Tripoli. Thus did Hester show that she was not just a Queen in name, but had the power of a ruler as well.

On 18th July 1816 Hester set off on a visit to Antioch. The reason given was that she wanted to consult with John Barker over her financial affairs, but locally it was thought that she wanted to congratulate in person those who had taken part in the Ansary

Antioch. Hester visited Antioch ostensibly on business connected with the disappearance of Colonel Boutin; but it was rumoured that she went in order to avoid having to meet the Princess of Wales, who had recently arrived in the Holy Land for a visit to Jerusalem.

expedition. In fact, the reason was simpler — she wanted to avoid the Princess of Wales. This fine lady was on a visit to the Holy Land, and had made herself unpopular by trying to land, without official permit, at Jaffa — the nearest port to Jerusalem — instead of Acre, the official seat of government. When she eventually landed at Acre and complained to the Pasha, he politely pointed out that it was she who was at fault, for having tried to get in "at the window instead of the door". In the event, since Hester was a queen in the eyes of those around her, it would be better to be discreetly absent, so that the necessity of inviting the Princess to Mar Elias need not arise.

Loustaunau was for ever prophesying an extraordinary future for Hester. She was to be a queen, a real queen of the Orient. Europe would succumb to revolution and chaos, but she, Hester, was destined to lead a crusade in reverse, a crusade that would purify Europe of all its evils, and substitute instead the perfect society. Hester would then be acclaimed Queen of both the East and the West.

She returned to Mar Elias in the autumn, and one of her first visitors was the son of Firman Didot, the famous Paris printer. Already, earlier that year, the first of those many travellers who were to call at Lady Hester Stanhope's house had arrived. He was William Bankes, a donnish and self-opinionated young man, and a writer friend of his called Silk Buckingham.

They were, like Didot, the first of a large flood of visitors. Hester would not receive them unless she approved of them; and if any of them wanted to go to Palmyra, she had an understanding with Nasar to let through only those who bore a special letter from her. "If there comes to me", she wrote, "a great man, on whom I can rely, and whose word you may trust as my own . . . I will send him with two seals; but if another sort of person, I will send him with one." William Bankes had one.

On 15th November 1816 a small boy came running into the village of Abra, where Meryon was still living, shouting, "I bring you good news". The good news was that her servant Giorgio, who had been sent off to England nearly eighteen months ago, was back again with Mr. Newberry, a surgeon who was to replace Meryon, and twenty-seven cases, none of which were opened by the Turkish custom officers because of Hester's position.

England had gone to the head of the once humble Greek serving boy. While denigrating everything English — he compared English palaces to Turkish prisons — he took great pride in the fact that an English princess had given him a silver chain when he had delivered a letter from Hester. Yet, at the same time, he considered the chain a mean piece of jewellery. He swaggered about the place, until everybody was quite sick of him.

Meryon meanwhile was busy driving about the countryside introducing Newberry to the people with whom he would have to deal. Newberry was a correct and somewhat fastidious man, and was horrified to discover when sharing a room for the night with Meryon, that the latter did not bother to undress, but merely curled up, fully clothed, on the mat he always carried with him. Newberry undressed properly down to his shirt and despite Meryon's warning got into the bed provided. It was an open invitation for the fleas and by morning he was so badly bitten that it looked as though he had caught measles.

The time came for Meryon to leave. He went up to Mar Elias on the evening of Friday, 17th January 1817, had dinner with Hester, and at 2 a.m. on 18th January 1817, said good-bye to her, Miss Williams and Newberry. He went back to Abra for a short rest and, soon after sunrise, mounted his horse and "departed from Abra (may I be excused for saying it?) amidst the tears and good wishes of the peasants, who followed me with blessings to the end of the village".

He was accompanied by Beaudin, the cook. "Our provision mule", he recorded, "was better stocked than usual, and we made an excellent dinner on cold pasty of gazelle-venison, tarts and plum-cake, besides cold fowls, and some other good things, with which Miss Williams was desirous of making my last day's travelling in Syria agreeable."

They arrived shortly at Beyrouth, where Beaudin left him to return to Mar Elias. Meryon went on to England, carrying with him numerous letters from Hester. His departure had, in fact, been delayed by the writing of these letters. Many, except the most private, were written by him at Hester's dictation, for during the past year the job of official letter writer had been added to all his other jobs. Did he wonder sometimes whether the stiff Mr. Newberry would be so accommodating?

Hester had not cried at his departure. Indeed, in the letter she wrote to her cousin, General Richard Grenville, she had only this to say for the small man who had served her so well, even, on a number of occasions, at the risk of his life: "The Doctor who is the bearer of this, is a good sort of slow dull man, he was a great fop and fool when he first came into the East, but I have cured him of these failings, having a sort of impediment in his speech, he is an unpleasant man to converse with, but he is *honest*, tho' nothing will ever make him *bright*".

Hester enclosed a letter, written in Meryon's handwriting, for Michael. It was intended as a farewell letter to "Dearest B". She had heard of his engagement, which in fact, was only a rumour, and of his father's bankruptcy. She said that she would not accept any more of his money, and then defended her earlier acceptance of financial assistance on the grounds that it was all used to "educate" him, explained some of her political feelings, gave him some good motherly advice about the future, and ended the letter sadly: "Adieu, Farewell, my once dearest B! I must call you so no more . . . ." But it was not entirely the end of the affair. Soon after Meryon had left, Hester learnt that her father, that eccentric 3rd Earl, had died on 15th December 1816. The news had taken some months to reach her. She wrote, once more, for the last time to Michael:

May 1st 1817.

"I thought dear B that I had written to you for the last time by the Dr., but a late event obliges me again to address you. The death of my poor father will put me in possession, (next Decr) of a certain sum of ready money. I have therefore ordered Mr. Coutts, when he receives that money, to replace in yr father's hands every shilling placed by him or you, to my account since you left me. This is my *irrevocable determination* so save yourself the trouble of combating it as it will be useless . . . ."

After a few more lines this untypical short letter from Hester ended, and with it her long love affair with Michael Bruce.

PART THREE

THE QUEEN

CHAPTER SEVENTEEN

DAR DJOUN

Brothers had said that she would pass seven years in the desert. It was now exactly seven years since she had left Portsmouth, and all those years had been spent wandering in a "desert", either literally or figuratively. Now the time was approaching for the final part of the prophecy to come true: her coronation as Queen.

With Meryon's departure (he had always been the advance guard in her wanderings) and the final break with Michael — she would never, never take another full time lover — the time had come to settle down. She was forty-one and had travelled enough, but she would never go back to that England she now hated so much. She would not even go to Paris for fear of meeting some of the despised British ministers. As long as a year earlier she had written to the Marquis of Buckingham:

> "The grand-daughter of Lord Chatham, the niece of the illustrious Pitt, feels herself blush, as she writes, that she was born in England — that England, who has made her accursed gold the counterpoise to justice; that England who puts weeping humanity in irons, who has employed the valour of her troops, destined for the defence of her national honour, as the instrument to enslave a free-born people . . . ."

The "free-born" people were the French. The French army was now "the bravest troops in the world", the British ministers were "those insensate dolts of our day". She was a very different person now from the exuberant girl riding through the rain at Walmer, at Pitt's side, inspecting and encouraging the troops training to fight the now "bravest troops in the world". It was her "insensate" hatred of the ministers who had followed Pitt that had slowly made her include the whole of England in her strong disapproval.

Then Loustaunau never stopped mixing his prophecies of her future glory with extravagant praise for the deposed Napoleon and the wretched fate of the French nation. And now a new and even crazier prophet had come to her. Metta, who had started off as a servant, had revealed that he possessed a magic book of prophecies. He would consult the book on all occasions, and once read out: "And the Messiah shall ride a horse born saddled."

This seemed to be an impossibility, for how could a foal arrive in the world already saddled? Hester had a fine string of mares in her stables at Mar Elias. One of them was a beautiful mare, a gift from her "friend" the Emir Beshir, ruler of the Druses, whom she visited frequently. The mare was said to have descended in a direct line from a pure-bred in King Solomon's stables. And one day, in 1817, this particular mare gave birth to a foal that had a deformed spine. The discoloration of the deformity made the strange foal look as though it was born with a saddle. Though Beshir laughed heartily at her, Hester was convinced that this was a miracle, and a sign from heaven of her future.

Had not fate always seemed to push her to this very place, at this particular moment of time? She had not set out for the Lebanon seven years ago, but had merely thought of taking a holiday, as so many people of her rank did, for the good of her health. Yet, slowly, inexorably, unavoidably, one event after another had edged her towards these high mountains where now her destiny was to be fulfilled.

These extraordinary ideas and her habit of talking endlessly about them did not endear her to Newberry, nor did her continual ranting against England. He had served as a surgeon at the Battle of Waterloo, and he did not share her hatred for her country. Unlike Meryon he was not prepared to perform duties not normally allocated to a medical man. Elizabeth Williams now took over the job of writing Hester's letters.

Moreover, Newberry never took to the East after that first disastrous encounter with the fleas, and was soon involved in all kinds of disputes. On 26th July 1817, Beaudin, Hester's household comptroller wrote to Newberry:

> "The Sheik Beshir commands me to write to you in order
> that you sh come here and say before him and his wife the
> words you said to her Ladyship before me at Jeboa — and if
> you do not chuse to come it will be a sure proof that you
> have told a lie: and perhaps the Shaihk [sic] will take means
> to make you come. The bearer has orders to provide horses
> for you."

Newberry refused to do as he was commanded, and wrote to Hester
asking her to intercede on his behalf, stating that he would resist
"to death" rather than obey. Hester, probably annoyed by the
petty squabble, wrote back sharply:

> Sir, you might as well cool your absurd and violent passion
> and reflect that this is an affair of justice, neither you nor the
> Shaihk's wife have any right to give it to be understood that I
> keep a spy in the house of another and the Shaihk's wife as
> well as yourself must prove her words, for it rests between
> you who told the untruth . . . .

Soon Newberry told Hester that he wished to return to England
and did so in 1819, along with Mrs. Fry.

Hester had kept up a correspondence with Meryon during the
time Newberry was with her, and, although he had now officially
left her service she asked him from time to time to carry out little
services for her, as the following letter, dated June 1818 shows,
when she asked him to send out:

> ". . . Surtout quelques petites lampes et lanternes d'etain
> qu'il sont propre à se servir avec de l'huile, ou bien des
> Cocked Hats, comme ça   . . .   a sort of tea saucer
> with a little sort of thing like a snuff box in the middle which
> when open protects the wick for travelling."

Now left alone with Elizabeth Williams, Hester wrote to Meryon
suggesting that he should come back to her. He was not doing very
well in England, and in July 1818 noted in his diary:

"During this month I made up my mind to rejoin Lady Hester Stanhope. This as far as regarding my settling in life was utterly destructive of it. I was yearly losing ground from not having passed my examination at the College of Physicians in order to become a fellow."

So, in 1819, he left London for the second time for the East. What happened then cannot be ascertained for certain. The usually voluble doctor was remarkably reticent in the preface to his memoirs. Of the visit, all he would say was:

"I again revisited Syria, but I found that her Ladyship had in the meanwhile completely familiarised herself with the usages of the East, conducting her establishment entirely in the Turkish manner, and adopting even much of their medical empiricism. Under these circumstances, and at her own suggestion, I again bade her adieu, as I then believed for the last time."

No one knows what really happened, nor whether this was the real reason for Meryon's hurried departure. There had been rumours for some time that Hester had taken another lover, had even married a handsome Arab. She herself always maintained that the Arabs always looked upon her neither as a man nor as a woman, but as a special person.

Rumour continued, however, that she had replaced Michael. Three years earlier, on 6th April 1816, Madame Ney, then much enamoured with Michael, wrote him about the fact that he was then still sending her money:

"According to what you yourself told me, she renounced you and even gave herself to others. Even though she must be well aware that you know of this, she had the impudence to reproach you, and the lack of delicacy to allow you in part to keep her."

On the 21st August 1816, Madame Ney wrote again to Michael, noting: "Although she belongs to another man it is you who are obliged to support her."

Then there was the mysterious business of Loustaunau junior.

This young French captain, son of Hester's mad, old prophet, came out to Lebanon in 1819 in search of his father. He was a good-looking but coarse young man, who, as rumour has it, captivated Hester — although at forty-three she was now nearly twenty years older than he. The affair, if it really happened, for it may have been just another of her protective ventures, and due to the need to have somebody young whom she could influence, was of short duration. Captain Loustaunau died of over-eating and was buried at Mar Elias. Hester, who believed that he and she were soul mates, retired once more to Meshmushy.

From time to time, during her various trips around Mount Lebanon, Hester had travelled through the village of Djoun. On a nearby mountain stood the local manor house of Dar Djoun. It belonged to a Damascus merchant called Joseph Seweyah, who was prepared to let it on a repairing lease for £20 a year. It was a sprawling mass of one-storey buildings set upon the flat top of the orange-shaped mountain. Mar Elias was too small and too near the sea for Hester's liking, so she accepted Joseph Seweyah's conditions, and, soon after Meryon's second departure, moved into her new domain. She kept on Mar Elias, a short distance lower down the slope of Mount Lebanon, and left the half-mad Loustaunau there. But she took up with her his son's body and had it reinterred at Dar Djoun; for they were soul-mates, and she wished, when she died, to be buried next to him.

When she had settled into the new domain, she began altering it, building a maze-like construction that eventually consisted of forty rooms, linked by dark corridors. There were inter-connecting walks, shaded by trellis work, jasmin-shaded arbours, and inner courtyards — there was even a prison. There were hidey-holes and eavesdropping recesses, where servants or the guests could be spied upon. The whole was enclosed by a formidable wall, and the exits and entrances were so arranged that nobody could leave or arrive without being seen. This meant that the personnel and servants were virtually prisoners of the place, and that Hester could reign over them like an absolute monarch.

At the same time she bought a number of houses in the village itself, and had them made up and repaired for any refugees from famine or persecution who might come to their Queen for protection. She was in absolute control of her building work, and was guided not by architectural or aesthetic considerations, but by supernatural and superstitious beliefs. On one occasion, for example, she had a newly-built room immediately pulled down. When the builder asked what was the matter, she retorted that it was his business to obey her instructions without question. The construction had taken place during a bad aspect in her horoscope, and if she had left the room as it was, she believed she would have died.

Just as at Walmer years before, so now she created a garden at Dar Djoun. She brought the same imperious energy to this project as to all her ventures, and soon the bare bald top of the humped mountain began to show signs of an English—oriental garden. English creepers, jasmin and honeysuckle grew side by side with oriental plants. A marble fountain was placed in the middle of it, a terrace was built, and from Hester's room, its only approach, a view of low hills and a distant glimpse of the sea completed the idyllic vista. Only the very privileged were allowed to visit the secret garden.

After the war there was a period of unrest and civil disturbance, particularly in those areas where there had been no fighting. The ideas of liberty, carried through Europe with the "tricolours" of revolutionary France, survived both Napoleon and the allied victory. They were particularly potent in the vast multi-racial Turkish Empire. In 1821, the Greeks rose up against the Turks and there were large-scale massacres of Turkish peasants living in predominantly Greek areas. In revenge the Turks hanged, on Easter Day 1821, outside his palace, and in his full robes, the Patriarch of Constantinople, head of the Greek Church.

The European powers were in a quandary. The Tsar of Russia, Alexander I, was deeply religious, and had at the time of the Congress of Vienna formed, with Prussia and Austria, the "Holy Alliance". He had envisaged it as a Christian movement to avoid future wars; but Metternich had seen in it a means for suppressing future revolutionary movements. He was obsessed by the conviction that a French Revolution type of uprising must not be allowed to take place in Europe, since he believed it would lead to a new European war.

(right) Turkish general's uniform probably dating from the time of the Green War of Independence. The Turkish soldiers fought well when they were in the valleys or plains, but when faced with mountain or desert were disconcerted by the harsh conditions.

The Holy Alliance was therefore always at hand to suppress any uprising, particularly in those states where an absolute monarchy, or something like it, was in existence. In theory, therefore, the Holy Alliance should have come to the help of the Turks in their effort to contain the revolutionary uprising of the Greeks, but in practice it would be impossible for so Christian a movement as the Alliance to support a non-Christian government slaughtering Christians.

Although Britain had been careful to remain outside the Holy Alliance, she had agreed to join, with Russia, Austria and Prussia, a Quadruple Alliance, a purely defensive arrangement. (It was this apparent joining up with the repressive elements in Europe that had so incensed Hester.) But faced with the problem of having to choose between Greeks and Turks, the Holy Alliance did what many such organizations do — nothing. Popular feeling, however, was entirely on the side of the Greeks. Volunteers in their thousands rushed to help the Greek insurgents, among them many famous people such as Byron.

Metternich did all he could to isolate the Greeks and prevent help reaching them. He was afraid that if they were successful against the Sultan, revolutionary movements among the discontented and restless people in other parts of Europe might be encouraged to take the same course. But although he was able to isolate Greece politically, he could not prevent the influx of volunteers, and, thanks mainly to them, the Turks were not, for some time at least, able to regain the territories captured by the Greeks, particularly in the Morea.

Repercussions of the general unrest in the Turkish Empire were felt around Hester's lonely fortress, mainly in the form of preventive repressive action by the local pashas against possible uprisings led by local dissident rulers. During these confused years Hester continued to write to Meryon, even though he had now taken a five-year post as personal physician to Sir Gilbert Heathcote at 400 guineas a year.

Hester was becoming more and more involved in the daily events surrounding her. Nearly eighty letters dating from around this time and written either to her or at her dictation in old-fashioned Arabic have lain at Chevening untranslated for over 120 years. Recently they were handed over, along with all the other Stanhope papers, to the County Library in Maidstone, Kent.

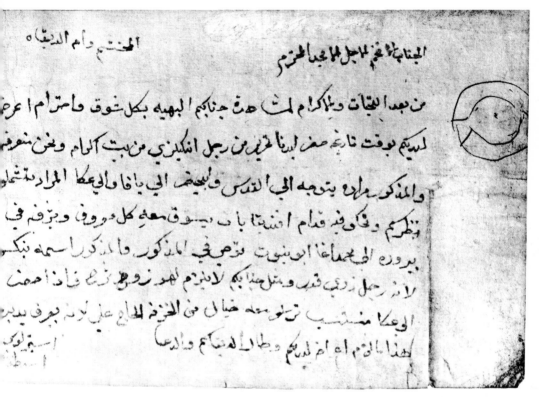

Facsimile of a letter written in Arabic by Hester. It affords a pass through neighbouring lands to William Bankes, when on a visit to her. (*Frank Hemel*)

These have, by kind permission of the Curator, Dr. Felix Hull, been translated for the first time.

Many of them refer to minor domestic matters, such as acknowledgement for an order for wine, a shopping list and the purchase of pistols from abroad. There is also a letter thanking her for gifts of a barometer, wallpaper and felt. It would appear that the working of the barometer was beyond the comprehension of the writer, that it had broken and that it was being returned.

There were a number of letters to do with her servants, who frequently gave her a good deal of trouble. There is a request for a position in her household; and a letter from the authorities asking her to send details of a slave in her household. On the other hand, there is a letter from one of her slaves, asking for her help in obtaining the release of his sons, who had been arrested by an agent of the Sublime Porte. There is no confirmation whether she was successful or not, but, knowing her determination, character and position, it is more than likely that she was.

There are, not unnaturally, letters concerning the plague. One correspondent writes of the need to disinfect a house. There are two documents, possibly sequels to the above request, certifying that a house had been disinfected.

Then there are references to her political activities. A Jewish Rabbi, for example, asks her to arrange the release of his servants, who have been taken from him. Another letter asks her to send in a list of her servants' names and anyone under her protection, so that the occupying troops — probably the Egyptians — will not arrest them. There is too a formal letter "complaining about the protection in her house of 45 supporters of Abdullah Pasha, who has been banished from the country, and who can cause trouble to the authorities". This is a reference to her invariable practice of giving shelter to those who were fleeing tyranny. She never acceded to any such requests from the authorities, even when her house was surrounded by hostile troops and not only her means of subsistance but also her very life were threatened.

There are, too, among these letters, many of a social type. One man, who was going to Egypt, asked Hester to ". . . take my wife into your house and protect her until my return, when I will reimburse you for every penny spent". Another, enclosing a number of gifts, tells her that he is sending her ". . . many gifts of food as an apology for my inability to visit you when my ship called at Jaffa".

There are light-hearted moments, such as in one letter referring to an invitation from Hester to taste some special French wine at her house. In another letter a person invites her to his house should she ever be in the area. Other communications for permission to take a fortnight's holiday, and for a gift for Ramadan. There is also one inquiring after her health. Further there is her official letter of introduction and protection to travellers moving through her territory or visiting territories where she has some influence.

On 21st April 1821 Hester wrote to Meryon:

"A terrible civil war has broken out in this country — about eighty thousand men in arms in Mount Lebanon, troops and inhabitants. . . . Do not write, or send any boxes, or anything; for God knows, if all these people come bundling down in a stream, you may imagine, we shall not be in a very secure situation."

Just over a year later, on 9th June 1822, she was writing to him again:

"You can have no idea of the state of things, and next month all will be bloodshed from one end of the country to the other. I have made my place at Jûn compact and secure from stragglers, but the expense, the fatigue, the worry of all this, the horrid stupid idle people I have about me, the distress and dangers of my friends, has been too much for me. Also, Williams got a hurt on her side moving a box: — I feared an abcess, but, thank God, an Arab doctor dispersed it, and she is now quite well, only thin and weak. I would not allow her to stir her arm for nearly three weeks, and I worked like a slave. I have had neither rest, air or exercise for eight months. Constant worry and fatigue with a constant fever which has hurt my eye-sight, split my nails, worn away the gums from my teeth, of which however I have not one decayed in my head; but I feared a fortnight ago, all would come out — not loose, but they were half bare, although better now, having rubbed them with a root which cooled my mouth."

It was in this year that Meryon got married, but Hester still hoped that he would be able to break his employment with Sir Gilbert Heathcote and come out to her. There was only Elizabeth Williams with her now, and Hester was worried about her constant companion. In a letter, dated 30th January 1823, she wrote:

"What wd become of poor W if anything sh happen to me? What means will she have of departing who can she confide in poor soul? This thought pains me more often than I can express."

By 1823 plans were discussed about the doctor's return and on 12th April 1823, Hester wrote:

"It was always my contention, were you not as fortunate in

the world as I should wish, to have offered you and your daughter to return to this country, when I had wherewithal to make you comfortable."

But he was either unable or unwilling to get away at that time, and when he told her this, she replied on 27th July:

"I take very cooly your not coming, as I do all things, however important, which concern my own comfort. Williams cried about it a good deal, for she looked forward to being released from the care of medicine, about which she knows nothing, and she was mortified to find that I was right in my suspicion. I often used to say to her: 'It is not too sure that the doctor will come: he is a very weak character — a child may flatter and turn him. Talking and acting are two different things'."

The feeling that he had put his own interests before hers continued to torment him during the whole of the following years. Even as late as 17th August 1825 she wrote to him:

"You have accused yourself of "vile interest". I cannot admit any such motive. I have ever known you to be honest, and perhaps too liberal: but a man without future, and who has a child to provide for, cannot always act as he would wish."

It was in this year that James Stanhope committed suicide. He had married, romantically, in 1820, Lady Frederica Murray, daughter of the Earl of Mansfield. When she died after the birth of her second child in 1823 James never got over his grief. His death, which Hester heard about six months after it had happened, meant the almost final cutting of her connections with her own family. Mahon, now the 4th Earl, had not communicated with her for nine years, ever since he had come into the title in 1816, when she had written what he later described as a "most cruel and insulting letter" in which, among other things, she wrote:

"Far be it from me ever to wish to be upon friendly terms with you, should you still persist in the perverse opinions which have lowered you in the eyes of those you most courted, and deprived you of their *real* confidence."

So "Incomparable Mahon" was gone (they never in fact ever communicated with each other again) and there was only Griselda left, and she and Hester had never been close.

When Meryon wrote to her telling her of James's suicide she wrote back to him in July 1826 and had only this to say about her brother's death: "I received yesterday your letter of the 29th March. Alas, alas, alas! – More I cannot say".

By now, however, Meryon was at last professionally free to join her, and, on 23rd January 1827 he set off with his wife and daughter to join her. His progress was, to say the least, slow. The first four months were spent in Calais, partly waiting for the weather to improve, partly to deal with some property matter. By June they were in Pisa, where he found three letters from Hester, written in January 1827. They informed him of the trouble she was having with a certain X, as she called him, who pretended to be the representative of the Dukes of Sussex and Bedford. They, so X claimed, along with a number of other eminent men, were prepared to pay off all her debts.

By July, Meryon and his family were waiting in Leghorn for an appropriate ship. Another letter awaited him, written from Djoun as late as 29th May 1827. In it she told him to forget all she had said about X, mentioned her brother, James, and then went on to give the doctor, who was now approaching forty, his instructions:

> "Land, if possible, at Sayda [Sidon], and, on reaching the harbour, leave your family in the ship, take an ass at my farrier's and come here to Djoun . . . I cannot express my gratitude. May God reward you hereafter . . .! I hope Mrs. M has plenty of rings on her fingers, as that is very necessary in this country, and the greatest of possible ornaments in the eyes of women."

"Mrs. M" was, however, a quiet and somewhat reserved lady, who shared many of Mrs. Fry's views of foreigners; she both hated and feared them. And Meryon, no doubt suitably provided with rings for his wife, set sail with his family on the "Fortuna" for Cyprus on 7th September 1827.

It was an unfortunate choice of name for the ship, for on 15th September 1827 a tall-masted Greek schooner bore down upon them. She had twelve guns, and a crew of sixty or eighty fierce looking Greeks. Her Captain ordered Lupi, the Italian captain of the "Fortuna" to come aboard. Lupi had no illusions about the outcome of the encounter — the Greeks were after plunder. "Make yourself as smart as possible", he told Meryon, "assume an air of authority, and pass yourself off as a consul."

This Meryon did in the quarter of an hour that passed before a Greek lieutenant and twenty men boarded the ship. Four friars who were on a pilgrimage to the Holy Land began surreptitiously to hide their money among the folds of their ample habits. The Greek lieutenant was very polite, and taking Meryon for somebody special informed him that Cyprus, with its large Turkish community, was being blockaded. No doubt the "Fortuna" was full of contraband goods. It would be necessary to search her.

"You, being an Englishman", he said, "will meet with no molestation; the English are our friends, and we are not incapable of gratitude." Then, holding the bill of lading in his hand, the lieutenant marked off each item as it was hauled up. Among them were a number of large trunks, each with a cross on it, belonging to the four friars.

As one Christian to another, the Greek lieutenant told the friars that these religious receptacles would have to be opened too. Out of the sacred containers appeared, most unexpectedly, boxes of chocolates, almonds, bottles of rum, Bologna sausages, as well as men's and women's clothes of the finest cut and large quantities of money in various denominations. The Greeks began to shout and dance with excitement, while the friars fell on their knees and prayed. All the money hidden in the habits was shaken out.

Wine was found in the hold and was drunk. The Captain was pinioned and his life threatened unless he told where he kept the ship's money. The Captain cried out to Meryon for help, and while the latter appealed to the lieutenant, Mrs. Meryon, despite the presence of her infant daughter, rushed courageously forward and saved the man's life.

After a good deal of confusion, the lieutenant and his men abandoned the ship, leaving its occupants to spend a miserable night after a meal of hard biscuits and water. Much to the passengers alarm the lieutenant returned in the morning, but only to ask in the politest possible way whether they had spent a comfortable night. He also begged the Captain to hand over a box of jewels listed on the bill of lading, an oversight during the confusion of the previous day. The jewel-case was reluctantly handed over, whereupon — after shaking Meryon by the hand as if they were old friends — the polite pirate left.

The ship returned to Leghorn on 12th October 1827 and remained there in quarantine until 17th November. It was while Meryon and his family were there that news of the battle of Navarino reached them.

This was the battle that never was, for although the Greeks and Turks were murdering each other with great enthusiasm, neither was officially at war. But by the Treaty of London in 1827, France, Russia and Britain agreed that pressure should be brought on the Sultan of Turkey to make him recognize Greek independence. A combined Anglo-Russian-French fleet was sent to the Mediterranean. At the Bay of Navarino, it met the combined Turco-Egyptian fleet, and a chance shot started the unofficial battle. By the end of the day the Turco-Egyptian fleet was utterly destroyed.

What with this, the bad weather and the nervous breakdown Mrs. Meryon suffered after the pirate incident, it was decided to put off the journey to the Holy Land until the spring.

Meanwhile Hester was having even more trouble with her erstwhile friend, the Emir Beshir. He had given orders that no one, under pain of death, was to have anything to do with Dar Djoun. This meant that even essential stores, such as food and water, which were brought up by mule, were threatened. Hester, however, refused to be intimidated, and eventually the Emir was ordered by the Porte to stop harassing her.

The Battle of Navarino, however, added to her problems, for although she herself lost none of the respect of the Turkish authorities, other Europeans in the area were not so fortunate. There was enormous indignation at the high handed way the combined Anglo-Russian-French fleet had destroyed the Turco-Egyptian ships, and many Europeans and their sympathizers found their way to that perpetual refuge for the persecuted — Dar Djoun. Once again Hester was handing out large sums of money she hadn't got to those in need.

When she heard about Meryon's abortive attempt to reach her, she wrote, on 23rd March 1828:

"I must say, it would be very imprudent to bring women or children into this country at the moment, and a great source

Emir Beshir, the ruler of the Druzes, a clever but cruel man. At first he was a friend of Hester, but later he bacame jealous of her increasing power and influence. (*Frank Hemel*)

of fatigue and vexation to me; for they could not be comfortable under the present circumstances of the times. What I should propose is, that, when you have settled your business, you immediately set off alone with a Dutch passport in case things should turn out ill before you arrive. Leave Mrs. M. at Pisa where she could remain very comfortably until you return."

War or no war, she was determined to get Meryon back, preferably without the encumbrance of his wife and child. The use of a Dutch passport was a subterfuge English and French travellers prudently adopted, in order to hide their real identity for a while after the Battle of Navarino.

Meryon, however, had to attend to business in London. In June 1828, he went to London, and returned to Pisa in October. He had now decided to take his family back to England in the spring, and join Hester then. But in December Meryon heard that Elizabeth Williams had died through neglect while ill, also that Hester had been very ill and was in a weak state. He was so upset that he set off immediately, despite his wife's pleas, to Leghorn and booked a passage on a ship due to sail to Beyrouth. Mrs Meryon did not wish to be left behind, but on the other hand her fear of pirates was so great that she could not bear the idea of setting off again. So the ship sailed without them.

Nor could Meryon, despite all his efforts, convince her to move when the spring arrived. It was not until August 1829 that she finally agreed to move, and this time it was not to Beyrouth, but back to England. She had, however, finally agreed that Meryon should leave her in England, and go out to Syria on his own. But when they reached Paris her old fears returned. She did not want him to go on his own, for fear that he would catch the plague or something almost as bad. So, once again, the plans were changed: she would, after all, accompany him, and they set off for Marseilles in order to find a boat. Having got that far, however, it took Meryon almost a year to persuade her to make the journey and it was not until 3rd November 1830 that they finally sailed on a 220-ton ship called "The Belle Sophie". They travelled in greater comfort than three years earlier, for they had a state-room.

At last, on 8th December 1830, Meryon disembarked at Beyrouth. Meryon, on Hester's instructions, put on the old faded

Turkish suit and Arab cloak he had worn on his two journeys to Palmyra, and sent a message to Hester to tell her that they had arrived. Her reply was somewhat typical of her. She would, she said, be delighted to welcome him but would prefer not to meet his wife or daughter. They were, she said, his and not her responsibility. However, she had, she told him, put a cottage in the village of Djoun at their disposal, and had allocated two of her native servants to them. When they were finally within two miles of Dar Djoun they were met by Hester's secretary. He took charge of Meryon's family, and the doctor hurried on alone to the great fortress-house, arriving there at noon.

Hester greeted him with tremendous pleasure, even kissing him on both cheeks. This astonished him, for in all the time he had been with her, she had never even taken his arm. Further surprises were in store. She insisted that he sat on the sofa beside her, again something she had never done before. Finally, she served him with sherbet, coffee and a small cup of orange-flower water; all marks, in the Eastern mind, of great respect.

He had not seen her for ten years. Now, at fifty-four, she looked much the same as she had done before. Even his experienced doctor's eye could see little medically wrong with her. There was no sign of the many illnesses, including failing eyesight, she had written about in her numerous letters. She was indeed bright-eyed and sparkling, although she sometimes wore prince-nez, which, clamped on the bridge of her nose, gave her voice a somewhat nasal intonation. She was dressed in a completely Eastern way, although Meryon noticed she was not as smart as she used to be. The Turkish man's clothes did, however, hide her excessive thinness, and, although there were some lines on her face they could not be seen in the dim light of the room. In fact, she looked remarkably attractive.

Then she started on one of the marathon talking sessions that were a feature of her life now, and the afternoon drifted away. When dinner came there was no trace of European habits. She sat on her sofa, Meryon on a rush chair opposite. An unpainted deal table, covered with a small tablecloth stood between them. Cutlery consisted of two spoons (which alone remained, the rest having been stolen by her servants) and two black-boned knives and forks. There were two plates, one on top of the other, in front of each of them, and in the middle of the small table three yellow earthenware dishes containing respectively a pilaf, an Irish stew of sorts and a boiled fowl.

As soon as the simple meal was over Meryon tried to get away, saying that he was afraid his family would begin worrying about him. This, as can be imagined, had no effect on Hester whatsoever. She went on talking as before. It wasn't until midnight that he finally managed to escape after a continuous twelve-hour session with his aristocratic patient.

He found his wife sitting disconsolately among her still unpacked trunks. Hester's secretary was still with her, but his presence had not been much of a help. He had spent most of the time telling her gory tales of how people on foot had been attacked late at night by the wolves and hyaenas that roamed the countryside. It took all of Meryon's tact and persuasiveness to reassure his wife that he had in fact returned safely to her.

The pattern of life at Dar Djoun was simple if exacting, and was entirely geared to Hester's way of life. She was in all matters supreme Queen of the place and of the surrounding countryside. Although the village was officially ruled by the Emir Beshir, it was really under Hester's control. Nobody could come or go without her permission, for all the mule and camel drivers were in her service, and the local people looked upon her, rather than the Emir, as their ruler. This fact still rankled with Beshir.

But simplicity was now the keynote of her way of life. Her bed consisted of planks nailed together on low trestles. A mattress, seven feet long and four and a half feet wide, was laid on the planks. There were neither mosquito net nor sheets, only Barbary blankets. Her pillows were, however, of Turkish silk, and she was very fussy about the way this strange bed was made. She kept the two native girls who served her making and remaking it.

The room itself was as austere as the bed. It had a cement floor covered with a drab carpet and three windows, one boarded up. There was no table in it. A jug and basin stood in one of the curtainless windows, and apart from a large box covered with green calico at the end of the bed the room was bare. Her two personal maids took it in turn to sleep in the room with her.

She got up between two and five o'clock in the afternoon, and would then begin one of her long one-sided "conversations" if she could find anybody to listen to her. This would consist of an almost continuous monologue on every kind of subject: astrology, magic, philosophy, politics, the state of the world, the meaning of life, her own glorious past and the failings of her listener, particularly if, as in Meryon's case, he was a doctor.

She could talk in this way for eight to twelve hours at a stretch, pausing only to issue new orders to her staff in a rough and impatient way. Meryon noticed that she was very much more bad-tempered than earlier and was never satisfied with anything. She would call for food at all hours. A maid would hold a tray in front of her and, if it were dark, shade the candle so that the light did not flicker in Hester's eyes. She grumbled all the time she ate. She would quite often wake the whole house up in the middle of the night and get everybody moving about, working as busily as if it were full daylight.

She was extremely untidy. The niches in the walls of her rooms were filled with odds and ends: writing paper, a few books (for she hardly ever read, and then mainly books on magic) tied up in handkerchiefs, plates on which lay scissors, a pair or two of the the spectacles Meryon had earlier sent to her, pins, sealing-wax, blotting paper and accounts books.

She refused to have any kind of clock or watch anywhere near her, "because", she said, "I cannot bear anything that is unnatural; the sun is for the day, and the moon and the stars for the night, and by them I like to measure time". Nevertheless, she did not scruple to ask Meryon the time by his watch.

At times she seemed tireless, carrying on, with that extraordinary and terrifying attention to detail she had shown in Wales, all kinds of mental activities from dictating long letters to local pashas on how they should rule their domains, to working out cunning ways of catching out a servant suspected of cheating her. At last, some time in the early hours, she would fall asleep, and Meryon could return to his fretful wife.

Some time went by before Hester found that she could invite Mrs Meryon to visit her. An audience, for such it was, was arranged for a certain morning. An ass was sent to the village to bring her up to the house. Doctor Meryon introduced his wife formally to Hester in the drawing-room, then left the room. Hester rarely entertained more than one person at a time.

The meeting lasted three hours. It was not a particularly satisfactory one. Hester, as usual, talked without stopping. Mrs. Meryon was bored and resentful. On leaving, she committed, through ignorance, a gaffe that in Hester's eyes was unforgivable. It was an Eastern custom to robe a departing guest as a sign of honour. Hester had called for a magnificent Turkish cloak in gold brocade, and a finely embroidered muslim turban. With her own hands, she had placed the cloak over Mrs. Meryon's shoulders, and wound the turban around her guest's head. This done, the guest should have thanked her and then left. Mrs. Meryon, thinking that this was some kind of childish dressing-up game, took the cloak and turban off before leaving, and left them on a table.

Meryon was obliged, as usual, to spend the rest of the day and evening listening to Hester talking. When, at last, it was time to go, soon after midnight, he found that a terrible storm had broken over the countryside. The continuous thunder echoed round the mountains. The heavy tropical rain never ceased. When he at last made his way to the cottage, he found his wife almost in hysterics. Unaccustomed to such a storm she had thought the end of the world had come, but she could speak to nobody to allay her fears, for the servants only spoke Arabic.

Real trouble did not, however, start until 25th January 1831 when Hester decided to send Meryon off to Damascus to help cure an old friend of theirs. Mrs. Meryon, however, refused even to consider the idea of letting her husband go to Damascus. Apart from the danger of getting the plague, she could not bear the idea of being left alone with her daughter among people with whom she could not communicate.

Hester summoned Mrs. Meryon to come to her at once. A second and rather more painful interview took place between the two women. First, Hester tried to point out that if Meryon refused to go, his career would suffer. Then she reverted to magic, saying, apparently with complete conviction, that she knew sorcerers who could make hair grow on Mrs. Meryon's face and cover the wretched woman's body with blotches. Mrs. Meryon was neither frightened nor flattered. She said that if her husband wished to go, she could not stop him, but it would be without her consent.

Mrs. Meryon's defiant attitude reduced Hester to acts of petty vindictiveness. On one occasion she sent Fatoom, one of Hester's two personal maids, to the Meryon's cottage to insult them at breakfast. "I and the rest of the servant", yelled Fatoom in Arabic, "can contain ourselves no longer, to think that you and Madam, there, should be the cause of my lady's falling ill. She is worried to death by you — people that have the insolence to disobey her commands!" Luckily Mrs. Meryon could not understand what was being said. Meryon took the girl by the arm, shoved her out of the room, and shut the door on her; but the girl continued to yell abuse at them, in full hearing of the village.

On 3rd February 1831 Hester and Meryon had a stormy meeting. At the end of it he told her that he would return to England with his family, adding that he had come out there for no good at all. She scathingly compared him to a hen-pecked, half-bred horse, saying:

> "I have given a good deal of advice to many persons, in whom I have taken an interest, and you are the last of my disciples whom I thought I could make something of. But it is like cutting the hair off the legs of half-bred horses: it grows again, and you may often get a kick in the face for your pains. You know what a good opinion they had of you in this country, which I kept up; but your conduct now has spoilt all; for when a man gives his beard to a woman, it is all over with him. Remember my words, and write them down."

This state of partial warfare continued for the next few months. The villagers were so afraid of Hester that they hardly dared bring the daily provisions to the doctor, his wife and daughter. Meryon and his wife were virtual prisoners of Hester. He had no money and Hester never paid what was due to him. Eventually, however, he managed to have some money sent out to him, but still had to face the problem of persuading somebody in the village to supply them with mules. The villagers were far too afraid of Hester to do so, nor would the consuls in Sidon dare to go against her wishes.

Then suddenly, at the beginning of April 1831, she relented, and at last gave the doctor permission to leave. On 6th April 1831 she called him to her bedroom. She lay on her huge bed, apparently in an exhausted state. They took tea together, and discussed various matters, including her debts, which at this point had reached £14,000. As she was paying approximately 20%, or £2,800 per annum on them, she had no chance, on her pension of £1,200 a year, to pay them off. On the contrary, they just went on accumulating. Then towards midnight she sent him to the next room to replace the list of her debts in Elizabeth Williams' writing desk, which had been moved there after the latter's death.

When the doctor returned to Hester's room he found the door bolted. One of Hester's maids was on duty outside the door. She said that in order to spare them both a painful farewell Hester had decided to see nothing more of him.

The next day, Meryon, his wife and daughter set off for Sidon, mounted on asses. Their luggage was carried by camels. They reached Sidon about midday and received an unfriendly welcome because news of the quarrel had reached the town. The following day they set sail. The unpredictable Hester astonished them all with a final, quixotic and baffling gesture: she sent them ample provisions for the journey.

CHAPTER EIGHTEEN

RETREAT

In 1832, the year after Meryon's departure, Egyptian forces captured Acre and overran Syria. Mehemet Ali had quarrelled with his nominal overlord, the Sultan of Turkey. The ruler of Egypt had been led to understand that he would be given control of Syria in exchange for his powerful help to the Sultan in suppressing the Greek rebellion. The fact that after the battle of Navarino Greek independence became inevitable was of no importance. A promise was a promise. Since the Sultan refused to honour it, the Egyptians who, under their wily Albanian leader, were stronger than the Turks, took what they considered to be theirs anyhow.

To Hester, the change-over meant little. Mehemet Ali was as much a friend as the surrounding Turkish governors and officials. It was just a question of exchanging one friend for another. To the local inhabitants, however, war brought, as usual, chaos, misery, destruction and death. Once again the road to Djoun and its mysterious and dominating fortress-house became crowded with refugees. Once again Hester, always sensitive to the hardships of ordinary people en masse, if not individually, gave them food and shelter. The newly arrived Egyptian overlords did not dare dispute her authority any more than the Turkish governors had done before. And when the Sultan finally made friends again with his powerful and aggressive underling, Mehemet Ali was allowed to keep Syria — and life at Djoun went on much the same as before.

This was the time when the Hester Stanhope legend reached its height. News of the strange Englishwoman, who ruled a kingdom in the midst of the turbulent war-torn Turkish Empire with absolute authority, became the subject of conversation not only of those who still remembered her personally, but of the general public both in and outside Britain.

No traveller would undertake a visit to the Holy Land without including in his or her itinerary an attempted visit to Dar Djoun. Not all were successful. It depended on how they wrote out their application form to Hester. A young American lawyer called Stephens, who was later to unravel with the English architect Catherwood the mysteries of the Maya civilization, made the mistake, because he was in a hurry, of actually naming the day he would like to call on Hester. She did not even bother to answer his letter.

Lamartine, the great French poet and writer, was more crafty. In an extremely flattering and flowery letter, he asked whether he and perhaps a few friends could have the honour to pay their respects to her, who was acknowledged as one of the marvels of the East, at a time of her choosing. He would, he added, understand if she did not wish to see him for he, too, appreciated "le prix de la liberté et le charme de la solitude".

However, she did wish to see him, and indeed gave him two interviews, which was rare for her, showed him round her luxurious and secret garden and introduced him to her two favourite mares, Laila and Lulu.

He was delighted with the reception he had been given, and went away to write it all up in his projected book, "Voyage en Orient". He might not have been so pleased with himself if he could have known how Hester, herself, was later to describe him:

> "With his straight body and straight legs he pointed his toes in my face, and then turned to his dog, and kissed him and held long conversations with him. Think of his getting off his horse half a dozen times to kiss that dog, and take him out of his bandbox to feed him, on the road from Beyrout here! The very muleteers and servants thought him a fool."

A more sensitive and thoughtful visitor was Kinglake, the author of "Eothen". He had, he recalled, been brought up on Hester's fame. "I know", he wrote, "that her name was made almost as familiar to me in my childhood as the name of Robinson Crusoe, both were associated with the spirit of adventure; but whilst the imagined life of the caste-away mariner never failed to seem glaringly real, the true story of the Englishwoman ruling over Arabs always sounded to me like a fable."

While the best contemporary descriptions of the strange fortress-house with its sombre maze-like corridors, its compelling pipe-smoking owner and elaborate Eastern customs are to be found in "Voyage en Orient" and "Eothen", every single traveller who managed to obtain an audience added his or her contribution to the build up of the picture of this strange woman.

So powerful was her effect on visitors that one, Sir Thomas Gore-Browne, writing to his daughter over fifty years later on 2nd October 1885, recalled:

> "We were fed and detained in a kiosk while the Astrologer ascertained that we had got red hair and were not born under a hostile star to hers. This over, we were conducted through various apartments filled with retainers & at last reached one occupied as I thought by a middle-aged chief but which proved to be Lady Hester herself.
>
> "Here we remained until 2 p.m. listening to her marvellous conversation in which she told us Eastern Tales as wonderful as those of the Arabian Nights interspersed with the most graphic accounts of Beau Brummel, Mr. Pitt & George IV, then Prince Regent. Her conversation was the most interesting I have ever listened to in my life.
>
> "She had an Arab horse, strangely marked with a saddle mark, on which the Saviour was to ride escorted by her, when he should reappear which would be shortly after I saw her.
>
> "Ibrahim Pasha had recently conquered Syria from the Sultan and desired her to give up some deserters who had taken refuge with her. This she promptly and personally refused whereupon Ibrahim applied to the Consul General in Egypt — the Consul wrote to Lady Hester on gilt-edged paper and with much circumlocution to which she replied as follows: 'Consuls are for trade not for the nobility', signed 'HS'."

So Hester continued to reign over her little kingdom, receiving her visitors and trying to get rid of the refugees, who even when comparative peace had returned to the Holy Land turned her house and village into a refugee camp. It was not until the beginning of 1836 that she managed to get rid "of the last of eighteen persons of one family, all orphans and widows" whom she had saved.

It was in August 1836 that Meryon, now living with his family at Nice, received a letter from Hester, begging him, as an old friend, to return to her and help her in the matter of her Irish inheritance. It appeared that she now believed that she was, and indeed had been for many years, entitled to the revenue from a property in Ireland. It had been concealed from her, but a young lawyer, who had met some Irish cousins of hers, assured her that the money was hers by right.

Meryon feared that this was another X case, another Ascalon. For a woman as shrewd as she was in many matters and who, in her own estimation, was a political genius, she was extremely naïve where finance and treasures were concerned. Perhaps, in her desperate financial circumstances, she grasped eagerly at any miraculous solution to her problems. But once again he responded to the call. He engaged a governess, as much to be a companion for his wife as a protector for his daughter, and on 6th June 1837, his fifty-fourth birthday, set off from Marseilles once again for the Holy Land.

They landed at Beyrouth on 1st July 1837. A terse letter from Hester showed at once that she had not forgotten the battles of six years earlier. She would be pleased to see Meryon — indeed she had sent for him — but she was not prepared to receive Mrs. Meryon. She suggested that Mrs. Meryon and the children should be left behind at Beyrouth, while Meryon came to Djoun alone.

Meryon, however, provided with a double green marquee, travelled by night (because of the heat) to Sidon. There had recently been an earthquake which had so damaged Sidon that no house could be found for the party. However, the French Consul kindly said that they could pitch their tent under the shade of some trees in his orchard.

On 4th July 1837 he went up to Djoun and met Hester again. She was now sixty-one, a tall, gaunt haggard-faced woman, with a terrible racking cough; she smoked without cessation. Her large bed, where she spent more and more of her time, still had the same Barbary blankets on it, but now they were covered in the smouldered holes where the hot tobacco had fallen upon them. The floor, apparently unswept for months, was covered in tobacco ash, cobwebs and dust. How she had not managed to set herself on fire was a mystery to Meryon.

Yet she retained the same imperious manner, and indeed talked to Meryon as if he had been away six weeks instead of six years. The main purpose of her conversation appeared to be to persuade Meryon to keep his wife and children as far away from Djoun as possible. On the following day – he had spent the night at Djoun – a letter arrived for him from Sidon saying that his wife and family were in a great state of terror and distress, and could he come at once. This convinced Hester that, however much she disliked the idea, Mrs. Meryon would have to be within reasonable distance of Djoun. She suggested, therefore, that Meryon should move into Mar Elias, which she had still kept on. It had been extensively damaged in the January earthquake but was serviceable enough. It was within a few hours ride from Djoun, near enough for the doctor to be summoned when required, but far enough away to prevent Mrs. Meryon calling.

His family's distress had been caused by the appearance, in the middle of the night, at the entrance of the tent, of a horrifying-looking scarecrow of a man, who gibbered and shook his arms at Mrs. Meryon. Her screams brought the children, governess and servants to her side. It turned out that the man was an escaped prisoner and, far from wishing to harm them, was begging for help. But with nobody speaking, to Mrs. Meryon's way of thinking, any civilized language, she could hardly be expected to know this.

Next day they travelled up to Mar Elias, where the half-crazy 82-year-old General Loustaunau told Meryon how the earthquake had occurred. He was sitting under the verandah of the quandrangle, reading the Bible as usual, when his chair began to tilt. He looked up from the book and saw that the wall opposite him was rocking while a cloud of dust rose from the roof beyond it. Then everything was quiet again.

He was unhurt, but the damage was considerable. The store-room ceiling had collapsed, Hester's old bedroom was cut in half and the kitchen roof had gone. The flower-bed in the centre of the courtyard had been lifted up two feet, but the palm-tree and rose bushes planted in it still grew on their new and elevated site.

However, some of the rooms were untouched, notably the drawing-room and bathroom. With a little bit of ingenuity Meryon was able to make a reasonably comfortable flat among the ruins. He installed his family, and once again set about the almost impossible task of combining his medical services to his employer and keeping his frightened family happy. In the evenings, when he got back to Mar Elias — he could when necessary spend the night at Dar Djoun — he would write down, busy Boswell as he still was, the more interesting items she had told him.

Mar Elias was rendered even more miserable when a woman, whom Hester intended to engage, was sent to stay there. She contracted a mysterious illness, or possibly had a brain tumour, and went mad, dying after a fortnight of agony for herself and all within earshot. So upset was Mrs. Meryon, that she refused to stay on at Mar Elias any longer. But Hester could not help the doctor find alternative accommodation. She had advised him not to bring his family, and if he had done so against her advice, it was for him to make the best of matters.

When his daughter, Eugenia, wrote to her suggesting that she might come up and help at Djoun during her father's temporary absence owing to a slight indisposition, Hester wrote back a letter beginning:

"I was pleased to find, my dear Eugenia, that you inherit your father's goodwill towards me. I must thank you and Mademoiselle Longchamp for your kind offers of assistance, but I must decline them, having taken a determination not to have anything more to do with the doctor's family than if it did not exist in the country. I should forget my situation and rank in life were I to condescend to dispute and make daily explanations to my inferiors . . . ."

However, she also wrote to Meryon, saying that when his business with her was finished he could go to Beyrouth, Cyprus or Europe if he pleased.

Winter came early and wet that year, the rain penetrating the flat Syrian roofs. Cracks brought on by the intense summer heat could not close up in time to prevent the continual dripping of water. In Hester's bedroom pans were laid across the floor to catch the drops. The wind howled around the fortress-house and snow on Mount Lebanon was deeper than it had ever been before.

Hester spent day after day in bed, smoking endlessly, seized with sudden terrible fits of coughing, while complaining continuously about the insolence of the servants, their cynicism and their uncaring disregard for her, who was, after all, their Queen. "If I happen to fall asleep", she said one day to Meryon, "there is not one would cover my shoulders to prevent my taking cold." When, during one of these long diatribes against her staff, Meryon suggested that she sacked some of them, she retorted haughtily, "Doctor, think of my rank".

She still had great hopes that the Irish inheritance would solve all her problems. She had written to Sir Francis Burdett in England, asking him to make enquiries for her. Daily she expected his letter telling her the good news of her life-saving fortune. But the days turned into weeks and Christmas would soon be there. Sometimes she would get out of bed for an hour or so and sit on an ottoman couch in an alcove of her bedroom.

"I believe it will do me good to cry", she told Meryon one day. Her weeping was more like a wild howling. It seemed to Meryon that there was nothing feminine about it. But, however painful, it did her good, and she was able then to pick up the "conversation" where she had left it, and tell the ever-patient, ever-listening Meryon more tales of the glorious days when she was with her brilliant uncle, William Pitt.

The attacks of coughing came more frequently. She would be seized with a sudden spasm in the throat and chest. "Some water, some water", she would beg, gasping for breath. "Don't leave me, doctor", she would shout, "I can't bear to be left alone a moment." The doctor believed she had consumption, as there had been much of it on the Stanhope side of the family; but today doctors faced with her symptoms, her thinness and the fact that she smoked continuously, might have come up with another answer — cancer of the lungs.

The new year came, and still there was no news of that Irish inheritance. Everything depended on it. She had managed to keep some of her creditors at bay by the promise that they would be paid as soon as the money had arrived. Then one day Abella, a Maltese who acted as English Consul at Sidon, came up to Dar

Djoun with a letter. As Hester was not on speaking terms with any consuls, except Guy, the French Consul, she refused to receive him, and told Meryon to collect whatever the man had brought. But Abella was adamant. His instructions had been to hand Hester the letter himself. However, Meryon managed eventually to persuade him to hand over the letter. He took it to Hester, who was convinced that this was from Burdett, telling her that all her financial troubles would now be over. It was, however, from Colonel Campbell, the Consul-General for Egypt and Syria, informing her that, in order to repay some of her debts the British Government had decided to suspend payment of her yearly £1,200 pension.

Behind this apparently brutal, though gently conveyed, message from Campbell, were three years of intensely embarrassing negotiations on the part of the Consul-General. Without her realizing it, Hester and her debts had become a factor in the complicated diplomatic relationships between Great Britain, the Sultan and Mehemet Ali.

The trouble went back to 1832 when Mehemet Ali and his victorious Egyptian troops had pushed on, after taking Syria, to Turkey, and threatened Constantinople. The Sultan had appealed to Russia, and Constantinople had been saved. But by the Treaty of Unkiar Skelessi, in 1833, the Sultan agreed that in the event of war the Dardanelles would be closed to all warships except those of Russia. This meant that the Russian Fleet could emerge from the Black Sea, do whatever it liked in the Mediterranean, and then, if necessary, retreat in the Black Sea without fear of pursuit. As a result the European powers felt a growing antipathy towards Russia.

By 1838 the young Queen Victoria was on the throne of Britain, and Palmerston was her Foreign Secretary. Once again it seemed that Mehemet Ali was about to attack the Sultan, and this time he would be supported by France. Palmerston wanted to prevent a war; for if Mehemet Ali were successful, then French influence, broken since Napoleon's day, would be re-established in the area. If the Sultan won, then Russian influence would be further extended. Palmerston wanted to woo the Sultan from the Russians and establish an independent Egypt, under Mehemet Ali, in exchange for a promise from the latter that he would no longer threaten the Sultan.

In these delicate negotiations it was important for Palmerston to remain on the best of terms both with the Sultan and Mehemet Ali. Even such a minor matter as Hester's debts had its significance. As Mehemet Ali, whose friendship for Hester was no longer as warm as before, pointed out to Colonel Campbell — whenever British merchants brought claims for payment against his subjects, the Government immediately brought pressure to bear on the debtor concerned, and the debt was quickly repaid. Surely it was little enough to ask that the reverse should also be true?

Hester could not, however, be expected to understand this. To her, this was the final treason of those terrible statesmen who had followed the great William Pitt. She did not fly, as usual, into a temper, but her anger, cold and controlled, was even worse to witness. No one was spared, not even the young Queen Victoria herself.

"My grandfather and Mr. Pitt", she said, scathingly, "did something, I think, to keep the Brunswick family on the throne, and yet the grand-daughter of the old king [George III] without hearing the circumstances of my getting into debt, or whether the story is true (for it might be false), sends to deprive me of my pension in a foreign land, where I may remain and starve. If it had not been for my brother Charles, and General Bernard, the only two who knew what they were about, when the mutiny took place against the Duke of Kent at Gibraltar, she would not be where she is now; for her father would have been killed to a certainty."

After a while, she returned again the the theme of the "Old King" who had written down on paper: "Let her have the greatest pension that can be granted to a woman." Now his ungrateful grand-daughter and her cruel Foreign Secretary had deprived her of her legitimate pension. "I think", said Hester, "I shall take the bull by the horns, and send a letter to the Queen."

Next day, 30th January 1838, she suffered a return of the convulsive attacks of coughing that seemed almost to pull her apart. At the same time she learnt, through her eavesdropping system, that her secretary was trying to find out whether she was consumptive, and how much longer she would live. In order to show that there was nothing the matter with her, she managed, by a tremendous effort of will, to get up and stagger into the garden, where she sat in the pale January sunshine for a while.

This gave Meryon the chance to supervise the cleaning of her room. It was very much in need of it. Everything was covered with dust and cobwebs. There were bundles of linen, calico and silk scattered over the floor. Clothes and papers lay in corners and under the few bits of furniture. Hester had refused to let the servants clean her room, for fear they would steal the last few of her personal possessions. As it was, she shouted to Meryon, from the garden, to watch the cleaners and see that they stole nothing.

The outing, however, made her worse. When she got back to her room, she began striding up and down, shouting, "You had better leave me to die". She wanted to go back to her own country, by which she meant Arabia, and there, she said, "with not a rag on me, I may be fed by some good-natured soul, and not such cannibals, as these servants!" She ranted against Meryon: "You are not a man, to see me treated in this manner." But when Meryon, unable to withstand the abuse any longer, left her to Fatoom, her

Meryon, Hester's doctor for many years. He gave her great service and devotion, putting her far above his own comforts. When, after she died, he published his memoirs on her, he was bitterly attacked, especially by the Stanhope family.

native servant, she rang for him to come back. Her mood had changed now to one of fear and sorrow. "Don't leave me", she begged.

The following day she returned to the question of writing to the Queen. For a while she considered the possibility of writing to the newspapers and asking for a public enquiry. She felt sure that if the British people knew the situation they would soon force the Government to restore her pension. She only had £20 in the house, and she had already given thirty shillings to a begging leper, and another thirty shillings to an impoverished shopkeeper. Even in her present dreadful financial state her generosity to those who were worse off did not slacken.

Finally, on 12th February 1838, while smoking her usual pipe, she dictated the following letter to Queen Victoria;

Jôon, February 12, 1838

Your Majesty will allow me to say that few things are more disgraceful and inimical to royalty than giving commands without examining all their different bearings, and casting, without reason, an aspersion upon the integrity of any branch of a family who had faithfully served their country and the house of Hanover.

As no inquiries have been made of me what circumstances induced me to incure the debts alluded to, I deem it unnecessary to enter into any details upon the subject. I shall not allow the pension given by your royal grandfather to be stopped by force; but I shall resign it for the payment of my debts, and with it the name of English subject, and the slavery that is at present annexed to it: and, as your Majesty has given publicity to the business by your orders to consular agents, I surely cannot be blamed in following your royal example.

Hester Lucy Stanhope.

It was the letter of one Queen to another, of a senior queen to a junior one, in need of being taught a lesson: it was also a challenge. In a further letter to Abercrombie, the Speaker of the House of Commons, she elaborated on this theme: "Your magnificent Queen has made me appear like a bankrupt in the world, and partly like a swindler; having given strict orders that one usurer's account must be paid, or my pension stopped, without taking into consideration others who have equal claim upon me. Her Majesty has not thrown the gauntlet before a driveller or a coward. . . ."

She wrote to the Duke of Wellington, and to others. When all the letters were duly copied out by the patient, but now almost exhausted Meryon, she began sealing up the letters. This was, she explained to Meryon, a matter of great importance. The sheet of paper should be folded over exactly in the middle (it was before the days of envelopes) and the sealing-wax and seal correctly applied.

Even at this moment she could not resist a side attack on Meryon's character and ability: "Doctor", she said as she held the wax to the candle, "you never now can seal a letter decently: you once used to do it tolerably well, but now you have lost your memory and all your facilities, from talking nothing but rubbish and empty nonsense to those nasty women; and that's the reason why you never listen to anything one says, and answer 'yes' and 'no' without knowing to what."

She was meticulous about the way letters were to be addressed: "Where's the one to the Queen? Write Victoria Regina — nothing else — in the middle." For the Speaker's letter she instructed Meryon to write: "To the Right Hon. James Abercrombie, with three et ceteras, Carlton Gardens." Seated on a rush-bottom chair in front of a rickety card table, Meryon, a pair of glasses on his nose, wrote out the famous names by candle light. They came to the Duke of Wellington's letter: "You must begin — To His Grace the Duke of Wellington, K.G.", said Hester. Meryon wrote out the name, while Hester watched him continuously.

"What's that?", she asked suddenly, "show it me." She picked up the letter, put on her glasses, and exclaimed: "Good God, doctor, are you mad? — what can you mean? — what is this vulgar ignorance, not to know that 'His Grace' should be in one line, and 'The Duke of Wellington, K.G.' in the other: what people will fancy I am got among? Why the lowest clerk in the Foreign Office would not have made such a blunder. This is your fine Oxford education!" Even when the letter was finished, she was not contented. "How many et ceteras have you put?" asked Hester. "What! Only two? I suppose you think he's a nobody!"

The niece of the great William Pitt, accustomed to sending out from Downing Street beautifully addressed and sealed envelopes, wanted to show that even in the "reduced circumstances" in which she was now forced to live she still knew the intricate delicacies of etiquette.

Finally the last of the letters were addressed. Hester consulted the oracles and the stars to find out which day and hour would be most auspicious for their dispatch, and gave Meryon his instructions. He, in turn, roused Ali Hayshem, Hester's confidential messenger, out of his bed and handing the packet of letters to him repeated Hester's instructions: "You are to take this packet, and start at sunrise precisely — not before and not after — and to take care you deliver the letters into Mr Guy [the French Consul at Sidon]'s hands before sunset: for it is Friday, and Friday is an auspicious day."

It was three o'clock in the morning. The letter-writing session was over. It was now a question of waiting for the replies. The doctor could at last get some sleep.

CHAPTER NINETEEN

THE FINAL ESCAPE

Spring came and Hester's health improved. She was able to get up and go into her beloved garden. Though she was physically stronger her temper remained as short as ever. When Meryon remonstrated at her violent language to him, she retorted, "If you were a duke, I would use exactly the same language", and, without apparently noting the incongruity, held a long diatribe on the sweetness of her nature. Meryon put up with it all as well as he could, glad that the terrible winter illness, whatever it really had been, had left her.

But sometimes the attacks of coughing and the paroxysms returned. After one of these, on 8th March 1838, she said to Meryon, after complaining as usual about the behaviour of the servants:

> "I had a very bad night, and whether I shall live or die, I don't know: but this I tell you beforehand, that if I do die, I wish to be buried like a dog, in a bit of earth just big enough to hold this miserable skin, or else to be burnt, or thrown into the sea. And, as I am no longer an English subject, no consuls, nor any English of any sort, shall approach me in my last moments; for, if they do, I will have them shot. Therefore, the day before I die, if I know it, I shall order you away, and not only you, but everything English; and if you don't go, I warn you beforehand, you must take the consequences. Let me be scorched by the burning sun —

frozen by the cold blast — let my ashes fly in the air — let the
wolves and jackals devour my carcase; — but . . . ."

She had now grown so excited that another attack of coughing
seized her. It was a quarter of an hour before she was calm enough
to speak again. But in the evening when Meryon came to see her
again, she was unusually gentle: "Take your chair", she said, "here
by the bed — turn your back to the window to save your poor
eyes from the light — never mind me: there — I'm afraid I have
overworked them by so much writing." "However", she added in
her usual practical way, "but I know, if you did not write for me,
you would be writing or reading for yourself." Even in this gentler
mood she could not resist a mild dig at the doctor: "You are just
like my sister Griselda."

Queen Victoria's high-handed attitude, as Hester conceived it,
still rankled. "Although the Queen may think herself justified in
taking away my pension", she declared, "I would not, even if I
were a beggar, change places with her."

And still Hester waited anxiously for a reply to her various
letters.

Although, thanks to Lamartine and others, she was now a
famous institution, she had not allowed visitors to call on her
because of the depressed state of her financial affairs. They were
turned away, much to their annoyance, after they had made the
hard journey to Djoun.

But on 20th March 1838, while she was resting on a sofa in a
small white alcove in the garden, she received a letter from a
German prince named Prince Pückler Muskau. It was written in
such a flattering and respectful style that she decided that she
would ask him to visit her as soon as she was better. She also
received a letter from an old friend of hers, Lord Ebrington, telling
her that he was on a committee investigating pensions, and that he
would like to help her regain hers. Her reply, dictated by pride,
was sharp and rude: "You tell me that you are on the committee,
and that, whatever I have to say respecting my pension, I had
better write it to you: I have nothing to say. You can hardly
suppose that I would owe a pension to the commiseration of a
pettifogging committee, when I refused Mr. Fox's liberal pro-
position of securing me a handsome income by a grant of
Parliament . . ."

Hester entertaining a visitor, probably Dr. Meryon, at Djoun. She is smoking a pipe. Her black slave is bringing coffee. She could and often did sit up all night talking (*Frank Hemel*)

She ended this letter, which was, in fact, an attempt on the part of an old friend to rescue her from official censure and her own stubbornness, with her usual attack on Queen Victoria: "New-coined Royalties I do not understand, nor do I wish to understand them nor any of their proceedings."

There was trouble once again in the neighbourhood. The Druses, who through treachery had earlier been overrun by Turkish troops, now rebelled. The mountains were once again full of fighting, and the refugees once more found shelter and safety in and around Djoun.

But this did not prevent Prince Pückler Muskau from arriving at Dar Djoun at about five o'clock in the afternoon of Easter Sunday, 15th April 1838, accompanied by two European servants. He was a handsome man of fifty, whose object in visiting Djoun was to pay homage to the "Queen of Palmyra", and to write an account of his visit in a book he was planning, on the lines of Lamartine's "Voyage en Orient".

Prince Pückler Muskau brought a much needed touch of glamour to the decaying and decrepit stronghold at Dar Djoun. Something almost of the atmosphere of the old days returned to the sombre, sprawling rooms, the ferrety corridors and the claustrophobic enclosures.

He was a swashbuckling sort of man who wore a huge Leghorn hat, lined with green taffetas, that set off very well his fair skin. Blue trousers, a carelessly-draped shawl and a pair of thin Parisian boots completed the outfit. The boots were chosen with particular care. Ever since Lamartine's book had stated that Hester judged a man's breeding by the arch of his feet, every visitor tried to give the impression of having well-shaped feet.

He brought with him a considerable cortège, among which were two Abyssinian slave girls; one, aged seventeen, named Mahbooby (Aimée) was his concubine, the other, aged twelve, fetched and carried for him. The buying and selling of slaves was quite normal throughout the Turkish Empire, and Hester had long accepted the custom. There was, anyhow, little difference between a slave and a servant in that part of the world.

Pückler Muskau also brought with him an elegant young man, Count Tattenbach, whose exact function in the Prince's household was somewhat ill-defined. A chameleon completed the picaresque appearance of the group. Unlike Lamartine's dog, however, it managed to remain invisible.

Hester was really quite excited at the sight of such a handsome man. Her old preference for good-looking men returned, and in a moment of endearing vanity she said to Meryon: "You know he will be writing about me; and, although I do not care what he says of my temper, understanding, doings, and all that, I shouldn't like him to say anything about my person, either as to my looks, figure face or appearance."

The Prince, although he had some difficulty in making out sometimes what she was saying, was delighted to be there. He was supposed to be going on to the Emir Beshir, Hester's old enemy—friend, but first feigned illness, which meant that he had, much to his annoyance, to swallow some of Hester's black dose of salts which she had administered to anyone with any illness at all.

(left) Prince Pückler visited Djoun in 1838, the year before Hester's death. With his swashbuckling air he brought a touch of glamour and excitement to the huge rambling domain. (*Frank Hemel*)

Then he put off his visit to Beshir again. Hester took great pleasure in sending messages to the Emir, for in the eyes of the Druses it showed that the Prince placed Hester above the Emir. When the Prince finally did leave he handed Hester £25 to be divided among the servants.

During all this time Mrs. Meryon, her daughter and companion were not invited up to Dar Djoun to meet the Prince. Hester had remained true to her original declaration. As far as she was concerned the doctor had come there alone. Whether his family were at Mar Elias, Nice or England was no concern of hers.

Mrs. Meryon had accepted the situation more philosophically than during the first visit. There were a number of reasons for this. She had a companion with her, she was not harassed by Hester's servants as she had been at Djoun. Then Charles had told her that he was collecting material for a book about Lady Stanhope. Since everybody wrote about her, even after a few days' visit, why shouldn't he, who had known her, on and off, for twenty-eight years? Finally, although he was a famous doctor around Mount Lebanon, he had trouble finding work nearer home. Even though they were not paid much, they at least lived free.

Now it was Meryon who was keenest to leave. The long impossible hours, the strain of living a "double" life, and the fact that he was now over fifty-five, all urged him to leave. He spoke to Pückler Muskau of his longing to return to a quieter form of life. The Prince was frankly horrified: "But you will not leave my lady whilst she is so ill?", he asked. That, of course, was the trouble. The question tormented Meryon day and night, but he could find no answer to it.

Though Hester was prepared, in fact happy, to receive a German Prince, she refused to allow any Englishmen who had any connection with the hated Government in England to visit Dar Djoun. A certain Member of Parliament, called Dr. Bowring, arrived by steamer to Sidon (the 3rd Earl's much ridiculed prophecy that the ships would one day be propelled by steam had now come true), and asked to visit Dar Djoun. Hester sent Meryon down to tell him that she would not see him. Bowring was furious. He felt that as a Member of Parliament he had a right to meet a Government pensioner like Hester. He appeared to be unaware of Palmerston's instructions and Hester's reaction. Meryon prudently decided not to mention Bowring's objections to Hester. He did not want to write more long letters about Hester's dispute with yet another politician.

Pückler Muskau had promised to write often to her, and to do his best to give her letter to the Queen the greatest possible publicity. From Damascus, on 9th May 1838, he wrote as follows:

> Dearest Lady Stanhope
> Avant tout comment va votre santé? J'esp ere que mon bavardage et mes importunités de vous faire dicter de jolis histoires n'ont pas au moins empiré votre maladie. Si cela etait j'en serai desolé, car tout le plaisir aurait été pour moi, et toute la peine pour vous.
> J'ai passé depuis 6 jours au camp d'Ibrahim Pascha ou j'ai été reçu avec un peu de méfiance, et où Messieurs les Druses nous ont fait quelques petites visites. Mais ils sont aux abois. On leur a coupé l'eau et detruit toutes leurs citernes, de manière que je crois toute l'affaire sera finie en quelques jours, tout au plus en quelques semaines.

This was followed by another, undated, but probably of the same period:

> Milady,
> Vous êtes bonne, charmante, naturalle, sans affectation comme sans prétentions, telle enfin que je savais que vous deviez être malgré toutes les disparatés que les voyageurs, et surtout l'abominable race des voyageurs auteurs, ont debité sur votre compte. Voilá le coté noir de la celebrité!

Finally, from Aleppo, on the 25th July 1838:

> "Dearest Lady Stanhope,
> I am sorry to inform you, that the insertion of your letter to the Queen in the Allgemeine Zeitung met with some unexpected difficulties, and I shall now make an attempt to have it appear in some French paper."

Meryon, once again, began thinking of leaving. He was torn between Pückler Muskau's outcry and Hester's derisive shout of, "You are of no use to me: what good do you do me? I was just as well without you". Although Meryon did not really believe this, he knew that when he was away she turned for help to a local man called Lunardi. Lunardi was not a qualified doctor, but years earlier had been so impressed by Meryon's skill that he had become a willing pupil. When Meryon left Lunardi had set himself up as a local doctor, and, unqualified though he was, practised with considerable success. More important still, Hester trusted him. But, of course, he could not perform those many other tasks, scribe, confidant, book-keeper and general messenger, that Meryon did. Meryon was being driven to the edge of a nervous breakdown.

The lack of news from England made Hester uneasy and irritable. It was some months now since she had written to Palmerston and the Queen. No reply had yet arrived, and there was still nothing from Sir Francis Burdett concerning her Irish inheritance. Even Pückler Muskau, who had promised to look into her private affairs and report back to her, had failed to write. To add to her financial worries there were reports of fresh outbreaks of plague here and there. Though Hester declared that she was not afraid of it, Meryon frankly admitted that he was.

Into this confused situation strode the figure of Maximilian, Duke of Bavaria, who was travelling about the Holy Land. He had not had much luck. He had arrived in Jerusalem at the same time as the plague, and his personal doctor, a twenty-six year old German, had died of it in three days. Maximilian and his party hurried to Sidon, where they were immediately put into quarantine as suspect plague carriers because of the illness of their New York-born negro servant, Wellington. However, it turned out to be typhus, and they were released from quarantine.

Hester invited Maximilian up to Djoun, and he gratefully accepted for Saturday 9th June 1838. The whole house was in an uproar, preparing for his visit. Hester had even sent a servant up to Dayr el Kamar, the Druse capital, to buy some beef, for this was the only place beef could be bought. Logmagi, her faithful attendant, sent fish, fruit and vegetables he had bought at Sidon. The last of the silver forks and spoons were brought out of their hiding place. The servants were dressed in their best clothes, and, for once, were not rebellious. Maximilian had a reputation for generosity, and they hoped to get a good tip.

But Hester had had a very bad night, and in the morning was running a high temperature. It was quite obvious that she could

Sidon. Maximilian, Duke of Bavaria, stayed here when he intended to visit Hester at Djoun. But her ill-health and his fear of the plague prevented the visit. Instead, he boarded an English ship, leaving his American Negro servant, Wellington, behind.

not entertain her guests. Meryon was sent off to tell the Duke that the outing was cancelled. He was very upset, but said that he would send Hester his portrait when he returned to Europe. When the doctor told her this, Hester said, "No; I must write to him and prevent his sending it".

Next day Meryon went down to Sidon, and was astonished to discover that Maximilian and his entourage had gone. An English steamer had providentially come into the harbour the evening before. The Duke had gratefully boarded it and set off as fast as he could — leaving poor Wellington behind. Meryon arranged for a dressing-gown, some warm socks and a pot of tea to be sent to him.

The heat was now torrid — books left on tables curled up, furniture split, May-bugs blundered clumsily about, and in the evening mosquitoes appeared in their hundreds. Another steamer came in, but there were no letters for Hester.

"Doctor, the die is cast", said Hester, "the sooner you take yourself off, the better. I have no money — you can be of no use to me — I shall write no more letters, shall break up my establishment, wall up the gate, and, with a girl and a boy to wait on me, resign myself to my fate — Let me have none of your foolish reasoning on the subject. Tell your family they must make their preparations, and in a fortnight's time you must be gone."

But Meryon still hesitated. He was not so concerned now with the state of her health as with the state of her finances. She was still borrowing from the generous French Consul, but that could not go on for ever. Unless the British Government relented, or Burdett was successful, he could not see how she could go on.

He was worried, too, about the Druse civil war. There were more and more troops of every kind in the countryside. At times the violent fighting came close to Djoun. There were reports of massacres and atrocities from nearby villages, and it was said that the Egyptians were advancing again. This was no place for a penniless, if autocratic, despot like Hester.

But she was utterly unmoved by the surrounding chaos. She was a queen destined for great events. She would triumph over illness, Palmerston's treachery, Victoria's youthful indifference, every-one, just as she had always done. She compared herself with the man in the Eastern story who had been flung into prison and condemned to death; but at the last moment the Sublime Porte at Constantinople had sent orders that the Pasha who had imprisoned him should have his head cut off, and the poor man was saved.

"So it is with me", she said; "I cannot be worse off than I am; I shall, therefore, when the next steamboat comes, see what it brings; and, if I hear no news about the property that was left me, I shall get rid of you and everybody, and of all the women; and, with one black slave and Logmagi, I shall order the gateway to be walled up, leaving only room enough for my cows to go in and out to pasture, and I shall have no communication with any human being."

Her reason for doing this, she declared, was to force Palmerston to apologize publicly for the harm he had done her. She would neither answer nor write any more letters. She would be a complete hermit. "This sort of life perhaps will suit me best, after all." She continued, "I have often wished that I could have a room in my garden, and, lying there with only some necessary covering, slip from my bed as I was into my garden, and after a turn or two slip back again: I do assure you I should neither be low-spirited nor dull."

It was not until nearly the end of June 1838, that the long awaited reply arrived from Palmerston. It had been written two months earlier. It was curt and cold:

Foreign Office, April 25, 1838.

Madam,

I am commanded by the Queen to acquaint you that I have laid before her Majesty your letter of the 12th of February, of this year.

It has been my duty to explain to her Majesty the circumstances which may be supposed to have led to your writing that letter; and I have now to state to your ladyship that any communications which have been made to you on the matter to which your letter refers either through the friends of your family, or through her Majesty's agent and Consul-General at Alexandria, have been suggested by nothing but a desire to save your ladyship from the embarrassments which might arise, if the parties who have claims upon you were to call upon the Consul-General to act according to the strict line of his duty, under the capitulations between Great Britain and the Porte.

I have the honour to be, Madam, your ladyship's most obedient humble servant,

Palmerston

In other words, Victoria, young as she was, was not amused at the condescending tone of Hester's letter, and Palmerston had no intention of doing anything to upset the Sultan.

A week later a letter at last arrived from Sir Francis Burdett. Though full of solicitude and affection, it showed only too clearly that Hester's claim on the Irish property would not hold up in law. Though Colonel Needham, who owned the original property, had left it to Pitt (the starting point of Hester's claim), Pitt died three days before Needham. Legally, therefore, the will was invalid.

There was now nothing to stop her immuring herself as she said she would. She sent Meryon down to Beyrouth on business, and while he was away got Logmagi to book a passage for him and his family for Cyprus, for she knew that he was putting off the decision to do so from day to day.

She sent for a mason to come up from Sidon to arrange for the blocking up of the gateway on Monday, 30th July 1838. Stones and materials had already been collected, and Hester had drawn up the plans herself. A wall was to be built completely hiding the gateway. There was to be a side opening just wide enough to allow a cow and a water-carrying ass to enter. Meryon, as a final macabre assignment, was put in charge of the work. The mason took two days to complete the job. A week later, on Monday 6th August 1838, Meryon took his farewell of her, for he and his family were leaving the next day.

"It is better that I should not see you tomorrow", he said, "even though I should not set off early."

"You do right", she replied, "let this be our parting."

"But you have no money", said Meryon, knowing that the obliging French Consul at Beyrouth had been dismissed by the French Government, "how will you do for your current expenses?"

For once, Hester allowed commonsense to rule her pride. "It's true", she replied, "I must thank you to lend me 2,000 piastres [£100] before you go, and I'll repay you as soon as I can."

She gave instuctions how the gold was to be put into a basket, under a cup and saucer and other items of no interest, and sent up to her via her personal messenger, Ibrahim. Meryon tried to get her to take more, but she replied: "Two thousand will do, and, if I want more, Logmagi, I am sure, will raise me as much."

Meryon and his family left at eleven o'clock next day. Both Mrs. Meryon and her daughter cried now that the day of departure had arrived. Zezeföon, one of Hester's personal black slaves watched, with a number of other servants, from the garden wall. There was no sign of Hester. The new wall blocked the entrance gate like a tombstone. The fortress-house, on its hill, grew smaller as they descended the slope.

They had covered about two miles when one of Hester's servants was seen running after them. The party halted, Meryon not knowing what to expect. Had some new drama occurred up at that strange place? Were they to return? But the man merely unloaded a bundle he carried on his shoulders. In it was a small Turkish carpet. It was, he explained, a present from her ladyship. She thought it might come in useful to cover the floor of the cabin on their ship.

Her letters to Queen Victoria, Palmerston and others appeared at last. They were published in "The Times" in the autumn of 1838 and public reaction was not favourable. She had lived away from the country too long. The Napoleonic Wars were something of the past, and a new era was beginning under the guidance of the young Victoria. Hester's high tone annoyed many, amused others. So much so, in fact, that Colonel Napier, who had once served with Charles Stanhope at Corunna, wrote on 7th December 1838:

Sir,

The correspondence of Lady Hester Stanhope recently published in the Times has given occasion for mirth with some unthinking people. It may in the end be found a serious matter.

This "crock-brained lady" as some of your contemporaries — falling with the true instinct of baseness, upon what appeared to them a helpless and afflicted woman — have called her, may appear, judged by English customs, somewhat wild in her views and expressions; but, in the East she is, as she well deserves to be, for her nobleness and virtue revered.

The letter concludes:

It may be asked, what have I to do with the matter? In early life I was an inmate of Mr. Pitt's house, when Lady Hester Stanhope was the mistress of it, and when those who now insult her would have been too happy to be allowed to lick the dust from her shoes. The hospitality, the kindness, the friendship I then experienced from Lady Hester, did not cease with Mr. Pitt's death, nor by me are they forgotten; nor is the friendship which subsisted between my family and her gallant brothers, Charles and James Stanhope, while they lived. I remain, Sir, your obedient servant,

W. F. P. Napier, Colonel
Freshfield,
Near Bath, Dec. 4

Hester retired behind the walls of Dar Djoun, declaring that she would never leave the place and that only the two black girls, Fatoom and Zezeföon, were to come near her. As outlined to Meryon, she now became a complete hermit. It was useless for travellers even to write to her for she would not answer their requests. Food and necessary supplies were pushed through the side opening of the wall and left there to be collected. Only Logmagi and Lunardi, her "doctor", were allowed near her to receive instructions and conduct consultations. For most of the rest of the time, she sat, as she had said she would, in her garden, looking at the mountains and staring down to the distant sea.

Now that she had lost all and been abandoned, as she imagined, by everyone, a strange kind of peacefulness took possession, for the first time in her life, of her restless spirit. It was as if, by deliberately cutting herself off from the outer world, she had also flung away its cares and worries. The wall she had built before the doorway of Dar Djoun was a symbol of this rejection of life, and the guarantor of the inner spiritual peace she had somehow achieved.

Only in one matter did she not carry out her own instructions. Despite her announcement to Meryon that she would not write any more letters — who was there, once he had gone, to dictate to? — she did, in fact, write to him about once a month. On 22nd October 1838, she wrote:

Dear Doctor,
I hope soon to hear of your safe arrival at Marseilles, and take the first opportunity of repaying you the 2,000 piastres, for the loan of which I am very much obliged to you. I enclose a bill on Coutts for £50 — twenty for you and thirty for commissions."

The letter then went on to list a number of objects she wanted Meryon to send out to her. They included dried cherries and Burgundy apricots, three wire-blinds to keep the flies out of the milk-room, and a supply of yellow and red earthenware. She asked for some French books to be sent out, as she had "found out a person who can occasionally read French to me".

On 9th February 1839 she wrote again but the news was practical. She had no one to write the words down for her, so she had to write her letters herself. Her glasses, she declared, hurt her. Her talk was of the wet weather, and of a hyaena that got into the garden. Though she had sworn she would not give Meryon any more advice, she did advise him not to return to England, but that, if he did leave Nice, to go to Switzerland.

On 11th March she wrote to him again, this time calm and philosophical: "I am content with the violence of my own character". She declared, "it draws a line for me between friends and enemies." She asked for a dozen new pairs of glasses to be sent out. She said that the Prophet, as she called General Loustaunau, was comfortable in his new quarters. She had had shrubs planted round the windows, and had even provided him with an excellent sofa.

On 6th May 1839, she wrote to Meryon:

> "The vapour is expected in a few days. I am much better, but not yet well enough to make a little drawing necessary to explain what I want to be made . . . Do not keep reproaching yourself about leaving me it did *not depend upon you*, had the business which you came for been happily persued I'd not have allowed you to remain near me a day longer."

It was the last letter she was to write to him.

On 6th June 1839, in answer to Lord Hardwicke, who had told her that if she returned to England, it might be possible to sell her property and pension (if she could get it back) for £20,000 and thus pay off her debts of £8,000 − £10,000, she wrote: "What you say about my coming to England I understand, and appears very reasonable, but I cannot, will never, go there but *in chains*, therefore that subject must never more be mentioned". Later, in the same letter, she added:

> "Do not be unhappy about my future fate. I have done what I believe my duty, the duty of everyone of *every religion*; I have no reproaches to make myself, but that I went rather too far; but such is my nature, and a happy nature too, who can make up its mind to everything but *insult*. I have been treated like a vile criminal, but God is great!!! When I have quite made up my mind about what I shall do, I shall let you know, but avoid bothering you and

boring you. My annuity will not do without the pension, and perhaps the two even not enough; but that is no one's business but mine."

A fortnight later she felt suddenly worse and sent for Lunardi, but he was away at sea and did not reach Beyrouth in time. News came down from the crumbling house the following day, 23rd June 1839, that she had died.

Immediately Moore, the Consul at Beyrouth, whom she included amongst her list of special hatreds, came riding out to Djoun, with a visiting American, the Reverend W. M. Thomson. In a letter to the 4th Earl, Moore wrote:

"The day before her decease she foresaw the approach of death, and said she should not outlive the next day. The impression was too well founded, as, about four o'clock of the day predicted, she breathed her last, preserving, till within a few minutes of her decease, all her faculties."

The American missionary also wrote an account of that visit. He subsequently published it in a book entitled "The Land and the Book". The relevant passages read:

"The English Consul at Beyrouth requested me to perform the religious services at the funeral of Lady Hester. It was an intensely hot Sabbath, in June, 1839. We started on our melancholy errand at one o'clock, and reached this place about midnight. After a brief examination, the Consul decided that the funeral must take place immediately. The vault in the garden was hastily opened, and the bones of General Loustaneau or his son, I forget which — a Frenchman who died here, and was buried in this vault by her Ladyship, were taken out, and placed at the head.

"The body, in a plain deal box, was carried by her servants to the grave, followed by a mixed company, with torches and lanterns, to enable them to thread their way through the winding alleys of the garden. I took a wrong path, and wandered for some time in the mazes of these labyrinths. When, at length, I entered the arbour, the first thing I saw were the bones of the General, in a ghastly heap, with the head on top having a lighted taper stuck in either eye-socket — a hideous, grinning spectacle. It was difficult to proceed with the service, under circumstances so novel and bewildering. The Consul subsequently remarked that there were some curious coincidences between this and the burial of Sir John Moore, her Ladyship's early love. In silence, on the lone mountain, at midnight, 'our lanterns dimly burning', with the flag of her country over her, she 'lay like a warrior taking his rest', and we 'left her alone in her glory'. There was but one of her own nation present, and his name was Moore.

"The people of Djoun, that village across the wady, made large profits from the liberality and extravagances of Lady Hester, and they are full of wonderful stories about her. Several of our friends at Sidon were in her service for years, and from them, and from others still more closely connected, I have had abundant opportunity to learn the character of this strange being. On most subjects she was not merely sane, but sensible, well-informed, and extremely shrewd. She possessed extraordinary powers of conversation, and was perfectly fascinating to all with whom she chose to make herself agreeable. She was, however, whimsical, imperious, tyrannical, and, at times, revengeful to high degree. Bold as a lion, she wore the dress of an Emir, weapons, pipe and all; nor did she fail to rule her Albanian guards and her servants with absolute authority. She kept spies in the principal cities, and at the residences of Pashas and Emirs, and knew everything that was going on in the country. Her garden, of several acres, was walled round like a fort, and crowning the top of this conical hill, with deep wadys on all sides, the appearance from a distance was quite imposing. But the site was badly chosen. The hill has no relative elevation above others; the prospect is not inviting, the water is distant, far below, and had to be carried up on mules. She, however, had the English taste for beautiful grounds, and spared neither time, labour, nor expense to convert this barren hill into a wilderness of shady avenues, and a paradise of sweet flowers, and she succeeded. I have rarely seen a more beautiful place.

"The morning after the funeral, the Consul and I went round the premises, and examined thirty-five rooms, which had been sealed up by the Vice-Consul of Sidon, to prevent robbery. They were full of trash. One had forty or fifty oil jars of French manufacture — old, empty, and dusty. Another was crammed with Arab saddles, moth-eaten, tattered and torn. They had belonged to her mounted guard. Superannuated pipestems, without bowls, filled one room. Two more were devoted to medicines, and another to books and papers, mostly in boxes and ancient chests. Nothing of much value was found anywhere, and the seals were replaced, to await legal action. The crowd of servants and greedy retainers had appropriated to themselves her most valuable effects. One of the wealthy citizens of Sidon is said to have obtained his money in that way. She told Mrs. Thomson that once, when she was supposed to be dying of plague, she could hear her servants breaking open her chests, and ripping off the embossed covers of her cushions. 'Oh! didn't I vow', said she, 'that if I recovered, I would make a scattering of them!' and she performed her vow to the letter. But each succeeding set, like the flies in the fable of the fox, were as greedy as their predecessors; and, as she finally died of a lingering disease, they had time enough to work their will, and nothing valuable escaped their rapacity. What a death! Without a European attendant — without a friend, male or female — alone, on the top of this bleak mountain, her lamp of life grew dimmer and more dim, until it went quite out in hopeless, rayless night. Such was the end of the once gay and brilliant niece of Pitt, presiding in the saloons of the master spirit of Europe, and familiar with the intrigues of kings and cabinets. With Mr. Abbott and his lady, she would sit out the longest night, talking over those stirring times of the last century, and the beginning of the present, with exhaustless spirit and keen delight. But nothing could tempt her back to England. At length her income was greatly curtailed to pay her numerous debts. She was furious, but unsubdued. In her mountain nest, and all alone, she dragged out the remnant of her days in haughty pride and stubborn independence.

"She could be extremely sarcastic, and her satire was often terrible. Many of her letters, and the margin of books which I purchased at the auction, are 'illuminated' with her caustic criticisms. There was no end to her eccentricities. In some things she was a devout believer — an unbeliever in many. She read the stars, and dealt in nativities, and a sort of second sight, by which she pretended to foretell coming events. She practised alchemy, and, in pursuit of this vain science, was often closeted with strange companions. She had a mare, whose backbone sank suddenly down at the shoulders, and rose abruptly near the hips. This deformity her vivid imagination converted into a miraculous saddle, on which she was to ride into Jerusalem as queen, by the side of some sort of Messiah, who was to introduce a fancied milennium. Another mare had a part to play in this august pageant, and both were tended with extraordinary care. A lamp was kept burning in their very comfortable apartments, and they were served with sherbet, and other luxuries. Nothing about the premises so excited my compassion as these poor pampered brutes, upon which Lady Hester had lavished her choicest affections for the last fourteen years. They were soon after sold at auction, when hard work and low living quickly terminated their miserable existence. Lady Hester was a doctor, and most positive in her prescriptions to herself, her servants, her horses, and even to her chickens, and often did serious mischief to all her patients. She had many whimsical tests of character both for man and beast, and, of course, was often deceived by both, to her cost. But we must end these random sketches. To draw a full-length portrait is aside from our purpose and beyond our power. She was wholly and magnificently unique."

CHAPTER TWENTY

NOT EASILY TO SUBMIT TO FATE

The auction did not raise enough money to pay off much of the large debt Hester left, nor did the little remaining money she had in England. But eventually the family settled matters; and it seemed that although she had been a "character" in life, she would soon be forgotten after death. Only Griselda, who was to live until 1851, and Mahon, now the 4th Earl, who did not die until 1855, survived her. Mahon had not had any communication with Hester since 1816, and Griselda and Hester had never really been close. Apart from a few references in books, it seemed as if there was no one to keep alive their sister's memory — except Meryon.

In December of the year that Hester died the 4th Earl learnt that Meryon was planning to publish his memoirs. He immediately wrote to Meryon asking him to stop publication. He felt sure that Meryon would not wish to be "the instrument of wounding the feelings of Lady Hester's relations and friends by a disclosure of family anecdotes and domestic dissension which ought to remain unknown to the world".

Meryon replied that he was fifty-six, poor and had a family to support. He had spent many years in her service, and had always been under the impression, even though in 1829 Hester had asked him to burn her letters, that she intended to make up for the fact that while she employed him, she was never able to pay enough to make it possible for him to save a penny. He wrote to the 4th Earl:

"It was her legacy to me, for she had nothing else to leave me, and I confess I have indulged the hope that the profits will, in a pecuniary sense, in part realise her good intentions towards me."

He added:

"Having on one occasion said that, had she chosen to write her own life, she might have paid her debts by it, she laughing observed, that she could never have patience to write a book, nor even to dictate one, but could tell me a few stories now and then to help me to write one with."

Nevertheless, in order to please her family, he ordered the publication to be stopped. Then, in 1843, "Colburn's New Monthly Magazine" began publishing some of Hester's letters to General Oakes, dating mainly from 1811 to 1817. As a result, on 3rd March 1843, Meryon wrote to the 4th Earl saying that he "takes the liberty of mentioning that he has nothing whatever to do with it". He was trying then to obtain the post of Consul in Cyprus, and had asked the 4th Earl to help. He was not, however, successful in obtaining the post, and now that some of Hester's private correspondence had, in fact, appeared, he could not see why he should not publish his book.

It appeared in 1845, six years after Hester's death. It was in three volumes (1,150 pages) and was entitled "Memoirs of Lady Hester Stanhope, as related by Herself in Conversations with her Physician, comprising her Opinions and Anecdotes of some of the most remarkable Persons of her Time".

It was reviewed at great length in the September number of that year by the "Quarterly Review", which began:

"The publication of private correspondence and other matters of a private nature touching individuals deceased, has more than once drawn from us remarks which we deemed it the bounden duty of those who exercise the function of Literary Police to make. The evil then complained of is clearly on the increase . . . ."

The self-appointed "Literary Police" then went on:

"We are once more brought to dwell on this subject by the appearance of a new feature which it presents in the disclosure, for the first time, by a *medical gentleman*, of the matters communicated to him during his professional attendance – his attendance too upon *a lady* – a lady of high rank, and with many high qualities – but unhappy, solitary, ill at ease in body and in mind, an exile among the wilds of Lebanon – having no one near her to whom she could speak of bygone days and buried friends and foes – nobody but this Physician."

There followed over twenty pages devoted to a detailed description of the contents of the three volumes. Towards the conclusion the Literary Police could not refrain from introducing a then topical political note:

"Some money lender complained that she was in debt to him, whereupon Lord Palmerston thought proper to issue his orders to the Consuls in the Levant that they should refuse to sign any certificate of her being alive, which ceremony was necessary in order to give her the right to draw her quarterly pension! The consequence was that, on a mere statement of one party, she was deprived for the last two years of a pension as much her right as his lordship's rent, perhaps as well earned as his lordship's salary. We verily believe this instance of official oppression is without an example, and we are curious to hear by what law it was justified, and what use Lord Palmerston or his colleagues could by law make of the Parliamentary pension which they stopped."

The "Revue des Deux Mondes" also reviewed the book at some length. It took a cooler look at the work, and complained mainly of the complete lack of literary style and expertise of the author:

"Le médécin de lady Stanhope vient de soumettre au procédé usuel des biographs anglais la vie, les conversations, les actes de cette femme extraordinaire. L'ouvrage n'est pas celui d'un homme d'esprit ou même d'une intelligence bien ordonnée; de mille ou douze cents pages gonflées par les ruses de la librairie et les redits d'un ecrivain qui tire au volume, à peine pourrait-on extraire cinq cents pages vraiment utiles. Peu importe; on aime ces longeurs, on s'engage avec plaisir dans ce marécage de mauvais style et d'anecdotes entassées pêle-mêle, tant elles éclairent bien cet étrange figure de la nièce de Pitt, reine de Tadmor, sorcière, prophétesse, patriarche, chef arabe, morte en 1839 sous le toit delabré de son palais ruineux, à Djôhoun, dans le Liban."

The 4th Earl, having been unable to prevent publication, obtained a copy of the book, and made a number of comments in the verges, contradicting or disparaging much that was written. Thus, in the margin of page iii of the introduction, the ex-Incomparable Mahon wrote:

"No apology for betraying & publishing private conversations & circumstances relating to family affairs."

Against Hester's tale (page 9, Vol. II) of the stilts and how she managed to persuade the 3rd Earl to buy a coach for her step-mother, the 4th Earl wrote, "all false". Whether this was a comment on Meryon's faithfulness as a reporter or his dead sister's veracity is hard to say. In all events, since the 4th Earl was five years younger than his sister, it is difficult to see how he could have been in a better position to remember the past than she.

Again, on page 19, against Meryon's observation that there was a "sort of resemblance between her and Mr. Pitt", the 4th Earl wrote: "None". On page 22, Meryon reports that Hester said: "Pitt used to say Tom Paine was quite right"; the 4th Earl wrote, "he could not have said so". The comments refer to about fifty pages; but even so, the great bulk of the book did not draw any observations. Meryon, anyhow, had been extremely discreet and made no mention, for example, of the real relationship between Hester and Michael Bruce.

The following year he followed up the first work with an equally large three-volume sequel entitled "The Travels of Lady Hester Stanhope", thus providing posterity with such a detailed account, sometimes day by day, even hour by hour, of his subject, that even Pepys's diary is less informative on it.

In the meantime Djoun was left to grow wild. The Pasha of Sidon had forbidden anyone to go near the place by day, and the fear of spirits kept marauders away at night. Ten years after Hester's death Eliot Warburton visited the place and left this account of his visit:

"The sun was setting as we entered the enclosure, and we were soon scattered about the outer court, picketing our horses, rubbing down their foaming flanks, and washing out their wounds. The buildings that constituted the palace were of a very scattered and complicated description, covering a wide space, but only one story in height; courts and gardens, stables and sleeping rooms, halls of audience and ladies' bowers, were strangely intermingled. Heavy weeds were growing everywhere among the open portals, and we forced our way with difficulty through a tangle of roses and jasmine to the inner court. Here choice flowers once bloomed, and fountains played in marble basins, but now was presented a scene of the most melancholy desolation. As the watchfire blazed up, its gleam fell upon masses of honeysuckle and woodbine; on white, mouldering walls beneath, and dark, waving trees above, while the group of mountaineers who gathered round its light, with their long beards and vivid dresses, completed the strange picture.

"The clang of sword and spear resounded through the long galleries, horses neighed among bowers and boudoirs, strange figures hurried to and fro among the colonnades, shouting in Arabic, English, and Italian, the fire crackled, the startled bats flapped their heavy wings, and the growl of distant thunder filled up the pauses in the rough symphony.

"Our dinner was spread on the floor in Lady Hester's favourite apartment; her deathbed was our sideboard, her furniture our fuel, her name our conversation. Almost before the meal was ended, two of our party had dropped asleep over their trenchers from fatigue; the Druses had retired from the haunted precincts to their village; and W., L., and I went out into the garden, to smoke our pipes by Lady Hester's lonely tomb. About midnight we fell asleep upon the ground, wrapped in our capotes, and dreamed of ladies, and tombs, and prophets, till the neighing of our horses announced the dawn."

But soon the whole place was torn down; and when the Reverend W. M. Thomson, who had performed the burial service in such strange conditions, revisited Djoun in 1857, he found, as he recorded in his book "The Land and the Book", that:

"A melancholy change has indeed come over the scene since first I visited it. The garden, with its trellised arbours, and shaded alleys, and countless flowers, is utterly destroyed; and not one room of all her large establishment remains entire. This, on the South-west corner, was the apartment in which Lady Hester wore out the three last dreary months of life; and this, on the east of it, was the open room, where we found the body, wrapped in waxed cloths dipped in turpentine and spirits. The whole of these premises were alive with her servants, and others assembled on this mournful occasion. Now, not a dog, cat, or even lizard, appears to relieve the utter solitude. The tomb, also, is sadly changed. It was then embowered in dense shrubbery, and covered with an arbour of running roses, not a vestige of which now remains, and the stones of the vault itself are broken and displaced. There is no inscription — not a word in any language, and unless more carefully protected than hitherto, the last resting-place of her Ladyship will soon be entirely lost. The history of this place is peculiar. It belonged to a wealthy Christian of Damascus, who built the original house, to which Lady Hester added some twenty-five or thirty rooms. At his death, soon after hers, the property was left to an only son, who quickly spent it all by his extravagance. He then turned Moslem, and not long ago hung himself in a neighbouring house. His Moslem wife — a low, vulgar creature — fearing that the Christians would one day deprive her of the place, tore down the buildings, and sold the materials to the people of Djoun. Thus the destruction has been intentional, rapid, and complete."

It was not until forty-two years after Hester's death that any member of the family visited the place where she had lived and died. This was her great-nephew, Philip Stanhope, and his wife. They travelled there in 1881 and found her tomb in a very ruinous condition, still with no inscription. They thought of providing one, but finally decided against it, as they could think of no way of preserving it, and believed that Hester herself had asked that no permanent memorial should be set up.

Sixteen years later, in the winter of 1895, the Duchess of Cleveland, who had been born in 1819, the youngest of the 4th Earl's three children, visited Djoun. She was seventy-six, and Hester's niece, but she never saw her, for she was only nine when Hester left England. In 1897 she published the first family account of her aunt under the title, "The Life and Letters of Lady Hester Stanhope". All Hester's letters and papers had been assembled in the great library at Chevening, and they were presented in chronological order, one after the other with linking passages between.

Of her visit to Djoun two year earlier, she had this to say:

"Now, alas! garden and terraces alike have disappeared; the ground has been let to a farmer, ploughed up and planted with mulberries. Only some of the olives and orange trees that she planted are left, and the exact place of her burial cannot be determined, as nothing remains of the vault. Dr. Abela brought us an old man who had been in her service as a boy, and was fourteen at the time of her death, who pointed out where he thought her grave had been, and showed us the point on (what had been) the upper terrace, where she used to stand and watch through her field glasses the ships passing on the distant sea — ."

With the turn of the century her grip on the imagination of writers and travellers was strong as ever. Frank Hemel's very detailed life was published in 1913. The year before, in 1912, her grave was found and the family erected a monument, which was kept up until the 7th Earl, last of the Stanhopes, died in 1967. Since then Chevening and all its responsibilities has passed to the care of the Trustees of the Chevening Estate. Many of Hester Stanhope's papers are stored, with the rest of the Stanhope papers, in the Archives of the Kent County Council library at Maidstone. Some of them, particularly those in Arabic, have never been seen let alone read by the general public except for those included here. Today her tomb can be seen in the olive grove that was once her garden. In the village of Djoun the only restaurant has been called after her (although in Arabic her name has become Lady Hester Stanhob).

In 1951 Brigadier Bruce, a great-grandson of Michael Bruce, published many of the letters which had passed between Michael and Hester and Michael's father, Craufurd Bruce. He had found them in an old sack, and like the Duchess of Cleveland before him, had published them with linking passages. Thus a great deal of the minutiae of Hester's life are known, yet she was remained an enigma. A number of biographers, notably Frank Hemel and, in 1933, Joan Haslip, have put forward theories to explain why Hester exiled herself the way she did.

In 1866 James Williams, formerly Minister of the United States, sent to the 5th Earl of Stanhope a long memorandum on Hester which he intended to include in the autobiography of his life. In it he had this to say of Hester's reasons for living in the Lebanon:

> "The death of her uncle, though it made no change in her social position, shut her out for ever from the attainment of that pre-eminence, the first fruits of which she had only tasted, while she was the intermediary between the dispensers and the recipients of patronage. Child of a race whose ambition to rule was combined with the capacity to govern — inheriting a large share of both, with no field to gratify the one or display the other — precluded by the inexorable laws of society from the indulgence of any aspirations beyond the ballroom and the nursery — we may readily conceive of the existence of causes which might impel 'a daring thinker' to seek to accomplish elsewhere a destiny forbidden to all of womankind in the land of her birth."

And later:

> ". . . We must go back to that tender period of her early youth when her father's house by a father's unkindness ceased to be her home, when, a little later, the memories of childhood brought only bitter images to her mind, and bitterness to her imagination, when the thread which connected infancy with age was suddenly broken; and when the last of her family who had protected and sheltered and

guided her, died and the family circle existed for her no more, and she could no longer delude herself with the belief that she had a home."

There have been suggestions that as she was not the expected eldest son, she tried to behave as if she had been. But though the early loss of her mother and the indifference of her stepmother may have influenced her when she was young, it seems far-fetched to believe that it was the driving power behind her for the rest of her life.

Pitt's death was undoubtedly a terrible blow, but she remained in London another four years after it. Charles being killed at Corunna with General Sir John Moore were two fearful blows, but there is no evidence that she left England never intending to return. Indeed all the evidence points to the fact that she intended, as she had done at the time of her 1804 Continental journey, to return eventually.

The advent of Michael Bruce made her take a definite decision not to return to England, for she feared it would harm him. Even when she sent him back, as she promised his father she would, she still kept the bargain she had made.

Meryon stated in the introduction to his memoirs that her reason for staying abroad was mainly financial. It is true that her £1,200 a year pension was not enough to offer her the life she wanted in England, and Craufurd Bruce's generous allowance to his son increased her income considerably; but when he had left, and she had lost it, she only once, in 1815, seriously considered leaving the Lebanon — but that was to France, not to England.

As she grew older she came more and more to love France, and less and less to love England. She had always despised the Ministers who had, in her estimation, denigrated both Pitt and Sir John Moore. Palmerston's cruelty in cancelling her pension convinced her of the evil in her own country. As she wrote to Lord Hardwicke in her last known letter, she would only return to England "in chains".

But by then she had been driven by chance to the mountain of Djoun in the Lebanon. She had not chosen the place; it had been chosen for her. Her first objective, Sicily, had been rendered unapproachable because of Napoleon's armies. She had liked neither Constantinople nor Egypt. The Lebanon, half-way between the two, was the obvious place. In later years, when she had plunged deeply into mysticism, and the occult, she became convinced that fate had indeed intended her to come there. It is hard, knowing her life, not to feel that she had grounds for this belief.

But she was not one to submit to fate easily. And here perhaps is the true secret of her life. She was, after all, a Pitt. In that family there existed a formidable power. It sent "Diamond" Pitt to India to make a fortune. It appeared, under the guise of political genius, in both the great First Earl of Chatham, and his brilliant younger son William Pitt. It appeared, too, in the extravagant waywardness of Camelford; and finally, reinforced by the Stanhope eccentricity, it appeared in Hester.

The struggle between so forceful and original a person as Hester and the cruelty of her fate could only result in some extraordinary and dramatic demonstration. Had she lived at the time of the Roman occupation, she might have been another Boadicea. Had women been admitted to Parliament during her lifetime, she might, just conceivably, have followed Pitt as Prime Minister. As it was, her character and her stars drove her to the unique position she established in the Middle East. So strong was the impression she made that even today, 150 years later, she is alive in the minds and words of men.

INDEX

Places visited by Lady Hester Stanhope are filed additionally under her name, as well as in their own right.

Abdella, Mr, 254-5
Abercorn, Lord, 72
Abercrombie, James, 258-9
Abu Ghosh, 157, 160
Acre, 160-1, 206-7
Adams, W. D., 84
Addington, Lord, 52-3, 65-6, 68-70
Aleppo, 165, 170
Alexander I, Tsar of Russia, 230
Alexandria, 144-5, 147
Ansary peoples, 217-18
Antioch, 218-19
Ascalon, 194, 196, 209-11
Athanasius, 188
Athens, 118-19

Baalbec, 198-200
Bankes, William, 220, 233
Barker, John, 170-2, 188-9, 203, 209-10, 213
Bastille, Paris, 25
Bathurst, Lord, 210
Beaudin (an interpreter), 206, 221, 226-7
Bebec, Bosphorus, 130-3
Bedouins, 169
Berlin Decree, 92
Beshir, *see* Emir of the Druze
Bessborough, Frederick, 152
Bessborough, Lady Henrietta, 74-82, 89, 92, 102-3, 150, 152, 215
Bethlehem, 156, 159

Bonaparte, Napoleon, 54, 57, 65, 70, 81-3, 92, 115, 172, 196, 208, 213, 215-16
Boulton, Matthew, 29
Boutin, Colonel, 217-18
Brothers, Mr (a fortune teller), 157, 176, 225
Bruce, Craufurd, 109-13, 123-5, 131, 133, 142, 161, 164, 169, 172-3, 175, 184, 186, 196, 202, 217, 287
Bruce, Michael, 109-21, 127, 131, 134, 137, 140, 170, 172, 176, 186, 187, 191-2, 202, 215-17, 221-2, 228, 287-8
Bruce, Brigadier, 287
Brusa, Turkey, 128-31
Buckingham, Marquis of, 225
Buckingham, Silk, 220
Builth Wells, 100-1
Burckhardt, Mons., 158, 161
Burdett, Sir Francis, 43, 254, 268, 271
Burton Pynsent, Somerset, 42-3, 51-2, 55
Byron, Lord, 118-19, 232

Cairo, 148-52
Calvary, 159
Camelford, Lord (Thomas), 47-51, 65
Campbell, Colonel, 255-6
Canning, George, 65, 69, 73, 89, 103

Canning, Stratford, 133-4
Castlereagh, Lord, 84
Cedars of Lebanon, 200
Chatham, Countess (wife of 1st Earl), 14-15, 22, 29, 36, 42-3, 55
Chatham, 1st Earl of (Pitt, the Elder), 12-13, 42
Chatham, 2nd Earl of, 85
Chevening, 3, 4, 9, 11, 16, 17, 19-22, 29, 31, 38-9, 232
Cline, Henry, 104-5
Constantinople, 115-16, 120-36 passim
Corinth, 117
Cumberland, Duke of, 72

Damascus, 165-6, 168, 171
Dar Djoun, 229-30, 239, 242-5, 248-9, 251-5, 261-79 passim, 284-6
Death of Lady Hester Stanhope, 276-9
Del-el-Kamar, 163-4, 196
Dervish Mustafa Aga, 203-9
Devonshire, Duchess of, 74
Djoun, see Dar Djoun
Dover Castle, 56
Druse peoples, The, 162-4, 197, 263

Earthquake, 252-3
Ebrington, Lord, 262
Egerton, Mr and Mrs, 51-4
Egypt, 134, 143-5, 147-53, 215
Ehden, 200
Eldon, Lord, 66
Elgin, Lord, 210
Emir of the Druze (Beshir), 162-4, 197, 226, 239-40, 243, 265-6
Eothen (Kinglake), 249-50

Farquhar, Sir Walter, 58, 64, 84-6, 103-4
Faydan peoples, 178, 180-1
Forster, Captain, 194, 196
Fox, Charles James, 66-9, 86
Fry, Mrs Ann, 112, 116, 121, 125, 138-9, 141, 143, 161, 175, 188, 227

George III, King of England, 66-9, 78
George, Prince of Wales, 67
Gibraltar, 105-8

Giorgio, the Greek, 175, 206, 214, 220
Glastonbury, Lord, 43-5
Gore-Browne, Sir Thomas, 250
Greece, 117-21
Grenville Family, 8, 43, 103, 217
Grenville, Louisa, see Mahon, Lady Louisa
Grenville, General Richard, 104, 221
Grenville, Thomas, 68-9
Grenville, William Wyndham (1st Baron), 68-70

Haddington, 8th Earl of, 44-5
Hafiz Aly, 127-8
Haifa, 207, 211
Hamah, 171-3, 175-7, 181
Hamilton, Grizel (grandmother and later Countess of Stanhope), 4, 5, 9, 13, 17, 22, 29, 32, 39, 42, 44, 88, 142-3
Hamilton, Rachel (her sister), 6
Hardwicke, Lord, 275, 288
Hassan, 174, 178
Hastings, Warren, 23, 31
Hawkesbury, Lord, 84
Heathcote, Sir Gilbert, 232, 235
Hill, Hon. Noel, 89-90
Hobhouse, John Cam, 114, 119
Holland, Lord, 28-9, 30
Holy Alliance (1815), 230, 232
Holy Land, see Syria under Stanhope, Lady Hester Lucy
Holy Sepulchre, 159
Hope, Captain Henry, 144, 162
Hull, Dr Felix, 233

Jackson, Francis, 43-54, 59, 64-5, 81
Jackson, T. J., 58, 63, 99
Jaffa, 153-4, 157
Jerusalem, 153, 157, 159, 204
Joyce, Rev. Jeremiah, 30-2

Kinglake, Alexander William, 249-50

Lamartine, Mons., 249, 262
Lascaris, Mons., 171-4
Latakia, 184-91
Lavalette, Count, 216-17
Lebanon, see Mount Lebanon
Letters found at Chevening, 232-6

Leveson-Gower, Lord Granville, 68-9, 73, 74-5, 77-9, 82, 89, 102
Liston, Mr Ambassador, 194, 206, 213
Literary Institute for the Ottoman Empire, 201
Louis XVI, King, 25, 28
Louis XVIII, King, 217
Loustaunau, General, 207-8, 213, 219-20, 226, 229, 252, 276, 277
Loustaunau, Captain, 228-9
Lunardi, "Dr", 268, 274, 276
Lupi, Captain, 237-8

Mahannah, Emir of the Anizys, 171-4
Mahon, Lady Charles (formerly Hester Pitt, 1st wife of Lord Charles), 3, 7, 13
Mahon, Lord Charles (later 3rd Earl of Stanhope), 3, 5-8, 12-20, 24, 25-32, 36, 41-2, 51, 143, 222
Mahon, Charles Banks (later 4th Earl of Stanhope), 18, 23, 45, 47, 51, 56, 81, 83, 89, 91, 93, 95, 236, 280-1
Mahon, Lady Hester, see Stanhope, Lady Hester Lucy
Mahon, Lady Louisa (formerly Grenville, 2nd wife of Lord Charles), 14-16, 18, 20-1, 32, 51, 88
Mahon, Lord Philip Henry (youngest son of Lord Charles), 16, 18, 23, 30, 38-46, 53-4
Malta, 107-16
Mamelukes, The, 152-3
Mar Elias, Hester's house called, 192, 194-7, 206, 213-15, 220, 229, 252, 253
Mauboug, Latour, 133-4
Maximilian, Duke of Bavaria, 268-9
Mehemet Ali, 147-8, 152, 248, 255-6
Melville, Lord, 67-8, 86
Memoirs of Lady Hester Stanhope (Meryon), 281-3
Meryon, Dr Charles, 17-144 passim, 173-8, 183-4, 188-90, 206-7, 214, 220-1, 227-8, 234-5, 241-52 passim, 257, 266, 270, 272, 280-1

Meryon, Eugenia (his daughter), 253
Meryon, Mrs (his wife), 237-47, 251-2
Meshmushy, 197, 215, 229
Metta (a prophet), 226
Metternich, Prince Clemens, 231-2
Misset, Colonel, 144, 148
Moira, Earl of, 67
Moore, General Sir John, 90-5
Moskowa, Princess of, 215-16
Mount Lebanon, 190-7, 229, 234
Muly Ismael, 181-2
Mustapha Aga Berber, 218

Napoleon, see Bonaparte
Nasar, son of Mahannah, 170-1, 174, 177-8, 180-1, 183
Navarino, battle of, 239
Nazareth, 160-1
Nelson, Admiral Lord, 81-2
Newberry, Mr, 220-1, 226-7
Ney, Madame, 228
Ney, Marshal, 215-16
Northumberland, Duke of, 152

Oakes, General Hildebrand (and letters to), 108, 110, 114-15, 125, 128, 131, 143, 147, 167, 172, 176, 211, 214

Palmerston, Lord, 255-6, 270-1, 288
Palmyra, 179-81
Paterson, Captain John, 95
Pearce, Henry, 127-8, 135, 137, 140, 150, 157
Perceval, Spencer, 165
Philadelphia, Nr Smyrna, 129
Pitt, Lucy (1st Countess Stanhope), 10, 11
Pitt, William, the Elder, see Chatham, 1st Earl of
Pitt, William, the Younger, 3, 12-13, 16, 18, 30, 35-7, 38, 44, 52, 55, 56-9, 66-73, 78, 81-6
Plague, 176, 183, 185, 188-90, 195, 234
Price, Rev. Rice and son Thomas, 101-2
Pückler Muskau, Prince, 262-8
Pynsent, Sir William, 42
Pyramids, 152

Quadruple Alliance, 232

Ramlah, 160
Revolution Society, 25-6
Rhodes, 137-8, 142-3
Romney, Lord, 32
Rose, George, 41, 58
Rosetta, 148-9
Royal Society, 19

St Antonio, Palace of, Malta, 111-15
St Vincent, Lord, 68
Saud of the Wahabys, 185-6
Scott, Sir William, 185
Seweyah, Joseph, 229
Shaykh Ibrahim, 158, 161
Shipwreck, 137-43
Sidon, 162, 188, 191, 269
Sligo, Lord, 109, 117-21, 127-8, 133,
    184-5
Smith, Sir Sidney, 208-9
Smith, William (MP), 35
Smyrna, 143-4
South Sea Bubble, 11
Stafford, Lady, 74, 81
Stanhope, Alexander, 9
Stanhope, Charles Banks, see Mahon,
    Charles Banks
Stanhope, Countess Grizel, see
    Hamilton, Grizel
Stanhope, Grizelda, 17, 22, 36-7, 56,
    88, 237, 280
Stanhope, Lady Hester Lucy (her
    places of visit):
  Egypt, shipwrecked on voyage to,
      137-43; itself, 134, 143-5,
      147-53, 215
    Alexandria, 144-5, 147
    Cairo, 148-52
    Pyramids, 152
  England and Wales, 4-115, passim
    Burton Pynsent, 42-3, 51-2, 55
    Chevening, 3, 4, 9, 11, 16,
        19-32, 232
    Wales, 99-102
    Walmer, 56-7, 59, 61, 63, 81
  Mediterranean
    Athens, 118-19
    Brusa, 128-31
    Gibraltar, 105-8
    Greece, 117-21
    Malta, 107-16
    Rhodes, 137-8, 142-3

Syria
  Acre, 160-1
  Antioch, 218-19
  Ascalon, 209-11
  Baalbec, 198-200
  Bethlehem, 156, 159
  Damascus, 165-6
  Dar Djoun, 229-45 passim,
      248-9, 251-5, 261-79
      passim, 284-6
  Del-el-Kamar, 163-4, 196
  Druses Territory, 162-4
  Ehden, 200
  Haifa, 207, 211
  Hamah, 171-7, 181
  Jaffa, 153-4, 157
  Jerusalem, 153, 157, 159
  Latakia, 184-91
  Meshmushy, 197, 215, 229
  Mount Lebanon, 190-7, 229,
      234, but see also Mars
      Elias, house at
  Nazareth, 160-1
  Palmyra, 179-81
  Ramlah, 160
  Sidon, 162, 188, 191ff, 269 and
      see also Dar Djoun
  Smyrna, 143-4
  Tripoli, 189, 201
  Tyre, 156, 162
Turkey
  Bebec, 130-3
  Brusa, 128-31
  Constantinople, 115-16, 120-2,
      123-36 passim
  Therapia, 124-5
Stanhope, James (1st Earl), 9-12
Stanhope, James (son of Lord
    Charles), 20, 23, 45, 47, 51, 56,
    81, 83, 84, 85, 89, 91, 95-6,
    102, 105, 108, 128, 150, 236
Stanhope, Lucy (daughter of Lord
    Charles) (later Mrs Taylor), 13,
    22, 34-5, 37, 38-9, 56, 88, 196
Stanhope, Countess Lucy, see Pitt,
    Lucy
Stanhope, Philip (2nd Earl), 4, 5, 9,
    18
Stanhope, Philip Henry, see Mahon,
    Philip Henry
Stanhope, 3rd Earl of, see Mahon,
    Lord Charles

Stanhope, 4th Earl of, *see* Mahon, Charles Banks
Stapleton, Mrs, 52-3
Stephens, Mr (USA), 249
Sutton, Nassau, 102-3, 105, 108
Syria, places visited in, *see* Syria *under* Stanhope, Lady Hester Lucy

Talleyrand, Mons., 28
Tattenbach, Count, 265
Taylor, Thomas, 35, 38
Therapia (Bosphorus), 124-5
Treasure at Ascalon, 209-11
Tripoli, 189, 201
Tyre, 156, 162

Valley of the Tombs, 180
Victoria, Queen of England, 255, 258

Walker, Robert, 29
Walpole, Horace, 4, 10
Walmer, 56-7, 59, 61, 63, 81
Warburton, Eliot, 284
Watt, James, 28
Wellesley, Sir Arthur (*later* Duke of Wellington), 84, 92-3, 103, 134, 152, 259
Wellesley, Lord Richard, 134
Wellington, Duke of, *see* Wellesley, Sir Arthur
Wharton, Duke of, 11
Wilberforce, William, 23, 66
Wilkes, John, 7
Williams, Elizabeth, 100, 105, 116, 215, 226, 235, 241
Wraxall, Sir N. W., 4
Wynn, Henry, 152

Zante, 116-17
Zaym (Sultan's delegate), 203-9